Getting Started with Gamma

Create Stunning Presentations with AI

Kiet Huynh

Table of Contents

CHAPTER I
Introduction to Gamma

1.1 What is Gamma?

1.1.1 The Vision Behind Gamma

In a world increasingly saturated with digital information, our attention spans are shrinking, and our expectations for high-quality, engaging content are rising. Whether you're a professional pitching to investors, a teacher preparing a lesson, or a content creator sharing ideas online, you know that **how** you present your message is just as important as **what** you say. This is the reality that gave rise to **Gamma**—a revolutionary platform that blends the power of artificial intelligence with elegant design to help anyone create stunning, interactive, and impactful presentations effortlessly.

But Gamma isn't just another presentation tool. It's the manifestation of a bigger idea: **making storytelling intelligent, accessible, and beautiful for everyone.** To understand Gamma, you first need to understand the deeper mission behind it—the vision that drives its development and future.

The Problem with Traditional Presentation Tools

Before Gamma came onto the scene, the most widely used tools for creating presentations were platforms like PowerPoint, Keynote, or Google Slides. While these tools have served millions of users for decades, they often require significant time, technical skill, and creative energy. Users are burdened with:

- Tedious formatting tasks

- Manual content organization

- A steep learning curve for design principles

- Limited support for storytelling structure

These tools treat presentations as static visual aids. They help you *display* information but do little to help you *communicate* ideas effectively or think through your message. That's where Gamma is different.

Gamma's Foundational Philosophy: Intelligence + Simplicity

Gamma's creators believe that content creation should not be a bottleneck. The vision behind Gamma rests on three foundational principles:

1. AI as a Thought Partner

Instead of just automating tasks, Gamma's AI is designed to act like a creative assistant—a *thought partner*. When you input a prompt or an idea, Gamma doesn't just fill space with meaningless text. It tries to:

- Interpret the context

- Suggest a coherent structure

- Provide relevant subtopics

- Generate visual elements that support your message

It's like brainstorming with someone who never gets tired, always has fresh ideas, and understands modern design standards.

2. Design Should Be Built-In, Not an Afterthought

In traditional tools, users often spend more time tweaking layouts, choosing fonts, aligning boxes, and picking colors than crafting content. Gamma flips this dynamic. By embedding responsive design principles into every output, it lets users **focus on message and story** while the platform handles the visual execution.

Instead of giving you an empty canvas, Gamma provides a **smart framework** that evolves with your content. You don't need to be a designer. Gamma *thinks* like one for you.

3. The Future of Content Is Interactive

Gamma also recognizes that modern audiences crave interactivity. Static slides are no longer enough. Presentations should behave more like websites—clickable, explorable, and nonlinear. This is especially true for:

- Pitch decks
- Reports
- Product overviews
- Educational content
- Personal portfolios

Gamma enables this with **interactive cards, nested blocks, and page linking**, all without the complexity of coding or web development.

A Tool for Everyone, Not Just the Tech-Savvy

Another part of Gamma's vision is inclusivity. Many AI tools are powerful but intimidating. Gamma intentionally keeps its interface **minimalistic and intuitive**, making it suitable for:

- Students
- Teachers
- Founders and startup teams

- Marketers

- Freelancers

- Internal corporate teams

- Designers and non-designers alike

Its onboarding process is simple, with a focus on guiding users to their first success within minutes. This isn't a platform that assumes you're an expert—it *makes you feel like one.*

Human + Machine = Better Storytelling

At its core, Gamma aims to redefine storytelling in the age of AI. It doesn't aim to replace human creativity—it aims to **amplify** it.

You bring the **insight**, the **emotion**, the **narrative**. Gamma brings:

- Speed

- Visual cohesion

- Structural logic

- Data visualization

- AI-generated suggestions

This synergy creates more than a presentation—it creates **a communication experience.**

Solving Real Problems in Modern Workflows

Gamma was designed not just with individual creators in mind, but also teams and organizations. It addresses modern work realities like:

- **Remote collaboration**: With real-time co-editing and commenting.

- **Content reuse**: Modular blocks make it easy to repurpose ideas.

- **Cross-platform sharing**: Works beautifully on web and mobile.

- **Live analytics**: Track viewer engagement and interaction.

The platform recognizes that presentation isn't just about a "show and tell" moment. It's about **ongoing engagement**, **measurable impact**, and **scalable communication**.

The Future Gamma is Building

Gamma's current features already set it apart, but its creators have their eyes on something much bigger. The vision extends into:

- Real-time data integration
- Deep integrations with productivity tools
- Personalized content recommendations using AI
- A library of expert-built templates and AI "brains" for niche industries
- AI that adapts to your tone, brand, and audience type

Eventually, Gamma could evolve into not just a presentation tool—but a **full AI-powered knowledge communication platform**. Think dynamic documents, smart content hubs, or even an AI that helps you rehearse for a talk by predicting likely audience questions.

A Community-Driven, Learning Ecosystem

Another vision that drives Gamma is creating a **supportive creative community**. The team behind Gamma believes in continuous learning and improvement. As such, they invest in:

- In-app tutorials
- Showcase galleries of user creations
- Webinars and workshops
- Community templates
- Feedback loops with users to shape the product roadmap

This makes Gamma not just a tool, but a **movement**—a place where creators uplift one another and help redefine the future of digital communication.

Conclusion: A New Era of Expression

The vision behind Gamma is ultimately about empowerment. It seeks to democratize design, simplify storytelling, and turn everyday people into powerful communicators.

With AI at its side, Gamma removes the friction between thought and expression. It lets you go from an idea in your head to a polished, interactive, engaging presentation in minutes—not hours.

Gamma doesn't just help you present. It helps you **connect, persuade, teach, inspire**, and most importantly—**create**.

1.1.2 Gamma vs. Traditional Presentation Tools

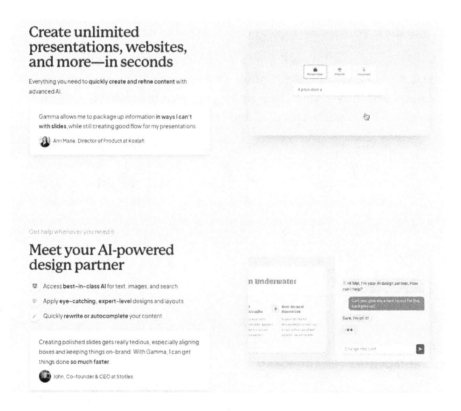

When it comes to creating presentations, most people immediately think of familiar tools like Microsoft PowerPoint, Google Slides, or Apple Keynote. These platforms have long dominated the world of digital presentations, offering slide-based templates, manual formatting, and limited interactivity. However, with the rise of AI-powered platforms, a new contender has emerged—**Gamma**. This section explores how Gamma redefines the presentation experience by comparing it with traditional tools across various dimensions such as workflow, design, interactivity, collaboration, and storytelling.

1. Gamma's AI-Centric Approach vs. Manual Design

One of the most striking differences between Gamma and traditional presentation software lies in **how presentations are created**. Traditional tools require the user to manually build their slides from the ground up—selecting fonts, adjusting layouts, resizing images, aligning objects, and ensuring consistent formatting. This process can be time-consuming and often distracts from the core objective: delivering a clear and compelling message.

Gamma flips this process on its head. With Gamma, **AI takes on the role of your design assistant**. Users can start with a simple text prompt describing the goal or theme of their presentation, and Gamma instantly generates a polished, visually cohesive presentation complete with titles, content blocks, illustrations, and layouts.

For example, instead of manually creating a sales pitch deck in PowerPoint, a user can type "Create a 5-slide presentation on our new AI marketing product" in Gamma—and in seconds, a draft presentation appears. The AI selects appropriate sections, suggests compelling language, and adds relevant visuals automatically. This **accelerates ideation**, reduces design friction, and empowers even non-designers to produce professional-grade content.

2. Slides vs. Cards: Rethinking Presentation Structure

Traditional tools organize content in linear slide formats. While effective in some contexts, slides often constrain storytelling and create **"slide fatigue"**, especially when used for long or content-heavy presentations.

Gamma introduces a fresh paradigm through the use of **"cards"**—modular, vertically scrolling content blocks that feel more like browsing a modern webpage than flipping through a deck. Each card contains a concise section of content and can include text, images, interactive elements, and multimedia. This structure encourages better segmentation of ideas and facilitates **smooth storytelling**, especially in digital-first environments.

Cards are **narrative-friendly** and highly adaptable. Users can reorganize them like building blocks, allowing for more **fluid navigation** and easier content updates. Unlike rigid slide transitions, cards in Gamma provide **continuous visual flow**, which feels more natural on mobile and desktop devices alike.

3. Design Freedom vs. Design Consistency

Design flexibility in PowerPoint and similar tools is a double-edged sword. While it offers total control, it also demands **significant effort** to ensure that a presentation maintains a coherent visual identity. This includes managing color palettes, typography, alignment, spacing, and more—details that often go unnoticed until something looks "off."

Gamma takes a **template-guided approach** where AI automatically applies consistent design themes across all content. From the very first prompt, Gamma ensures that fonts, color schemes, and visual styles align with the selected brand or theme. You don't need to worry about setting up headers, choosing fonts, or resizing images—Gamma does all of this **automatically and intelligently**.

Of course, customization is still possible. Users can tweak themes, swap out visuals, or apply their brand assets. But the starting point is already beautifully designed—giving users a creative head start instead of a blank canvas.

4. Static Slides vs. Interactive Experiences

Traditional presentations are often static, relying on the presenter to deliver context orally. While animations and transitions add flair, most tools offer **limited interactivity**.

Gamma brings **web-like interactivity** to the presentation format. Each card can include embedded content, such as videos, GIFs, forms, buttons, or clickable links. This makes Gamma presentations feel **more like microsites or web stories** than static slideshows.

Imagine presenting a product roadmap where each phase includes expandable cards with deeper information, or a pitch deck where investors can click to view embedded demo videos—all without leaving the presentation. Gamma empowers creators to offer **layered content**, enhancing engagement and catering to self-guided exploration.

5. File-Based Sharing vs. Live Publishing

Traditional slide decks are often shared via email as attachments or exported as PDFs. This creates challenges with version control, access permissions, and update notifications. It's also harder to track engagement with static files.

Gamma adopts a **live publishing model**, similar to how blogs or webpages are shared. Users can instantly generate a shareable link to a live version of their presentation—no need to download or attach files. And because the presentation is hosted online, any updates made by the author are **reflected in real time**.

Even better, Gamma includes **analytics features**, letting users see how viewers interact with their content—what they clicked, how far they scrolled, and how much time they spent. This data is invaluable for marketers, educators, and sales teams alike.

6. Desktop Software vs. Cloud-Native Accessibility

PowerPoint and Keynote are desktop-first applications that may require installation, licenses, or compatibility across devices. Google Slides, while cloud-based, still mimics the linear-slide paradigm and offers relatively basic AI functionality.

Gamma is **natively cloud-based**, accessible from any modern browser without downloads or installations. Your work is saved automatically in the cloud, and you can pick up where you left off from any device. It's also inherently **collaborative**, allowing real-time co-editing and comments—ideal for distributed teams or client-facing projects.

7. Templates and Themes vs. Smart Content Assistance

Traditional tools offer a collection of templates that users must manually adapt to their needs. While helpful, these templates are often generic and require significant effort to make them feel personalized or brand-aligned.

Gamma's AI can **tailor content to your intent**. Instead of picking a "Business Plan Template" and filling it in manually, you can just ask Gamma to "create a 7-slide business plan for a wellness startup," and it does the heavy lifting for you. The result is not only faster but often more **on-point**, thanks to natural language processing and dynamic layout generation.

This intelligence extends beyond just text—Gamma also helps find relevant images, organize ideas logically, and suggest section titles, making it a powerful co-creator for anyone building content.

8. Solo Creation vs. Team Collaboration

In PowerPoint or Keynote, collaboration is often clunky. While cloud integration has improved this, many users still face challenges with **multiple versions**, conflicting edits, or siloed workflows.

Gamma is built for the **modern collaborative workflow**. Team members can co-edit documents in real time, leave comments on specific cards, and assign action items directly within the workspace. Permissions can be managed with ease—granting view-only access, commenting privileges, or full edit rights depending on the user's role.

This **streamlined collaboration** makes Gamma especially powerful for teams in marketing, product, education, and sales—where fast, feedback-driven iterations are the norm.

9. Presenting Live vs. Sharing Asynchronously

Traditional tools emphasize **live presentations**, with the assumption that a presenter will narrate each slide in person or on a call. As a result, decks often lack sufficient context when viewed independently.

Gamma is designed for both **synchronous and asynchronous delivery**. Each card is self-contained and thoughtfully written, allowing viewers to explore the presentation at their own pace—even without a live presenter. This makes Gamma perfect for creating self-guided demos, online onboarding materials, or content libraries that remain useful beyond a single meeting.

At the same time, Gamma still offers a live presentation mode, enabling real-time delivery when needed. The dual-purpose nature of Gamma decks offers **flexibility that traditional slides can't match**.

10. Summary: Gamma's Competitive Edge

Let's summarize the key areas where Gamma outshines traditional tools:

Feature	Traditional Tools	Gamma
Creation Style	Manual, Slide-by-Slide	AI-Powered, Prompt-Based
Design Support	User-Dependent	Intelligent Visual Guidance
Structure	Slides	Modular Cards
Interactivity	Basic	Advanced (Clickable, Multimedia, Embedded)
Sharing	Files, Attachments	Live Links, Real-Time Updates
Collaboration	Limited	Real-Time, Cloud-Based
Presentation Mode	Live Focused	Live + Asynchronous
Analytics	Rarely Available	Built-In Viewer Tracking

Ultimately, Gamma reimagines presentations not just as a visual tool, but as a **dynamic communication experience**. Its blend of AI, modern design, interactivity, and collaborative features positions it as a next-generation platform—ideal for creators who want to stand out, communicate effectively, and work more efficiently.

1.1.3 Who Should Use Gamma?

Gamma is more than just a next-generation presentation tool—it's a revolutionary platform that redefines how we create, share, and experience content. Its intelligent features and design-forward interface make it a powerful option for a wide range of users, from students and entrepreneurs to marketers and corporate teams. But who exactly stands to benefit the most from using Gamma? In this section, we'll explore the different types of users who can take full advantage of Gamma's capabilities and explain how it aligns with their goals and needs.

1. Creators Who Want to Focus on Ideas, Not Slides

One of Gamma's core promises is to reduce the friction between your ideas and the final product. Traditional slide tools like PowerPoint or Google Slides often require a significant amount of manual formatting, alignment, and design work before your message can shine. Gamma, on the other hand, automates much of that busywork.

If you're a **content-first creator**—someone who cares more about the *message* than the *margins*—Gamma is perfect for you. The platform allows you to simply start writing or inputting ideas, and it takes care of the structure, visual hierarchy, and formatting using smart design algorithms and AI suggestions. It's like having a personal designer who understands your narrative.

2. Busy Professionals and Teams Who Need Efficiency

In the workplace, time is always a limited resource. Whether you're working on a **sales pitch**, a **project update**, or an **internal knowledge base**, the ability to create clear, engaging content quickly is a competitive advantage.

Gamma caters especially well to professionals who:

- Need to **communicate clearly and quickly**
- Frequently prepare materials for **meetings or client interactions**
- Want to collaborate **seamlessly with teammates** in real time

With AI-assisted content generation and responsive design, users can go from idea to ready-to-share presentation in minutes. Gamma also supports team workflows with real-time editing, comments, and version tracking—features that are vital for today's collaborative work environments.

3. Educators and Trainers Looking to Modernize Their Materials

For educators, instructional designers, and trainers, Gamma offers a dynamic and interactive way to share knowledge. Traditional slide decks can be static and linear, but Gamma presentations feel more like web experiences—with smooth transitions, clickable sections, and embedded media that keep learners engaged.

Educators can benefit from Gamma by:

- Creating **modular lesson content** that is easy to update and share

- Embedding videos, quizzes, and links directly into learning materials

- Encouraging interactive exploration, rather than one-directional teaching

Whether you're teaching in a classroom, hosting a webinar, or preparing onboarding materials, Gamma makes it easier to deliver knowledge in a visually compelling and flexible format.

4. Founders, Startups, and Pitch Deck Creators

Startups thrive on great storytelling. A well-designed, high-impact pitch deck can make the difference between a successful funding round and a missed opportunity. Gamma gives founders and startup teams an edge by combining persuasive design with lightning-fast execution.

Why startup founders love Gamma:

- It helps create **elegant pitch decks** without hiring a designer

- It ensures consistency across presentations and documents

- It enables quick iterations as business models evolve

With Gamma, you can focus on the story—your problem, your solution, your market—and let the platform handle the visual impact. You can even generate outlines or slide content from a few sentences using the built-in AI.

5. Writers, Bloggers, and Content Strategists

Not all storytelling happens on slides. Gamma also supports other formats like one-pagers, reports, and interactive documents—making it a strong alternative to traditional blogging platforms or Google Docs.

Content creators in media, marketing, or communications can use Gamma to:

- Build **interactive articles** that readers can explore non-linearly

- Create beautiful **content briefs** or **client reports**
- Share **web-like documents** that feel modern and professional

The no-code, design-smart interface empowers writers to focus on clarity and creativity while still delivering visually impressive content.

6. Marketers and Branding Teams

For those working in marketing or branding, Gamma offers the perfect combination of control and automation. With Gamma, marketers can stay on-brand while creating dynamic materials tailored to different audiences.

Marketing teams benefit from:

- **Template consistency**, ensuring all materials follow brand guidelines
- The ability to **embed video, forms, and social media** easily
- Responsive design for **mobile and desktop presentation**

Whether you're preparing a launch campaign or summarizing analytics in a report, Gamma makes it easy to produce engaging, on-brand collateral that drives results.

7. Students and Academic Presenters

Students and researchers are often expected to present their ideas and findings in a professional manner, even if they don't have access to advanced design tools. Gamma levels the playing field by providing smart layouts and AI help that make academic work shine.

Gamma helps students by:

- Generating outlines and summaries for complex topics
- Suggesting design improvements without needing design knowledge
- Supporting citations and data integration with ease

From book reports to thesis defenses, Gamma makes academic presentations feel polished and impressive.

8. Event Planners and Public Speakers

Events thrive on smooth storytelling. Whether you're speaking at a conference or organizing a workshop, Gamma gives you a way to structure and deliver your content in an engaging, interactive format that's easy to adapt to different audiences.

Public speakers use Gamma to:

- Create **narrative-driven slides** that guide their talk

- Share materials digitally before, during, or after events

- Keep presentations flexible and dynamic for live feedback

9. Knowledge Managers and Internal Communications Leads

Organizations often struggle with how to document, organize, and share internal knowledge in a way that's intuitive and scalable. Gamma excels at this, turning internal documents into interactive knowledge hubs that are both beautiful and easy to use.

Gamma is great for:

- **Wikis, SOPs, and team handbooks**

- Sharing updates or reports in a non-linear format

- Making internal comms more accessible and digestible

10. Anyone Curious About AI and Modern Productivity

Finally, Gamma is perfect for people who just want to explore what's possible with **AI-powered creativity tools**. If you're curious about how to make better presentations, communicate ideas more effectively, or level up your digital productivity, Gamma is a great starting point.

Even if you're not a designer, writer, or businessperson, Gamma's ease of use and intelligence make it an exciting tool for anyone who wants to express themselves more effectively.

In Summary

Gamma is designed to serve a broad and diverse user base, but the common thread is this: **people who want to communicate clearly and beautifully, without spending hours fiddling with formatting**. Whether you're leading a company, teaching a class, building your career, or sharing your voice with the world, Gamma gives you the tools to do it better, faster, and more creatively.

In the next section, we'll walk through the step-by-step process of setting up your Gamma account so you can start creating your own AI-powered presentations right away.

1.2 Setting Up Your Account

1.2.1 Signing Up

Getting started with Gamma begins with creating your own account. The sign-up process is straightforward and designed to get you building AI-powered presentations in minutes. In this section, we'll guide you through every step of signing up for Gamma, choosing the right sign-in method, understanding your account options, and setting up a profile that gets you ready to dive in.

Why You Need an Account

Before anything else, it's important to understand why signing up is necessary. Gamma is a cloud-based tool. That means all your presentations, content drafts, and project settings are stored online and accessible from any device. By creating an account, you'll unlock:

- **Persistent Storage** of your work

- **Access to AI tools** like content generation and auto-layouts

- **Real-time collaboration** with others

- **Analytics and presentation sharing features**

- **Theme and style customization**

Having an account also allows Gamma to save your preferences and personalize suggestions, making your work faster and easier every time you return.

Step-by-Step Guide to Signing Up

Step 1: Visit the Gamma Website

Start by going to https://gamma.app. You'll land on Gamma's clean and inviting homepage, featuring a call-to-action like **"Get started for free"** or **"Try it now"**.

Click the **Get Started** button. This will open the sign-up/sign-in interface.

A new medium for
presenting ideas.
Powered by AI.

Beautiful presentations, documents and websites.
No design or coding skills required.

Sign up for free

Step 2: Choose a Sign-Up Method

Gamma supports multiple sign-up options. As of now, you can choose between:

- Google Account

- Microsoft Account

- Apple ID

- Email and Password

Here's a breakdown of each method:

Using Google, Microsoft, or Apple

If you prefer simplicity and speed, choose a single sign-on method:

- Click the relevant button (e.g., "Sign up with Google")

- Select your account from the popup window

- Grant the necessary permissions (basic profile access)

- Gamma will automatically create your workspace and log you in

Tip: This method is recommended for professionals using Gamma for work or school. It simplifies access and automatically links your identity and contact info.

Using Email and Password

If you'd rather sign up without linking a third-party account:

1. Click "Sign up with Email"

2. Enter a valid email address

3. Choose a secure password (Gamma will show password strength)

4. Accept the Terms of Service and Privacy Policy

5. Click **Create Account**

You'll receive a verification email. Open it and click the confirmation link to activate your account.

Security Note: Use a strong, unique password. Consider enabling two-factor authentication (2FA) in your email account to further secure your Gamma workspace.

Step 3: Set Up Your Profile and Workspace

Once your account is activated, you'll be guided through a brief onboarding process. Here's what you'll encounter:

Choose a Display Name

Your display name is how you appear to collaborators. You can enter your full name or a nickname.

Create a Workspace

A **workspace** is your personal or team area where presentations and documents are organized. You can name it something like:

- "My Projects"

- "Marketing Team"

- "Client Decks"

- "ABC Corp Workspace"

You can create multiple workspaces later if you need to organize different projects or teams.

Set a Workspace URL (Optional)

Gamma may allow you to customize your workspace URL (e.g., yourname.gamma.app) for easier access. This is useful if you're sharing links frequently or want to brand your workspace.

Understanding Your User Dashboard

Once onboarding is complete, you'll land in your dashboard. At a glance, this area shows:

- Your recent presentations
- Templates and AI prompt options
- Import options from Notion, Google Docs, or Markdown
- Workspace settings and team management
- Access to help guides and Gamma's blog

This is the command center for everything you'll do in Gamma.

Troubleshooting and Common Issues

Didn't Receive the Verification Email?

- Check your spam or promotions folders
- Make sure you typed your email address correctly
- Resend the confirmation link from the sign-in screen

Using a Work or School Email?

Some domains may block third-party emails. If your organization has strict security settings, try using a personal email or contact your IT team.

Can't Sign Up with Google/Microsoft?

This is usually related to browser settings. Try:

- Disabling browser extensions (especially privacy blockers)

- Enabling third-party cookies

- Trying a different browser

Tips for a Smooth Start

- Bookmark your workspace so you can easily return later.

- Use a profile photo for easier collaboration and sharing.

- Invite a teammate early to explore Gamma's real-time editing features.

Managing Your Account Settings

Once signed up, you can modify your account by clicking on your profile icon in the upper-right corner. From there you can:

- Change your email or password

- Adjust your notification preferences

- Upgrade or downgrade your plan

- Add payment information (for premium features)

- View usage statistics and AI token limits (if applicable)

Pro Tip: Set up your preferences before diving into presentation creation. Things like default themes and sharing settings can save time later.

Free vs. Paid Account Options

Gamma offers a free tier with many powerful features, but depending on your usage, you may want to explore a paid plan. As of writing, tiers include:

Plan   Key Features

Free   Unlimited presentations, AI prompts (limited), basic templates

Pro   Enhanced AI credits, advanced branding, analytics

Plan Key Features

Team Collaboration tools, admin controls, shared workspaces

You can view the latest pricing and plan comparison on their <u>Pricing Page</u>. https://gamma.app/pricing

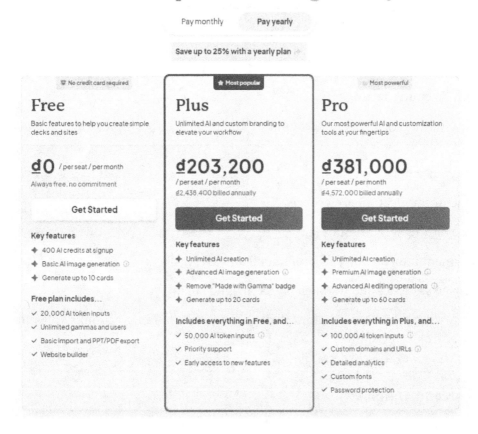

Final Thoughts: Ready to Create

You're now officially a Gamma user! From this point forward, you'll have access to one of the most innovative AI presentation tools available today. Signing up is just the first step— but it unlocks a world of creative possibility.

In the next section, we'll walk you through creating your very first Gamma presentation—using AI prompts, beautiful layouts, and intuitive tools that make your content shine.

1.2.2 Navigating the Dashboard

Once you've successfully created your Gamma account, the next step is becoming familiar with your workspace—specifically, the **Gamma Dashboard**. This is your central hub for creating, editing, organizing, and accessing all your presentations and documents. In this section, we will explore every component of the Gamma Dashboard, ensuring you're confident navigating and leveraging its features to streamline your workflow.

Understanding the Layout of the Dashboard

When you log into Gamma, you are greeted by a clean, minimalist interface. This simplicity is intentional—Gamma is designed to reduce cognitive overload and make the creative process seamless. The dashboard consists of the following primary areas:

1. Sidebar (Navigation Panel)

2. Main Workspace Area

3. Top Toolbar

4. Templates & Quick Start Options

Let's go through each of these in detail.

1. Sidebar (Navigation Panel)

Located on the **left-hand side**, the sidebar is your access point for navigation across all major parts of the Gamma platform.

a. Home

This brings you back to your main dashboard view—where all your presentations, recent documents, and quick actions are centralized.

b. My Workspace

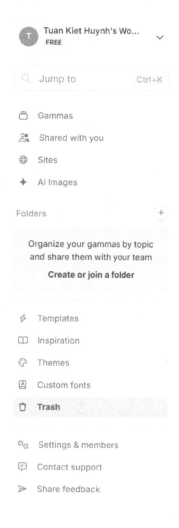

This section shows all of your personal files. If you're part of a team or organization, your workspace may also display team-shared files and folders.

• You can filter by document type: presentations, documents, drafts, etc.

• Files are shown with previews and last-edited timestamps.

c. Templates

Clicking this opens up Gamma's extensive template library. Templates are categorized based on purpose—pitch decks, portfolios, lesson plans, reports, and more.

You can bookmark your favorites, preview them, or start directly from one.

d. Trash

This area contains deleted presentations or documents. You can recover or permanently delete items here.

e. Settings & Preferences

Located at the bottom of the sidebar, this leads to account settings including:

• Profile information

• Notification preferences

• Workspace management

• Billing (if on a paid plan)

2. Main Workspace Area

The central part of the dashboard displays your documents in a grid or list view, depending on your preference.

a. Document Cards

Each card shows a thumbnail preview, title, creation date, last edit, and quick actions like:

- Open
- Share
- Rename
- Duplicate
- Move to Folder
- Delete

b. Sort and Filter Options

You can **sort by**:

- Last opened
- Last edited
- Recently created

- Alphabetical order

You can also **filter by type**, such as AI-generated presentations, manually created files, or collaborative documents.

c. Folder Organization

Gamma allows you to organize your content using **folders**. You can:

- Create new folders

- Drag and drop files

- Share entire folders with collaborators

Tip: Use **naming conventions** like ClientName_Pitch_2025 or Q2_Report_TeamA for efficient organization.

---

3. Top Toolbar (Command Center)

Running across the top of the dashboard is a toolbar containing **high-level actions and tools**.

a. Search Bar

This intelligent search allows you to look up documents by title, keywords, content inside slides, collaborators, or tags.

It's **real-time and typo-tolerant**—a great feature if you're managing dozens or hundreds of presentations.

b. New Document Button

Clicking this opens a dropdown menu:

- Create New from Prompt

- Choose a Template

- Start Blank Presentation

- Import from File (PDF, PowerPoint, etc.)

c. AI Quick Start Panel

Sometimes Gamma will suggest starting points based on your **recent activity**, **trending topics**, or **popular use cases**. Clicking one of these takes you directly into the editor with a pre-filled draft.

d. Account Menu

Click your profile picture to:

- Switch between workspaces
- Access account preferences
- Log out

4. Templates & Quick Start Options

One of the most powerful features of Gamma's dashboard is the ability to **jumpstart your creativity** using AI or professionally designed templates.

a. AI Prompt Generator

Found prominently on the dashboard, this is where you can simply type something like:

- "Create a presentation on climate change for high school students."
- "Make a pitch deck for a startup in the fintech industry."

The AI will instantly generate a multi-slide draft presentation. You can tweak the tone (professional, casual, educational), format (slides, doc-style), and length.

b. Use Case Templates

Examples include:

- Team Status Updates
- Internal Documentation
- Fundraising Decks
- Weekly Recaps
- Learning Modules

Each template is editable and serves as a springboard for personalization.

Customization Options on the Dashboard

Gamma allows subtle customization of your dashboard to make it feel personal and efficient:

- Switch between light and dark modes
- Pin favorite documents for quick access
- Change your default font or color scheme (for premium accounts)
- Set a default template for new presentations

Collaboration from the Dashboard

The Gamma Dashboard also enables real-time collaboration, even before opening a specific document:

a. Shared With Me Section

You can see all the files where you've been added as a viewer, commenter, or editor.

b. Comments & Mentions Overview

Gamma notifies you of any mentions or comments in a centralized alert system accessible via the top toolbar.

c. Activity Feed

Track who has edited what and when—especially helpful when collaborating on important decks.

Keyboard Shortcuts on the Dashboard

For power users, Gamma supports keyboard shortcuts on the dashboard:

- **Cmd/Ctrl + K**: Quick search bar
- **N**: New presentation
- **F**: Create a new folder

- **Cmd/Ctrl + / (forward slash)**: Show all shortcuts

These boost your efficiency, especially if you work with Gamma frequently.

Mobile and Tablet Dashboard Experience

While the desktop version offers the fullest experience, Gamma has a **mobile-optimized dashboard**:

- Accessible via browser or mobile app (Beta)
- Supports viewing, sharing, and light editing
- AI Prompt Generator still functions on mobile
- Great for on-the-go approvals or quick edits

Tips for Staying Organized on the Dashboard

To avoid digital clutter, here are best practices:

1. **Use folders early**—don't wait until you have 100+ files
2. **Label consistently**—standardize how you name decks and reports
3. **Archive old documents**—move unused files to a dated archive folder
4. **Leverage pinned files**—keep your active projects on top
5. **Color code templates** (available in future features roadmap)

Summary

The Gamma Dashboard is not just a launchpad—it's the **operational core** of your entire content workflow. With an elegant, user-friendly design, powerful AI integration, and smart organization features, Gamma empowers you to manage presentations efficiently and creatively.

By mastering how to navigate this dashboard, you'll significantly reduce friction in your creative process and focus more on what truly matters: **crafting impactful content with ease**.

1.2.3 Understanding the Workspace

Once you've signed up and familiarized yourself with the basic layout of the Gamma dashboard, it's time to dive deeper into the **Workspace**—the central hub where all of your creative work happens. Think of the Workspace as your digital studio: it's where you create, edit, collaborate, and manage your presentations or documents powered by AI.

In this section, we'll take a guided tour of the Gamma Workspace, explore each key component, and discuss how to navigate and personalize it for your needs. Whether you're using Gamma for solo content creation or as part of a team, a strong understanding of the Workspace will dramatically improve your productivity and experience.

Overview of the Gamma Workspace

When you log into Gamma, you're greeted with a clean, minimalist interface designed to reduce friction and help you focus on your ideas. The Workspace is split into three primary areas:

1. The Sidebar Navigation Panel

2. The Main Workspace Area

3. The Top Action Bar

Each section plays a unique role in how you interact with your presentations or pages. Let's look at each component in detail.

1. The Sidebar Navigation Panel

Located on the left-hand side, the Sidebar Navigation Panel is your control center for managing documents and navigating different spaces within Gamma.

Key Elements of the Sidebar:

- **Home**: This brings you back to your dashboard where all your recent documents and presentations are displayed. It includes filters for sorting and organizing work.

- **Spaces**: Spaces are like folders or workspaces for organizing different projects. For example, you might create one Space for "Client Pitches," another for "Internal Training," and so on. Spaces can be shared with teams or kept private.

- **Templates**: Access Gamma's library of built-in templates. These templates span use cases like business proposals, investor decks, educational content, and one-pagers. This is a great place to jump-start your projects.

- **Shared with Me**: See presentations or documents others have shared with you. Collaboration is a core Gamma feature, so this area helps you stay updated.

- **Trash**: Just like your computer, deleted items go here. You can recover them or permanently delete them.

Pro Tip: You can customize the Sidebar by collapsing it when you want more screen space or pinning key Spaces for quick access.

2. The Main Workspace Area

This is where the real magic happens. The Main Workspace is the canvas where your presentations or documents come to life. Gamma's unique hybrid format—somewhere between a slide deck, a web page, and a document—requires a slightly different way of thinking, but it's intuitive once you understand the flow.

Key Features of the Main Workspace:

- **Content Blocks**: Gamma uses blocks to structure content. These include text blocks, image blocks, embedded videos, tables, buttons, and even AI-generated content blocks. You can drag, drop, and rearrange them freely.

- **Canvas-Like Navigation**: Unlike traditional slide decks, Gamma's presentations are scrollable and fluid. You can create sections that behave like "pages" or "slides," but they flow together in a seamless reading experience.

- **Live Collaboration**: You'll see real-time cursor movements, typing, and edits from team members, making it easy to co-create with others without confusion.

- **Section Headers and Navigation Links**: Use headers to organize your content, and optionally create links to specific sections for internal navigation. This is especially useful in long documents or interactive presentations.

- **Customization Options**: Each block can be styled using context-aware tools. Gamma automatically suggests layouts and alignments, or you can tweak font sizes, background colors, spacings, and more.

Tip: Hover over any block, and a contextual toolbar will appear with quick editing options like duplicate, delete, move, or add AI suggestions.

---

3. The Top Action Bar

At the top of the Workspace, you'll find a sleek action bar that gives you quick access to essential features:

Key Buttons and Menus:

- **+ New**: This button lets you create a new presentation, page, or workspace. You can choose to start from scratch, use a template, or input a prompt for AI to generate content.

- **Undo/Redo**: Standard undo and redo functions to correct your last few actions.

- **Command Bar (Cmd + K / Ctrl + K)**: A powerful search bar that lets you quickly jump to documents, run actions, and use AI commands. Type "/" or use keyboard shortcuts to activate it.

- **AI Assistant**: This icon opens the AI helper panel, where you can type instructions like "summarize this section," "make this more formal," or "add bullet points for this paragraph." The AI responds in real time.

- **Share**: Click here to share your Gamma file with collaborators. You can set permissions like view-only, edit, or comment access.

- **Presentation Mode**: This transforms your scrollable document into a presentation experience with click-through transitions—great for live pitching or meetings.

- **More Options (:)**: This menu gives access to download, export, rename, duplicate, or delete the file.

Navigating Between Presentations and Pages

Gamma's interface is designed to handle multiple documents seamlessly. When working on multiple projects, you can:

- **Use Tabs**: Like a web browser, Gamma supports tabs at the top (in some layouts), making it easy to switch between files.

- **Favorites and Pinning**: You can pin frequently used documents to access them more quickly.

- **Search and Filter**: Use the universal search at the top of the dashboard to find presentations by title, tag, or keyword.

Personalizing Your Workspace

Gamma allows for customization to fit your style and workflow. Here are some ways to make the workspace yours:

- **Dark Mode vs. Light Mode**: Choose a theme that suits your eyes and environment.

- **Custom Branding**: If you're on a Pro or Team plan, you can apply your brand's colors, fonts, and logo to every presentation.

- **Workspace Organization**: Group your documents by Spaces, tag them with relevant categories, and archive older content.

Accessibility and Performance Considerations

Gamma is a cloud-based tool, which means your Workspace is accessible from anywhere with an internet connection. It's optimized for:

- **Browser Performance**: Compatible with Chrome, Safari, Firefox, and Edge.

- **Device Flexibility**: You can access Gamma on desktops, tablets, and even mobile browsers, though editing is easiest on larger screens.

- **Autosave and Version History**: Never worry about losing work. Every change is saved automatically, and you can roll back to previous versions if needed.

Common Workspace Tips for Beginners

- **Get Comfortable with Blocks**: Think of content in sections—title, subpoints, visuals. Use blocks to structure cleanly.

- **Try "/" Slash Commands**: Type "/" to pull up a list of commands, blocks, and AI tools while editing.

- **Use Templates to Learn**: Open a few templates and study how they're structured. You'll pick up best practices quickly.

- **Test Presentation Mode Early**: Always preview your presentation early to see how it flows and to catch formatting quirks.

Summary: Mastering the Workspace for Efficient Creation

Your Workspace is more than just a canvas—it's the core of your creative engine in Gamma. Understanding how to navigate it, structure your content, collaborate in real time, and take advantage of AI features is essential for efficient presentation building.

Once you've gotten comfortable with the Gamma Workspace, you'll find it not only speeds up your workflow but also encourages a more fluid and design-forward approach to communicating your ideas. With this foundation in place, you're now ready to start building your first presentation—AI-powered and visually stunning.

CHAPTER II
Creating Your First Presentation

2.1 Starting with a Prompt or Template

2.1.1 Using the AI Text Prompt

Creating a presentation has traditionally been a time-consuming process involving brainstorming, outlining, formatting, and revising. With Gamma's AI-powered presentation engine, you can now bypass much of the manual setup by leveraging its intelligent text prompt system. This feature allows you to generate an entire presentation structure simply by describing your topic in natural language.

In this section, we'll walk you through how to use Gamma's AI Text Prompt to create a polished, compelling presentation in just a few minutes. Whether you're preparing a pitch deck, a report, a lesson plan, or a personal portfolio, the AI prompt can be your creative partner.

What is the AI Text Prompt?

The AI Text Prompt in Gamma is a smart input box where you tell Gamma what your presentation is about, and the AI generates a structured slide deck based on your input. Think of it as asking an expert assistant to create a rough draft of your slides so you can focus more on refining the message and visuals.

Instead of starting from a blank screen, you start from a rich outline, complete with headers, descriptions, and sometimes even visuals, depending on your prompt.

How to Access the AI Prompt Feature

1. **Log in to your Gamma account.** If you haven't already created one, refer to [Chapter 1.2.1 Signing Up].

2. **Click "+ Create"** from the Gamma dashboard. This opens the creation options panel.

3. **Choose "Start with a prompt"** – usually shown as the first option on the screen.

4. **Enter your prompt** – this is a short, natural-language description of what you want to create.

Examples:

- "Create a presentation about the benefits of remote work"

- "Make a pitch deck for a startup that sells sustainable coffee"

- "Explain the history of the Roman Empire in a school-friendly format"

5. **Click 'Generate'** – the AI will take a few seconds to process and produce your initial presentation.

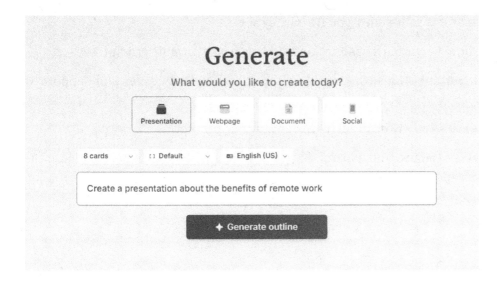

Tips for Writing an Effective Prompt

While Gamma's AI is quite intelligent, the better your prompt, the better the result. Here are some tips to help you get the most out of the AI:

- **Be specific**: Instead of saying "Make a presentation about marketing," say "Create a 10-slide presentation on digital marketing strategies for small businesses."

- **Define the audience**: Mention if the presentation is for executives, students, potential investors, or clients.

- **Add a goal**: For example, "Convince investors to fund a new app" or "Educate employees on cybersecurity best practices."

- **Mention tone or style** (optional): You can request a "friendly," "formal," or "data-driven" tone.

Example of a strong prompt:

"Generate a presentation that introduces a mental health awareness campaign targeted at high school students, focusing on social media impact and coping strategies. Make it informative and supportive in tone."

Understanding the AI Output

Once Gamma generates your slides, you'll typically see:

- **A title slide**: Featuring a headline and subtitle based on your prompt

- **Several content slides**: Organized by topic, each with a header and supporting content

- **Optional call-to-action slide**: If relevant to your prompt

You can now review, adjust, and expand on this outline. The goal isn't perfection on the first try—but a strong starting point to customize.

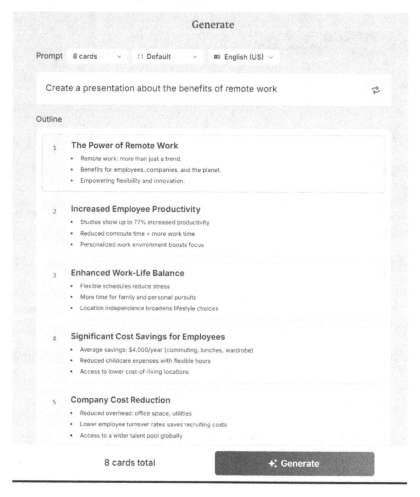

Customizing the Generated Content

After your presentation is generated, Gamma gives you the flexibility to edit every element. This includes:

- **Rewriting slide text** using the built-in AI or manual input

- **Changing the order of slides** by dragging and dropping

- **Adding or removing slides** to better suit your structure

- **Inserting media or visuals** to enhance clarity

The AI also includes suggestions on some slides, such as bullet points, image placeholders, or short summaries. You can use these as-is or tweak them for your unique voice.

Using Prompt Refinement

If the result isn't quite what you were expecting, Gamma gives you options:

- **Regenerate**: Click the "Try Again" or "Regenerate" button to get a new version with the same prompt

- **Refine prompt**: Go back to the prompt editor and add more details

- **Edit inline**: Manually adjust or highlight content you'd like the AI to improve

Prompt refinement is particularly useful if you're looking for a different direction or tone. For example, if your first prompt was too general, you might refine it from:

"Create a presentation about e-commerce"

To:

"Generate a 7-slide presentation about how small businesses can succeed on Shopify, including product selection, marketing, and customer retention strategies."

AI Collaboration vs. Manual Control

While the AI prompt speeds up the creation process, remember you're still the author. Use the AI's suggestions as a creative baseline, not a replacement for your voice or message.

Advantages of using the AI Prompt:

- Saves time on structure and layout

- Helps you overcome writer's block

- Offers fresh ideas and phrasing

- Provides a consistent visual aesthetic automatically

Limitations to be aware of:

- May generate generic content without detailed guidance

- Requires careful review for accuracy

- Not suited for highly technical or sensitive topics unless prompted precisely

To get the best outcome, think of the AI as your brainstorming buddy—it helps you get started fast, but your input will shape the final result.

Real-Life Examples

Let's look at how different types of users might use the AI Text Prompt:

- **Startup Founder**: Prompt: "Pitch deck for a subscription-based meal kit company"
Result: A deck including problem, solution, product, market opportunity, traction, business model, and team

- **Teacher**: Prompt: "Create an educational presentation on climate change for 6th graders"
Result: Simplified language, clear visuals, actionable insights, and interactive elements

- **Freelance Designer**: Prompt: "Portfolio overview of recent branding projects for agencies"
Result: Case study-based layout with space for images and client testimonials

Best Practices for AI Prompt Creation

- **Keep it short but informative**: A one-sentence description is fine, but a couple of lines will give more context.

- **Avoid overly vague topics**: "Make something cool" is too abstract.

- **Use prompts as a draft**: Don't aim for the perfect presentation in one go—focus on building from what the AI gives.

- **Explore different versions**: Sometimes regenerating gives a structure you hadn't considered.

Common Mistakes to Avoid

- **Not customizing the output**: Leaving everything AI-generated without editing may result in a lack of personality or alignment with your message.

- **Relying solely on the AI**: While helpful, it won't replace subject-matter expertise or thoughtful storytelling.

- **Overloading the prompt**: Too much detail can overwhelm the AI or lead to unexpected results. Try breaking complex ideas into stages.

- **Skipping the tone**: If your topic is sensitive or professional, be clear about the tone you want.

Summary and Key Takeaways

- The AI Text Prompt is a powerful tool to jumpstart your presentations.

- Clear, specific, and goal-oriented prompts yield better results.

- Always refine and customize the AI's output to align with your purpose and audience.

- Use prompt regeneration and editing features to iterate quickly.

- Think of the AI as a co-creator—it's there to help, but your voice and insight matter most.

By mastering this feature, you unlock one of Gamma's greatest strengths: the ability to go from concept to content in minutes, with AI as your creative partner.

2.1.2 Choosing and Customizing Templates

Creating a compelling presentation doesn't have to start from a blank slate. One of Gamma's greatest strengths lies in its **template-based system**, which helps users quickly structure and stylize their presentations while still allowing for flexibility and customization. Whether you're building a business pitch, an online portfolio, or a learning module, Gamma's templates can be your springboard to a polished, engaging output.

In this section, we'll explore:

- The benefits of using a template

- How to browse and select the right one

- Techniques to customize templates to reflect your goals, content, and brand

Why Use a Template?

Templates aren't just time-savers—they are **smart design blueprints** that solve many of the structural and aesthetic challenges in presentation creation. Here's what makes them especially valuable in Gamma:

- **Pre-built layouts**: No need to think from scratch about how to organize sections, visuals, or navigation.

- **Visual consistency**: Templates come with coherent font systems, color palettes, and component placements.

- **Best practices built-in**: Many templates are designed with communication principles in mind—clear hierarchy, readable text, and optimized slide flow.

- **AI adaptability**: Gamma's AI works well with templates, suggesting content and layouts based on the context you provide.

Using a template allows you to **focus on the message**, not just the design.

How to Access Gamma's Template Library

After logging into your Gamma workspace, you'll be presented with the option to:

1. **Start from scratch**

2. **Use a prompt**

3. **Choose a template**

To access templates:

- Click **"Start with a Template"** from the home dashboard.

- Alternatively, within an existing presentation, you can open the **"+ Add Page"** panel and choose a template for new slides.

From here, you'll enter Gamma's **template library**, a curated space filled with pre-designed formats across different categories.

Browsing Template Categories

Gamma offers a diverse range of templates tailored to different use cases. Some of the most common template categories include:

1. Business and Startups

- Pitch decks

- Investor presentations
- Startup overviews
- Company profiles

2. Marketing and Sales

- Product introductions
- Marketing proposals
- Campaign summaries
- Customer journey maps

3. Education and Learning

- Lesson plans
- Workshop presentations
- Case studies
- How-to guides

4. Personal and Portfolio

- Creative portfolios
- Résumés
- Blog-like presentations
- Visual storytelling

5. Internal Team Use

- Meeting agendas
- Project updates
- Strategy roadmaps
- Knowledge sharing docs

Each template is previewable—hovering over one will show you a preview of its slides so you can assess whether it fits your needs.

Choosing the Right Template

To choose the right template:

- **Clarify your goal**: Are you informing, persuading, educating, or documenting?

- **Think about structure**: Do you want a linear presentation, a microsite experience, or a storytelling format?

- **Visual preference**: Do you prefer bold colors, minimalistic designs, or a media-rich approach?

- **Time constraints**: Some templates are more ready-to-use than others. Pick what fits your timeline.

Pro Tip: If you're unsure, choose a general template like "Starter Deck" or "Simple Overview" — they're easy to adapt and great for beginners.

Customizing Templates to Make Them Yours

Once you've selected a template, the real power begins: customization.

Let's walk through the customization process step-by-step.

Step 1: Rewriting Text

Every template comes with placeholder text, which is there to guide your thought process. Start by:

- Replacing placeholder headings and subheadings with your own.

- Using Gamma's AI to help rewrite sections by highlighting text and choosing "Rewrite" or "Expand."

- Keeping your tone consistent—decide whether you want to sound formal, friendly, educational, or persuasive.

Tip: If you're unsure how to phrase something, let Gamma's AI generate or refine it.

Step 2: Replacing or Inserting Images and Media

Templates come with default visuals, but they're just suggestions. You can:

- Click on any image and replace it from Gamma's built-in **image library**, or **upload your own.**

- Use the **GIF search** to add some liveliness.

- Embed videos from YouTube or Loom for multimedia-rich slides.

- Add diagrams, charts, or logos as needed.

Pro Tip: Try using visuals that match your brand colors or thematic tone. Gamma helps by suggesting relevant image replacements via AI.

Step 3: Adjusting Layouts and Blocks

Templates are made up of **"blocks"**—modular content units such as headings, text areas, image containers, buttons, or embedded widgets. You can:

- **Move blocks** up and down, left or right (if the layout allows).

- **Add new blocks** by clicking the "+" at the bottom of a slide.

- **Delete** irrelevant blocks to declutter your content.

- **Duplicate** blocks you want to reuse for uniformity.

You don't need to understand HTML or CSS—just drag, drop, click, and type.

Step 4: Changing the Theme and Color Scheme

Even within a template, you're not locked into one aesthetic. Customize the visual identity:

- Click on the **"Theme"** panel in the top toolbar.

- Choose from dozens of **preset color themes** or create your own.

- Select your **brand fonts** for headings and body text.

- Change background colors or add gradient overlays.

If you have a brand style guide, you can match your template to it for visual consistency.

Step 5: Structuring Your Presentation

A good presentation follows a story arc. Use the template as a guide, but tailor the flow:

- Start with a **title or overview** slide.
- Move into **problem, solution, and evidence** (for pitches).
- Or go with **learning objectives, content, and takeaway** (for lessons).
- End with a **call to action** or summary.

You can rearrange pages anytime by dragging them in the sidebar.

Mixing and Matching Templates

Not everything needs to come from one template. You can:

- **Add pages** from other templates mid-project.
- Create **custom pages** that match the style of your chosen theme.
- Save modified pages as **"custom blocks"** to reuse later.

This is especially useful for recurring slide types like contact info, team bios, or product features.

Using Templates with Gamma AI: A Powerful Combo

Templates provide structure, but AI makes them smart. Together, they speed up content creation dramatically. Here's how you can combine both:

- Choose a **template for layout**
- Use **AI to generate** slide content for each page
- Use **"Rewrite," "Shorten," or "Summarize"** AI tools to polish and adapt your messaging

- Let the **AI assist with image suggestions**, layout tweaks, and even creating entirely new slides

It's like having a designer, writer, and assistant all in one.

Saving and Reusing Your Customized Template

Once you've customized a template to your liking, you don't have to redo everything next time.

- Click **"Save as Template"** to store your personalized version.

- Use it as a base for future presentations, keeping consistent branding and layout.

- Share it with your team so everyone is working from the same foundation.

Bonus Tip: You can also create different templates for different contexts—internal presentations, external decks, product overviews, etc.

Final Thoughts

Choosing and customizing templates in Gamma is both intuitive and powerful. Rather than wasting time wrestling with blank slides, you begin with a thoughtfully designed foundation and tweak it to fit your unique voice and purpose.

Whether you're a first-time presenter or a seasoned content creator, Gamma's templates offer the speed, elegance, and flexibility you need to bring your ideas to life—with style and substance.

2.1.3 Creating a Presentation from Scratch

Creating a presentation from scratch in **Gamma** allows for the greatest degree of creative control and customization. While Gamma's AI and templates offer an efficient starting point, there are times when you may want to build a presentation step-by-step with your own structure, voice, and design choices. Whether you're crafting a pitch deck, teaching material, a product walkthrough, or a personal portfolio, building from scratch ensures the final result is entirely yours.

This section will walk you through how to build a presentation from scratch using Gamma's intuitive tools and layout system, from setting up a new document to polishing and publishing it. Let's dive in.

Getting Started: Starting a Blank Presentation

1. **Accessing the Gamma Dashboard** Log in to gamma.app, and you'll arrive at your main dashboard. On this page, you'll see all your current workspaces and presentations. Click the **"+ Create"** button in the top-left corner or bottom-right floating button, and then choose **"Blank Presentation."**

2. **Naming Your Presentation** Gamma will prompt you to name your new document. Give it a title that reflects the purpose of your presentation. You can always rename it later by clicking on the title at the top of your workspace.

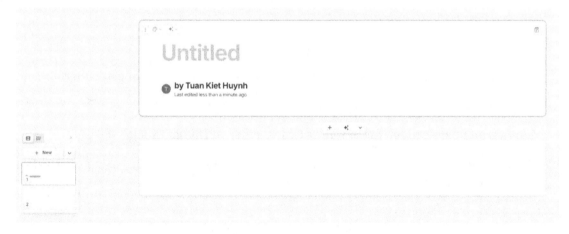

3. **Choosing a Layout Orientation (Optional)** While Gamma's layout is inherently responsive and web-friendly, you may choose a particular flow depending on

whether you want your content to feel more like slides or a long-form web document. You can adjust this by changing the **Page Type** settings.

Understanding the Gamma Building Blocks

When you start from scratch, you're essentially working with a modular content system. Gamma presentations are made of **Blocks**—think of them as intelligent content containers that can include text, images, embeds, charts, and more.

The key block types you'll use include:

- **Text Blocks** – Titles, paragraphs, bullet lists

- **Image Blocks** – Upload images or use AI-generated suggestions

- **Embed Blocks** – Videos, charts, links, social posts

- **Layout Blocks** – Columns, sections, and card-based designs

Each of these can be customized and rearranged with drag-and-drop precision.

Step-by-Step: Creating Sections and Slides

Let's walk through the process of building a slide-based presentation manually.

Step 1: Create the Title Slide

1. Click **"Add Block"** > **"Text"** > **"Title + Subtitle"** to create a strong opening.

2. Enter your main presentation title and subtitle or name.

3. Add an image or logo for branding by inserting an **Image Block**.

4. Optional: Add a call-to-action button like "Start" or "Let's Begin" using the **Button** element from the toolbar.

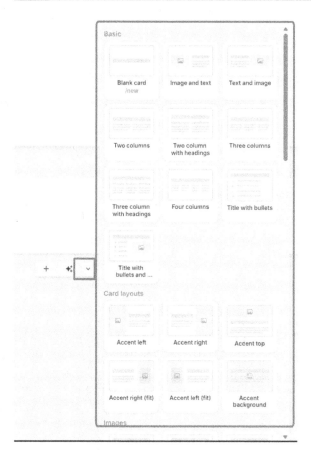

Step 2: Outline Your Content Structure

Before adding content, sketch an outline of your slides. Typical presentation structures include:

- Introduction
- Problem or Need
- Solution
- Key Features or Benefits
- Case Studies or Testimonials
- Pricing or Offer

- Call to Action

You can reflect this outline in your Gamma presentation by using **Section Headers** and separating each topic with a new slide or section.

To add a section title:

- Use **"Header"** blocks for new topics
- Use **Dividers** or new **Pages** to break up content

Step 3: Add Informational Slides

For each major point, create a new content block:

- **Text**: Use combinations of headers, paragraphs, and bullet lists.
- **Icons**: Use Gamma's built-in icon search to visualize key points.
- **Images**: Upload custom visuals or choose from built-in image suggestions or AI tools.
- **Layout Columns**: Display two- or three-column layouts for comparisons or side-by-side content.

To add a 2-column layout:

1. Click **"Add Block"**
2. Select **"Columns"** → choose **2 Columns**
3. Add text or images into each column

Step 4: Incorporate Visual Design

Gamma's built-in design tools allow you to control the look and feel of your presentation:

- **Themes**: Choose a theme or create your own to ensure consistent fonts and colors.

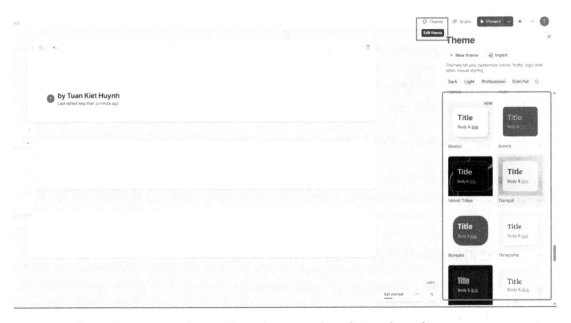

- **Color Palettes**: Match your brand or topic by editing the palette.

- **Typography**: Choose between modern, classic, or professional fonts depending on your tone.

Don't overcrowd slides. Instead, aim for simplicity—1 key idea per section—and support it visually.

Step 5: Add Interactivity

Gamma shines with its interactive content capabilities. Here's how to make your presentation more engaging:

- **Button Links**: Add a "Next" or "Back" button to control navigation.

- **Embedded Content**: Add YouTube videos, product demos, or Google Maps using the **Embed Block**.

- **Clickable Cards**: Present options or steps using linked cards that guide the user through the experience.

- **Internal Linking**: Link to other sections/slides to allow non-linear navigation (great for portfolios or product overviews).

Step 6: Organize and Rearrange Content

Once you've added several slides/sections:

- Use the **Outline View** or **Navigator** to drag and drop slides into the correct order.
- Combine slides or split sections using the contextual menu.
- Check for logical flow—does the story unfold naturally?

Gamma's smooth drag-and-drop system makes it easy to iterate and improve as you build.

Design Best Practices for Presentations from Scratch

Here are some tips to keep in mind as you design:

- **Consistency is Key**: Keep spacing, fonts, and colors consistent throughout.
- **Less is More**: Focus on clarity, not quantity—simplify your text.
- **Use White Space**: Don't be afraid to leave breathing room.
- **Balance Text and Visuals**: Alternate between narrative and visual-based slides.
- **Use Data Sparingly**: Only include charts if they truly support your message.

Polishing Your Presentation

Before sharing or publishing, review your work for:

- **Spelling and Grammar**: Use Gamma's built-in text editor or external tools.
- **Design Alignment**: Make sure everything aligns neatly—Gamma offers guides for precision.
- **Mobile and Web Preview**: Use the preview feature to see how your presentation looks on different devices.

You can also view your content in different **modes** (presentation, document, or page) depending on how you plan to share it.

Saving, Publishing, and Exporting

Once your presentation is complete:

1. **Click "Share"** in the top right

2. Choose whether to publish it publicly or share with select users

3. You can export as:

   o PDF

   o PowerPoint (PPTX)

   o Web link

   o Embeddable iframe

If you're collaborating, you can also invite team members to co-edit or comment on the project.

When Should You Build from Scratch?

While Gamma's AI and templates are time-saving, you may prefer to build from scratch when:

- You have a clear vision for your presentation flow

- You want complete creative control

- You're creating a custom client project or branded piece

- Your content is highly unique or non-linear

- You want to experiment with Gamma's full creative potential

Final Thoughts

Creating a presentation from scratch in Gamma is an empowering process. It allows you to build every block, define every transition, and control every moment of your audience's experience. As you become more comfortable with Gamma's modular system and design tools, you'll find that building beautiful, interactive, AI-enhanced presentations becomes second nature.

Whether you're making your first deck or refining a professional client pitch, starting from scratch gives you the freedom to design with purpose, creativity, and clarity.

2.2 Editing Slides and Layouts

2.2.1 Rearranging and Duplicating Slides

Creating an impactful presentation involves more than just typing content onto slides—it's about organizing your ideas clearly, logically, and in a visually appealing way. Once you've generated your initial draft in Gamma, whether through an AI prompt or by using a template, you'll likely need to fine-tune your slides. This includes **reordering them to improve flow** and **duplicating slides** when you want to reuse a specific format or structure.

In this section, we'll walk through the **how, why, and best practices** for rearranging and duplicating slides using Gamma's intuitive editing tools. You'll also learn tips for maintaining a clear narrative and how to make your workflow faster with these features.

📌 Why Rearranging and Duplicating Matter

Before diving into the *how*, let's explore the *why*. Rearranging slides allows you to:

- Create a **logical progression** of ideas
- Emphasize key points by placing them strategically
- Respond to **feedback or new insights** by adjusting the narrative
- Restructure long presentations into **digestible segments**

Duplicating slides, on the other hand, is extremely useful when you:

- Want to **reuse a design or layout** without starting from scratch
- Need to **highlight a different idea** using the same slide structure
- Are testing variations of content or design to see what works best
- Want to create **multiple language versions** of the same slide

Let's now look at how you can do all of this using Gamma.

☐ Navigating Gamma's Slide Structure

Before rearranging or duplicating slides, it's essential to understand how Gamma structures your presentation.

Unlike traditional presentation tools like PowerPoint or Google Slides, Gamma uses a **block-based layout**. Each presentation is built from a combination of "cards" or "pages," and within those, various layout blocks.

Slides in Gamma are stacked vertically in a scrollable format, and you can view all slides at once using the **Presentation Outline View or Sidebar View**.

☐☐ Rearranging Slides in Gamma

Step-by-Step: Rearranging Slides

1. **Access Slide List View**: On the left-hand side of your workspace, you'll find a vertical list of your presentation slides or pages. This is called the *Outline View*. It offers a quick way to understand the structure of your presentation.

2. **Click and Drag to Reorder**: To move a slide:

   o Hover over the slide thumbnail in the sidebar.

   o Click and **hold the slide** you want to move.

   o **Drag it up or down** to the desired position.

   o Release the mouse when you reach the correct spot.

3. **Observe the Visual Flow**: As you rearrange slides, Gamma updates the content instantly. You can **scroll through the full view** of the presentation to see how the new order impacts the story flow.

4. **Preview Your Presentation**: After reordering, click **Preview** to test how your presentation feels to a viewer. Does it flow well? Does the transition from one slide to the next make sense?

💡 Pro Tip:

Use Gamma's **Section Titles** to break your presentation into thematic segments. This will help you rearrange blocks of slides instead of doing it one-by-one.

☐ Duplicating Slides in Gamma

Sometimes, you may want to duplicate a slide to:

- Maintain consistent visual formatting

- Create variations of the same idea

- Make multilingual copies of the same content

- Save time when working with recurring sections (e.g., case studies, product features)

Step-by-Step: Duplicating Slides

1. **Select the Slide You Want to Duplicate**: From the Outline View on the left-hand side, locate the slide you'd like to copy.

2. **Click on the Three Dots (More Options)**: Hover over the slide thumbnail. Click the **"•••" icon** (also called the "More Options" menu) next to the slide title.

3. **Choose "Duplicate"**: From the dropdown menu, click **"Duplicate"**. A copy of the slide will immediately appear just below the original.

4. **Edit the New Slide**: The duplicate slide will contain all text, images, buttons, and layouts from the original. Simply click into it and begin editing your new version.

☐ Pro Tips:

- Rename the duplicate immediately to avoid confusion.

- Duplicates are great for **version testing**—keep one slide in the original format and tweak the duplicate to compare performance or feedback.

⚡☐ Using Keyboard Shortcuts for Efficiency

Gamma includes some **keyboard shortcuts** to speed up your workflow.

- **Duplicate a block**: Ctrl + D (or Cmd + D on Mac) when a block is selected.

- **Move slides**: While drag-and-drop is the main way, Gamma is developing keyboard-assisted navigation, so check for updates in the shortcut menu.

To view all shortcuts, press Shift + / or go to **Help > Keyboard Shortcuts** in the top right of the workspace.

☐ Rearranging and Duplicating Within a Slide

In Gamma, a single "slide" can contain multiple **content blocks** like headings, paragraphs, images, and columns. You can also rearrange and duplicate individual **blocks** within a slide, not just the slides themselves.

To Rearrange Blocks Within a Slide:

- Hover over the left edge of any block until the **block handle** appears.

- Click and drag the block up or down within the same slide.

To Duplicate a Block:

- Click the **three-dot menu** beside the block.

- Select **"Duplicate Block."**

This feature is especially helpful when building consistent layouts within the same slide—for example, listing features, testimonials, or FAQs.

☐ Maintaining Visual Consistency

When rearranging or duplicating slides, **design consistency** becomes even more important. Here are a few things to watch out for:

- **Fonts and Text Sizes**: Make sure duplicated slides keep consistent font choices and sizes.

- **Colors and Themes**: If you're using a specific visual theme, apply it uniformly across all slides, including duplicates.

- **Image Alignment**: Be mindful of image placement and alignment when duplicating visual-heavy slides.

- **Spacing and Layout**: Ensure padding and margins remain consistent for a clean look.

Gamma helps by preserving your existing layout styles when you duplicate, but always review before publishing.

📋 Checklist for Rearranging and Duplicating Slides

Here's a quick checklist to keep handy while working:

✓ Do the slides follow a logical narrative flow?
✓ Are call-to-actions (CTAs) placed at the right moments?
✓ Are duplicate slides updated clearly (titles, labels, content)?
✓ Have you avoided repetition that feels redundant?
✓ Is the design layout consistent throughout the slides?
✓ Have you previewed the full flow to check transitions?

📈 Real-World Scenarios

🖥️💼 Business Use Case:

A startup founder is creating a pitch deck. After writing out all their ideas using AI, they rearrange the slides to follow a classic pitch structure: problem > solution > product > traction > team > ask. They duplicate a product slide to tailor it for different investor groups (e.g., technical vs. market-focused).

🎓 Education Use Case:

A teacher creates a lesson presentation and wants to reuse the quiz format slide multiple times. They duplicate the quiz slide for different topics and update only the questions.

🚀 Summary

Rearranging and duplicating slides may seem like small tasks, but in Gamma, they are core components of building fluid, professional, and audience-friendly presentations.

By learning to quickly **reorganize your narrative** and **reuse strong designs**, you boost productivity and reduce friction in your creative process. Combined with Gamma's AI-powered tools, these editing techniques help you maintain both structure and flexibility—allowing your ideas to shine.

2.2.2 Adding Text, Images, and Media

Creating compelling presentations goes far beyond selecting a template. At the heart of any impactful slide is the content itself—the combination of thoughtfully crafted text, strategically placed images, and supporting media elements that work together to tell your story. In Gamma, these elements can be added, edited, and optimized with ease, thanks to its AI-enhanced, no-code interface. This section will walk you through every step of adding and managing content in your slides—from inserting a simple headline to embedding an engaging video.

Understanding Gamma's Content Structure

Before diving into the how-to, it's important to understand how Gamma organizes content. Each presentation is composed of slides (also known as "cards" in Gamma), and each slide is made up of *blocks*. Blocks are the foundational units of content and layout in Gamma. These can include text blocks, image blocks, media embeds, buttons, and more.

Unlike traditional slide software that relies heavily on manual placement, Gamma's blocks are *fluid*, automatically adjusting based on content and screen size—creating a web-like, responsive experience.

1. Adding Text to Your Slides

1.1 Types of Text Blocks

Gamma offers a few different types of text blocks to match your content needs:

- **Headings** – For slide titles or section titles.

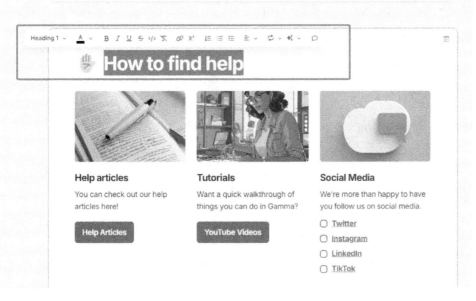

- **Body Text** – For paragraphs, explanations, or supporting information.

- **Bulleted and Numbered Lists** – For organizing ideas or outlining steps.

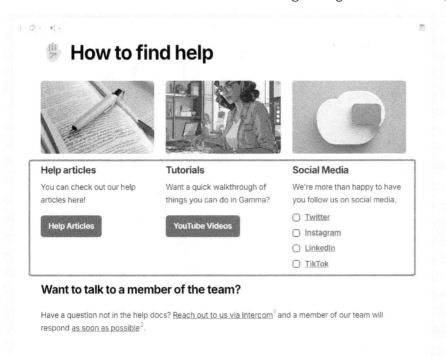

- **Quotes** – For emphasis or attribution.
- **Callouts** – Highlight key information using colored backgrounds or icons.

1.2 How to Insert Text

Step-by-Step Instructions:

1. Hover over an existing block or click the **+** icon to insert a new one.

2. From the block menu, choose **Text**.

3. Choose the type of text block you need (e.g., Heading, Body, List).

4. Click inside the block to start typing.

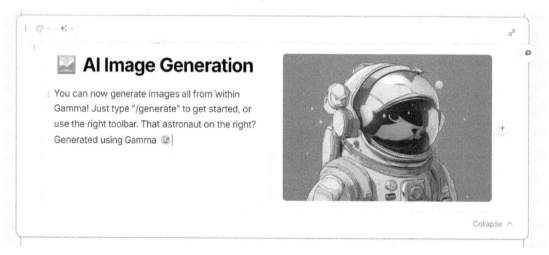

Gamma auto-formats your content depending on the type you choose, so you don't need to worry about spacing or alignment. It also provides keyboard shortcuts like:

- # followed by a space for headings
- - or * for bullet points
- > for quotes

1.3 Editing Text Styles

You can customize the appearance of your text by:

- Selecting the text and using the inline toolbar to **bold**, *italicize*, or **underline**.

- Changing alignment (left, center, right)

- Adding hyperlinks

- Using color and font style options from the style panel

1.4 Best Practices for Text

- **Keep It Concise**: Aim for one key message per slide.

- **Use Hierarchies**: Headings should stand out clearly from body text.

- **Focus on Readability**: Stick to legible fonts and avoid overloading with text.

- **Break It Up**: Use multiple blocks instead of long paragraphs.

2. Adding Images

Visuals are crucial to keeping your audience engaged. In Gamma, images are not just decorative—they're integrated into the design in a way that maintains a clean and responsive layout.

2.1 Ways to Add Images

Drag and Drop:

- Drag an image file from your desktop directly into the slide area.

Insert from Block Menu:

1. Click the **+** icon.

2. Select **Image**.

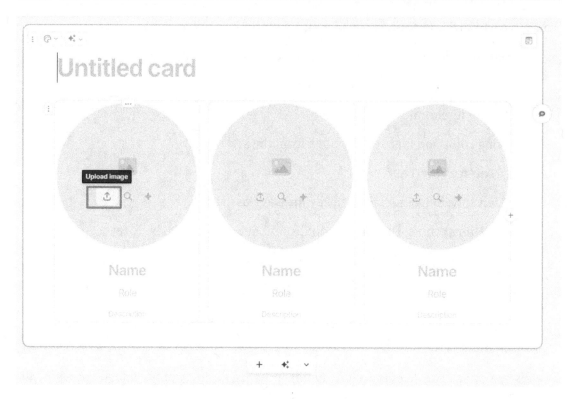

3. Choose from:

    o   Upload from device

    o   Search from Gamma's stock image library

    o   Paste an image URL

AI Image Suggestions: When you're using Gamma's AI to generate slides, it often suggests relevant images automatically, based on your text content.

2.2 Editing and Positioning Images

Once an image is inserted, you can:

- **Resize** by dragging the corners

- **Replace** with another image via right-click or toolbar

- **Adjust placement** by dragging the image block up or down

- **Add captions or alt-text** for accessibility

- **Wrap text** around images (auto-applied in some layouts)

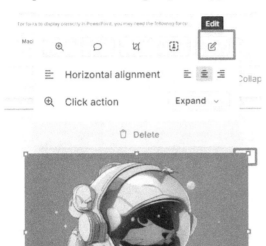

2.3 Using Gamma's Image Library

Gamma integrates with royalty-free image providers like Unsplash and Pexels, allowing you to:

- Search directly in the block
- Filter by category or theme
- Insert with one click

This is ideal for adding polished, high-quality images without having to leave the editor.

3. Adding Videos and Embedded Media

Interactive media makes presentations more engaging. Gamma supports embedded media including:

- YouTube Videos
- Vimeo Videos

- Loom Recordings

- Audio Clips

- GIFs and Animations

- Social Media Embeds (e.g., Tweets, LinkedIn posts)

3.1 Inserting a Video

To add a YouTube or Vimeo video:

1. Click the **+** icon.

2. Choose **Embed** or **Media**.

3. Paste the video link.

4. Gamma automatically detects and embeds the video into a responsive player.

For Loom: Loom integrates natively—just paste the link or use the Loom block to insert.

3.2 Customizing Media Layout

- Media embeds adapt to the width of the block container.

- You can set alignment (center, left, right).

- You can also insert a text block above or below the video for context or commentary.

3.3 Adding Audio

If you have an audio clip (e.g., a podcast snippet), Gamma allows audio file embedding through:

- Public audio URLs

- Spotify or SoundCloud links

Make sure audio files are hosted publicly; Gamma doesn't currently support uploading raw audio files directly.

3.4 Embedding Interactive Tools

Use embed blocks to add tools like:

- Google Maps
- Typeform surveys
- Calendly booking widgets
- Live documents (e.g., Google Docs)

This turns your slide deck into a dynamic, interactive microsite.

4. Combining Text, Images, and Media Effectively

Combining different content types well is essential for delivering a clean, coherent message. Gamma's layout engine helps ensure your content stays balanced and responsive, but here are some tips:

4.1 Use Layout Blocks

- Combine text + image side-by-side
- Use full-width media with centered call-to-actions
- Stack media above or below key messages

Use the pre-built layout options from the **"Layouts"** panel to speed up this process.

4.2 Maintain Visual Consistency

- Use a consistent style for headings and colors
- Avoid mixing too many media types on one slide
- Stick to a visual theme across the deck

4.3 Optimize for Engagement

- Use GIFs sparingly to highlight movement or emotion
- Videos should be under 2 minutes for best results
- Break longer content into multiple slides or cards

5. Accessibility and Performance Considerations

Gamma content is responsive and web-friendly, but here's how you can ensure accessibility and performance:

- **Add Alt-Text** to all images

- **Use Descriptive Titles** for each slide

- **Avoid Overloading Slides** with large files

- **Test Mobile View** using the built-in preview function

6. AI Assistance for Content Insertion

Don't forget Gamma's AI can help generate and place content:

- **"Add More" Button**: Suggests new blocks based on your previous text.

- **Auto-Caption**: Generates image descriptions.

- **Rewrite Tool**: Improves clarity or tone of your existing content.

Use AI as a helper—not a replacement—to speed up your creative process.

Conclusion: Mastering Multimedia in Gamma

Adding text, images, and media in Gamma is designed to be intuitive, dynamic, and powerful. Whether you're telling a story, pitching a product, or teaching a lesson, knowing how to use content blocks efficiently is a game-changer. With AI-powered assistance and a flexible design system, Gamma takes the heavy lifting out of multimedia creation, letting you focus on your message.

In the next section, we'll explore how to **save, preview, and publish your presentation**, ensuring that your content looks just as good when shared with the world.

2.2.3 Working with Layout Blocks

One of the most powerful features of Gamma lies in its unique **block-based design structure**, which provides both flexibility and clarity for users. Unlike traditional slide software that relies on freeform text boxes and manual formatting, Gamma organizes your content using **pre-built layout blocks**, allowing you to focus on the message while Gamma handles the design.

In this section, we'll take an in-depth look at how layout blocks work, how to customize them to suit your content, and best practices for using them effectively to create visually appealing and well-structured presentations.

What Are Layout Blocks in Gamma?

Layout blocks in Gamma are **modular content units** that can be added to any slide or page. Each block is designed with built-in formatting and structure, ensuring consistency throughout your presentation. Blocks help you build sections piece by piece — whether you're adding titles, bullet points, images, callouts, or comparisons.

This modular approach allows for more intuitive and scalable content creation. Instead of designing slide-by-slide, you build your story **block-by-block**, almost like building a web page.

Types of Layout Blocks

Gamma offers a variety of layout blocks tailored for different types of content. Understanding what each type does will help you choose the right one for your specific needs.

1. Text Blocks

These include:

- **Title and Subtitle Blocks**: Used for introducing a new section or concept.

- **Paragraph Blocks**: Ideal for elaborating ideas in a traditional narrative format.

- **Bullet Point Blocks**: Great for listing key takeaways, steps, or benefits.

- **Quote Blocks**: Useful for highlighting statements or testimonials.

2. Visual Blocks

These blocks allow you to bring images and media into your presentation:

- **Image Blocks**: Insert single or multiple images with automatic formatting.

- **Image + Text Blocks**: Combine visuals with explanatory text for storytelling.

- **Gallery Blocks**: Display multiple images in a grid or carousel.

3. Data Blocks

- **Comparison Blocks**: Display differences between two or more ideas side-by-side.

- **Table Blocks**: Insert structured data or comparisons.

- **Chart Blocks**: While still limited in Gamma compared to spreadsheet tools, you can add basic visualized data.

- **Progress or Stat Blocks**: Use percentages, counters, or KPIs to highlight achievements or goals.

4. Interactive Blocks

- **Button Blocks**: Add clickable buttons that link to other slides, documents, or websites.

- **Embed Blocks**: Include content like YouTube videos, Google Maps, or Forms directly into your presentation.

- **Link Cards**: Display external links in a visually appealing card format with preview images and descriptions.

5. Layout Enhancer Blocks

- **Divider Lines**: Add subtle lines to visually separate sections.

- **Spacer Blocks**: Adjust spacing between elements.

- **Containers**: Group multiple blocks together for easy movement and consistent formatting.

How to Add Layout Blocks

Adding a layout block in Gamma is as easy as clicking a "+" button.

Steps:

1. Hover over the area of a slide where you want to insert a new block.

2. Click the "**+**" icon that appears.

3. Choose the desired block type from the contextual menu.

4. Gamma will insert the block and allow you to start editing immediately.

You can also **drag and drop blocks** to rearrange them or use keyboard shortcuts for faster workflow.

Customizing Layout Blocks

Once a block is added, you can personalize it to match your content and design preferences.

1. Editing Text and Content

- Simply click on any text inside the block to edit it.

- Use **rich text formatting tools** like bold, italics, underline, bullet points, and hyperlinks.

- Keyboard shortcuts (like Ctrl+B for bold) are also supported.

2. Changing Block Styles

Each block can be customized with:

- **Text alignment** (left, center, right)
- **Font size and weight**
- **Background color or transparency**
- **Borders and padding**
- **Theme-based color palettes** to maintain brand consistency

Click the block, then choose the **"Style" or "Design" panel** on the side or above the block to access these options.

3. Adjusting Layout Orientation

Some blocks offer orientation choices — horizontal vs. vertical layouts, side-by-side content, or stacked columns. Gamma often uses **responsive design logic**, which adapts layout automatically for web or mobile viewing.

4. Replacing or Rearranging Media

If your block contains images, you can:

- Upload a new image
- Choose from **Gamma's stock photo library**
- Drag and drop files from your desktop
- Replace or reposition images within the block

Using Layout Blocks to Structure a Slide

A typical Gamma slide can include **multiple blocks** stacked vertically. Here's how to think about slide composition using blocks:

Slide Example: Introducing a Product Feature

1. **Title Block** – "New Smart Feature"
2. **Image + Text Block** – Showing a screenshot and short description
3. **Bullet Block** – Listing benefits or functionalities

4. **Quote Block** – User feedback or testimonial

5. **Button Block** – "Learn More" call to action

Using layout blocks in this way helps **tell a story visually**, with each block acting like a paragraph in your narrative.

Best Practices for Using Layout Blocks

✅ Plan Your Content Before You Build

Think of each slide as a "chapter" and each block as a "sentence." Have a clear idea of what you want to communicate before you start adding blocks.

✅ Be Consistent with Formatting

Use consistent block types for similar content. For example, always use the **same block style** for quotes or statistics across the presentation.

✅ Don't Overcrowd Slides

Gamma lets you build vertically, so don't cram too many ideas into one slide. Use more slides and let each block breathe.

✅ Use AI to Help Fill Content

When adding a text block, you can activate Gamma's AI writing assistant to generate, summarize, or rewrite text based on a prompt — saving you time and helping spark creativity.

✅ Use Containers for Complex Layouts

When combining multiple elements (e.g., side-by-side image + text + button), containers help maintain alignment and make group adjustments easier.

Common Mistakes to Avoid

✖ Using Too Many Block Types at Once

It may be tempting to try every block available, but this can lead to a chaotic layout. Stick to a few complementary types that suit your content.

✕ Forgetting Mobile Responsiveness

Gamma pages are often viewed as scrollable web experiences. Avoid blocks that rely on side-by-side text-heavy layouts that may not render well on smaller screens.

✕ Ignoring Alignment and Spacing

Proper use of spacer blocks and alignment settings ensures a clean, professional look. Don't rely on default padding—adjust it when necessary for visual balance.

Tips for Efficient Block-Based Workflow

- **Duplicate Existing Blocks:** Save time by duplicating a styled block instead of rebuilding it.

- **Use Gamma's Templates:** Pre-designed slides already contain optimized block arrangements—customize them instead of starting from scratch.

- **Drag-and-Drop Navigation:** You can reorganize entire blocks across your deck by dragging them from the slide navigator.

- **Copy-Paste Across Decks:** You can copy layout blocks from one presentation to another, preserving design and structure.

Conclusion

Mastering layout blocks is a key step toward becoming proficient in Gamma. These building blocks form the **foundation of your content structure**, providing visual clarity, modularity, and scalability. Whether you're crafting a sleek startup pitch, a product one-pager, or an interactive course module, layout blocks allow you to **focus on your ideas** while Gamma takes care of the formatting.

By using layout blocks effectively, you'll elevate your presentations from static slides to dynamic visual stories — faster, easier, and more beautifully than ever before.

2.3 Saving and Previewing Your Work

2.3.1 Auto-Save and Version History

When working with any digital content creation tool, one of the most important habits you can develop is saving your work regularly. Fortunately, Gamma removes the burden of manual saving through its powerful **auto-save** feature, allowing you to focus on creativity rather than file management. However, understanding how auto-save and **version history** work in Gamma is essential to working confidently and efficiently—especially when you need to revert or reference previous versions of your presentation.

This section will walk you through how Gamma handles saving, where to find version history, how to use it effectively, and tips for managing revisions in collaborative environments.

Understanding Auto-Save in Gamma

Gamma is a **cloud-native** platform, meaning all your content is automatically stored and updated online in real time. The moment you make an edit—whether it's adding a sentence, changing a color, or moving a block—Gamma begins saving those changes in the background.

How Auto-Save Works

- **Instant Sync:** Every keystroke, edit, or interaction is captured instantly. You don't have to press a "Save" button at any point.

- **No Manual Save Option:** Unlike traditional applications like Microsoft PowerPoint, there is no manual "Save" function. This reduces user error and the risk of data loss due to forgetting to save.

- **Cloud-Backed Reliability:** Your work is safely stored in the cloud, meaning you can access it from any device as long as you're logged in to your Gamma account.

This always-on auto-save ensures that even if your browser crashes, your latest changes are preserved. Still, it's helpful to know how to recover previous states—and that's where version history comes in.

Why Version History Matters

Although auto-save is convenient, it can sometimes record changes you didn't mean to make—or capture edits made by someone else on your team. Gamma's **version history** feature serves as a built-in time machine, letting you:

- View previous states of your presentation.

- Restore an earlier version if something goes wrong.

- Compare current and past content to understand how your ideas have evolved.

- Manage multiple collaborators editing the same file.

Version history is especially useful during the **drafting** and **feedback** phases of content creation, where changes can be frequent and sometimes experimental.

Accessing Version History

Gamma makes it easy to access your version history. Here's how to locate and use it:

Step-by-Step: Viewing Version History

1. **Open Your Presentation:** Navigate to your project from the workspace dashboard.

2. **Click the "..." (More Options) Menu:** This is usually located at the top-right of your screen, beside the share or publish options.

3. **Select "Version History":** A new panel or window will appear displaying a chronological list of saved versions.

🔍 **Note:** Each version is time-stamped and typically includes the name of the user who made the changes if you're working on a shared file.

Navigating the Version Timeline

Once you're inside the version history view, you'll see a list or timeline of all the saved iterations of your document. You can click through these snapshots to see what your presentation looked like at each point in time.

Key Features in the Version Timeline

- **Timestamps:** Clearly indicate when changes were saved.

- **User Activity:** In team environments, the system shows which user made each set of changes.

- **Live Preview:** You can preview a version before restoring it, ensuring you're reverting to the correct point.

- **Version Naming:** In some cases, you may be allowed to name important versions (e.g., "Final Draft", "Client Feedback Incorporated") for easier reference.

This functionality is especially helpful when collaborating with a team where multiple edits happen quickly.

Restoring a Previous Version

If you find that your current version is not working—or you simply prefer the way something looked before—you can easily roll back.

Step-by-Step: Restoring a Version

1. Open **Version History**.

2. Navigate to the version you want to restore.

3. Click on it to preview the contents.

4. Click **"Restore This Version"**.

✓ Once restored, that version becomes the **current live version** of your presentation. Gamma saves the restored version as a new entry in the history, so you never truly lose anything.

Best Practices for Working with Auto-Save and Version History

To get the most out of Gamma's saving and version control capabilities, consider the following tips:

1. Embrace Auto-Save, But Review Periodically

Trust Gamma's auto-save, but check your presentation periodically—especially after long editing sessions or collaborative inputs—to ensure everything looks the way you want it to.

2. Use Version History as a Creative Timeline

Sometimes the journey is just as important as the result. You can use version history to reflect on your creative process and even revisit discarded ideas that turn out to be useful.

3. Name Milestone Versions (If Possible)

If Gamma allows custom version names, use this to your advantage. For example, label important moments such as:

- "Initial Draft"

- "After Team Review"

- "Client-Approved Version"

This practice creates a navigable history of your project's development.

4. Restore With Care

Before restoring, always preview the version to ensure it contains what you need. Restoring automatically makes that version current, which can overwrite newer edits.

5. Communicate in Collaborative Workflows

If you're working with others, let your team know when you're making major changes or reverting to an earlier version. This avoids confusion and ensures alignment.

Common Questions About Auto-Save and Version History

Q1: Can I manually save my presentation?

No. Gamma is built on a fully automatic saving system. There is no manual "Save" button, and all changes are saved instantly to the cloud.

Q2: Can I download or export a specific version?

Depending on Gamma's export options, you may be able to download any version as a PDF or PPT. Always preview the version before exporting.

Q3: What happens if I restore the wrong version?

You can always go back again. Gamma records the restore as another entry in version history, so you can undo a restoration by selecting the next most recent version.

Q4: How far back does version history go?

Typically, Gamma maintains a generous backlog, especially for active projects. However, older or inactive files may have a limited history. It's good practice to periodically duplicate or export important versions.

Using Version History in Team Collaboration

In team environments, version control becomes even more crucial. Here's how Gamma's tools support collaboration:

- **See Who Made What Changes:** Gamma shows the editor's name with each version.

- **Coordinate Edits:** If you and your team are working on different sections, reviewing the version history can help avoid overwriting each other's work.

- **Conflict Resolution:** If conflicting edits occur, you can compare versions and decide which one to keep.

Final Thoughts

Gamma's auto-save and version history features are designed to empower creators to move fast, iterate freely, and recover from missteps without losing valuable work. Whether you're editing solo or collaborating with a team, these tools provide peace of mind and help maintain the integrity of your content throughout the creative process.

By understanding and using these features effectively, you can streamline your workflow and take full advantage of Gamma's intelligent platform.

✅ **Next Up:** In the next section, we'll explore how to **preview your presentation like a viewer**, check for errors, and get it ready to publish or share with the world.

2.3.2 Previewing Your Presentation

Previewing your presentation in Gamma is a critical step in the content creation process. While creating with AI can help you build presentations quickly and beautifully, it's the preview phase that allows you to evaluate, fine-tune, and polish your work before sharing it with your audience. This section will guide you through all aspects of previewing in Gamma, including what it is, why it's essential, how to use it effectively, and the best practices to follow to ensure your final product is audience-ready.

What Does "Previewing" Mean in Gamma?

In Gamma, **previewing** refers to the ability to view your presentation as your audience would see it — free from editing tools, overlays, and design grids. It allows you to experience the flow, readability, and visual impact of your content in its most authentic form.

Unlike traditional presentation tools where previewing often means entering a separate "slideshow" mode, Gamma's interface offers a more **fluid and web-like preview experience**. This reflects the modern, browser-based nature of Gamma presentations, which are meant to be interactive, scrollable, and responsive.

Why Previewing Is Important

Whether you're building a business pitch, a classroom report, or an interactive portfolio, previewing helps you:

- **Ensure content coherence**: Spot awkward transitions, text overload, or irrelevant visuals.

- **Check visual hierarchy**: Make sure the most important messages stand out.

- **Review interactivity**: Confirm that links, buttons, and embedded media function correctly.

- **Test user flow**: Understand how your audience will move from one idea to the next.

- **Evaluate mobile responsiveness**: Many Gamma presentations will be viewed on phones or tablets.

Skipping this step can result in sharing content that looks cluttered, disconnected, or confusing. Gamma's preview tool ensures your work is professional, clear, and compelling.

How to Enter Preview Mode

To preview your presentation in Gamma, follow these steps:

1. **Locate the Preview Icon**: In the top right corner of the editing interface, you'll find a small "eye" icon or a button labeled **"Present"**. This is your gateway to preview mode.

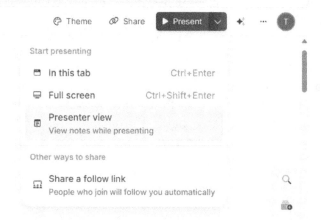

2. **Click the Preview Button**: Once clicked, Gamma instantly loads the presentation in its fully rendered state. This view hides all editing tools, sidebars, and toolbars.

3. **Interact as a Viewer**

   o Scroll naturally to explore your content.

   o Hover over interactive elements like buttons or links to ensure they behave as expected.

   o Click through any embedded navigation to test internal linking.

   o Play any embedded media or animations.

4. **Exit Preview Mode**: To return to the editing screen, click the "Exit Preview" or simply hit **Esc** (Escape) on your keyboard.

💡 **Tip**: You can also enter preview mode using keyboard shortcuts if enabled in your workspace settings.

Understanding the Preview Environment

Gamma's preview view mimics the final product across multiple platforms. Here's what you'll notice:

- **Scroll-based Layout**: Unlike slide-by-slide tools, Gamma treats your presentation more like a vertical story or webpage. This is ideal for narrative flow and modern storytelling.

- **Responsive Design**: Your preview adapts to various screen sizes. Resize your browser window to test how the content responds.

- **Embedded Functionality**: Embedded videos, audio clips, Google Docs, and surveys remain interactive and functional in preview mode.

Previewing on Different Devices

Gamma is designed to be **mobile-friendly**. You can preview your presentation on:

- **Desktop**: Full layout experience with wide-screen formatting.

- **Tablet**: Mid-sized layout; good for touch interaction testing.

- **Mobile Phone**: Essential for ensuring readability and navigation.

To simulate mobile views:

- Resize your browser window manually to a narrow width, or

- Use your browser's **Developer Tools (F12)** to toggle between device views (e.g., iPhone, Android).

▯ **Mobile-First Consideration**: Always ensure headings, text, and media elements are not too crowded on small screens.

What to Look for During Preview

When previewing your presentation, follow this mental checklist:

1. Flow and Navigation

- Are sections logically organized?

- Do transitions between points feel natural?

- Are navigation links working properly?

2. Visual Design

- Are fonts readable on all screen sizes?
- Are colors consistent and visually balanced?
- Is there sufficient white space?

3. Interactivity

- Do all buttons function as expected?
- Are external links opening in new tabs?
- Do embedded media elements play correctly?

4. Content Quality

- Is your messaging clear?
- Are there any typos or grammar issues?
- Is the tone appropriate for the audience?

5. Performance

- Does the presentation load quickly?
- Are animations smooth?
- Are large media files slowing anything down?

Real-World Example: Previewing a Startup Pitch Deck

Let's say you're building a pitch deck for a tech startup using Gamma. Your preview steps might look like this:

1. **Scan for narrative flow** — Do your slides tell a cohesive story from problem to solution to product demo to financials?

2. **Check for emphasis** — Are your investor highlights like traction metrics and team credentials easily visible?

3. **Test call-to-action buttons** — Do they lead to your contact form or Calendly page?

4. **Simulate a mobile viewer** — Can a VC read it easily from their phone during travel?

Troubleshooting During Preview

If something looks off during preview, don't worry. Here's how to fix common issues:

Issue	Solution
Text is overlapping or cut off	Revisit layout settings and increase padding or line spacing
Button not working	Double-check the link URL and test in incognito mode
Media not playing	Ensure you've embedded the correct URL and that the host platform allows it
Layout shifts on mobile	Simplify columns or use stacking layout blocks
Content feels too long	Consider splitting into sections or multiple presentations

Best Practices for Effective Previewing

- **Preview Early, Preview Often**: Don't wait until the end of your editing process. Preview after major content or design changes.

- **Get External Eyes**: Ask a colleague or friend to preview and give feedback.

- **Use a Checklist**: Create your own QA list based on your project goals.

- **Preview in Different Browsers**: Especially if your audience includes corporate users who may not be using Chrome.

- **Combine Preview with Share Testing**: Copy your presentation link and open it in a new browser window to simulate a real user experience.

When to Move On from Previewing

Previewing shouldn't be endless. Once you've reviewed content, fixed issues, and verified interactivity, you're ready to:

- **Publish or Share** your Gamma presentation

- **Export it** if needed (PDF, PNG, etc.)

- **Embed it** in a website or portfolio

- **Schedule or deliver** it in a meeting or event

Knowing when to stop tinkering is part of being a confident creator. Remember, Gamma is designed to help you produce professional presentations quickly — so trust the process and ship your work when it's ready!

Conclusion: Why Previewing Is Your Final Superpower

Think of previewing not as a final chore, but as a **final creative tool**. It's the lens through which your audience will view everything you've crafted — and it's your last chance to ensure that your ideas, your voice, and your design shine together in harmony.

With just a few clicks, you can transform a good presentation into a great one — simply by taking a moment to step into your audience's shoes.

So next time you finish editing in Gamma, don't rush to hit "Share" right away. Pause. Preview. Polish. Then present with confidence.

2.3.3 Publishing Options

Once you've created and fine-tuned your presentation in Gamma, the final step is to **publish it**—to make it viewable, shareable, and impactful. Publishing in Gamma doesn't just mean saving a file or exporting a PDF like in traditional tools; it opens the door to **web-ready, interactive, and intelligently structured content**. This section will walk you through all available publishing options in Gamma, along with step-by-step guidance, best practices, and strategic tips to make your work shine.

What Does "Publishing" Mean in Gamma?

In Gamma, publishing refers to making your content publicly or privately accessible outside the Gamma editor. When you publish a presentation, it becomes a **responsive webpage-like experience**, shareable via a simple link, embeddable in websites, or downloadable in traditional formats.

Unlike older tools where you need to convert your work for different channels, Gamma allows **multi-format publishing** with minimal friction. Whether you're preparing a client pitch, a classroom presentation, or an online portfolio, Gamma gives you flexible publishing modes tailored to your goals.

1. Publishing as a Web Link

Step-by-Step Instructions:

1. **Click on "Share"** in the top-right corner of your presentation.

2. Choose the **"Publish" tab** from the sharing options.

3. Select **"Generate Public Link."**

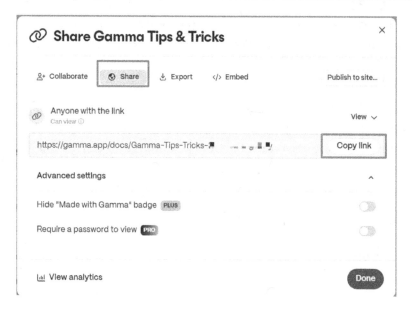

4. Choose your **privacy settings**:

   o *Public on the web*: Anyone with the link can view.

   o *Unlisted*: Only those with the link can access; it's not searchable.

   o *Restricted*: Only invited collaborators or authenticated users can view.

5. Click **"Copy Link"** and share it via email, social platforms, or embed it anywhere you like.

Benefits:

- Instantly accessible on all devices (mobile, tablet, desktop).
- Interactive elements remain fully functional.
- Perfect for real-time collaboration or asynchronous reviews.
- Seamless sharing in remote team settings.

Use Case Examples:

- A product manager shares a new feature roadmap with stakeholders.
- A marketing team publishes a campaign overview to clients.
- A teacher shares lecture slides with students via an LMS or class website.

2. Embedding Your Presentation

How It Works:

Gamma allows you to **embed your content** in external websites, blogs, portfolios, or internal dashboards using HTML code. This is ideal for showcasing content on your own platform while preserving the interactivity and layout of your Gamma presentation.

Steps to Embed:

1. Click **"Share"** > **"Publish"** and enable public access.

2. Click on **"Embed"** or look for the HTML <iframe> code.

3. Copy the embed code.

4. Paste it into your website's HTML editor or CMS (e.g., WordPress, Squarespace, Notion, etc.).

Customization Tips:

- Adjust **width and height parameters** for better layout control.

- Use **responsive containers** in your site to ensure it scales on all screens.

- Add titles or context around the embed to help viewers understand what they're looking at.

Example Use Cases:

- Designers embed a digital portfolio on their personal website.

- Nonprofits showcase reports and data visuals in blog posts.

- Startups add product decks to their investor pages.

3. Exporting as PDF or PowerPoint

Although Gamma is designed as a modern web-first tool, sometimes you need to **export your content in traditional formats**—for offline sharing, printing, or formal documentation. Gamma makes this easy.

Export Options:

- **Download as PDF**

  o Best for static, printable versions.

  o Maintains layout integrity.

- **Download as PowerPoint (.pptx)**

  o Allows further editing in Microsoft PowerPoint or Google Slides.

  o Useful for organizations that still rely on traditional slide software.

Steps to Export:

1. Click the **"Share"** icon in the top-right corner.

2. Select **"Download"**.

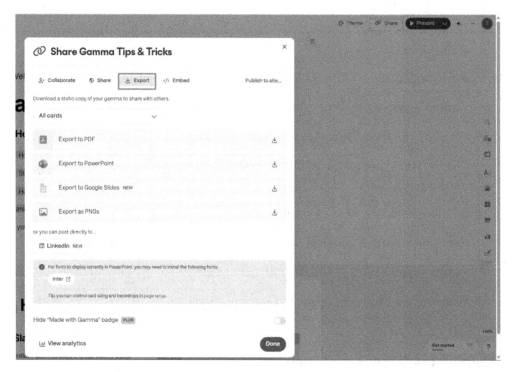

3. Choose your preferred format: *PDF* or *PPTX*.

4. Configure settings (e.g., page size, slide range).

5. Click **"Download"** and wait for the file to generate.

Best Practices:

- Use PDF for **archival or print sharing**.

- Use PPTX when **collaborating with teams** outside Gamma.

- Always preview before exporting to catch layout issues.

4. Creating a Shareable Microsite

Gamma's publishing system allows your presentation to become more than a deck—it can function as a **mini-website**. By linking sections or blocks, adding interactive elements, and grouping related decks, you can create a cohesive microsite experience.

Use Case:

- You're launching a new product and want to create a **one-page overview** with links to deeper details (e.g., feature pages, demo videos, case studies).

- You're preparing a portfolio that includes **multiple presentations**, each targeting a different audience.

Features to Explore:

- **Linking buttons or text** to other Gamma pages.

- **Navigation blocks** for multi-section experiences.

- Custom branding with logos, colors, and fonts.

How to Publish as a Microsite:

1. Structure your presentation like a website (home → sections).

2. Use interactive links/buttons to simulate page navigation.

3. Publish using the public link.

4. Embed on a custom domain (if supported by Gamma at the time).

5. Controlling Access and Permissions

Gamma gives you granular control over **who can see and interact** with your content. This is vital for protecting sensitive work or controlling information flow during product launches, client reviews, or internal briefings.

Access Levels:

- **Viewer Only**: Can see content but not comment or edit.

- **Commenter**: Can view and leave comments.

- **Editor**: Can make changes directly.

- **Owner**: Full access and permissions.

Password Protection (if available):

Some publishing modes allow you to **add password protection** to limit access even further. This is useful for sensitive financial reports, client presentations, or confidential documentation.

---

6. Real-Time Updates and Auto-Sync

One of the standout features of Gamma publishing is its **live-update capability**. When you edit a presentation that's already published via a public link or embedded somewhere, the changes are reflected **instantly**—no need to re-upload or resend anything.

How It Helps:

- Fix typos, update data, or add sections without resending a new file.

- Ideal for time-sensitive materials.

- Improves consistency across teams and platforms.

---

7. Choosing the Right Publishing Strategy

Ask Yourself:

- Is this for internal use or public sharing?

- Does the audience expect a polished static document or an interactive experience?

- Will people view this on desktop or mobile devices?

- Is further editing or collaboration expected?

Publishing Matrix:

Goal	Recommended Option
Client presentation	Public link + restricted access
Online portfolio	Embed in personal website
Offline review	Export to PDF
Team collaboration	Shared editable workspace
Product launch landing page	Microsite layout with internal links

Final Tips for Effective Publishing

- **Preview your content** before sharing widely.
- Always check how it looks on **mobile and desktop**.
- Keep your **link names descriptive** and organized.
- Track **viewer engagement** (if supported) to see what works.

Summary

Publishing your Gamma presentation is not the end of your creative journey—it's the moment it **comes to life**. Whether you're pitching a product, educating a class, or building a digital showcase, Gamma's publishing tools allow you to tailor the presentation to your needs. From a simple shared link to a fully interactive microsite, you control how your story is delivered.

Gamma turns the act of publishing into a **powerful extension of your content strategy**, combining accessibility, design, and interactivity in one seamless platform. Mastering these publishing options is key to creating work that doesn't just look good—but gets seen, shared, and remembered.

CHAPTER III
Enhancing Content with AI

3.1 Using AI to Generate Content

3.1.1 Generating Sections and Ideas

Creating compelling presentations is no longer a task reserved for design-savvy professionals. With Gamma's AI-powered content generation, even beginners can create structured, engaging presentations in minutes. In this section, we'll dive deep into how you can leverage Gamma's artificial intelligence to generate well-organized sections and content ideas with ease.

Whether you're working on a business pitch, a lesson plan, or a personal project, Gamma's AI helps you overcome the blank-page syndrome by providing structured outlines, creative suggestions, and fully-formed slides. Let's walk through how it works — and how to make the most of it.

Understanding the Power of AI in Content Generation

At its core, Gamma's AI is trained to understand user intent from minimal input. You give it a prompt — a topic, a goal, a rough idea — and it generates a multi-section presentation that can include titles, text, bullet points, and even suggestions for images or callouts. This dramatically speeds up the creation process while also helping you think through the flow and logic of your presentation.

Benefits of Using AI for Generating Sections and Ideas:

- **Time-Saving:** What used to take hours of planning can now take minutes.

- **Inspiration:** AI helps you think outside your typical patterns.

- **Structure:** It ensures a logical flow from introduction to conclusion.

- **Consistency:** Generated content follows clean, professional formatting.

Step-by-Step: Generating Sections with AI

Let's explore how to generate sections using Gamma's AI, step by step:

Step 1: Starting a New Presentation

1. From your Gamma dashboard, click **"Create New AI"**.

2. Select **"Generate"** from the available options.

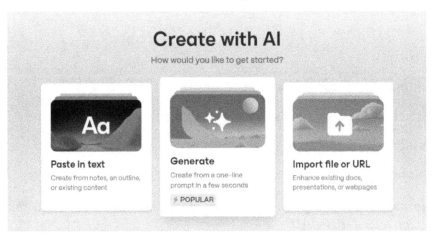

3. You'll be prompted to enter a **short prompt or topic idea**.

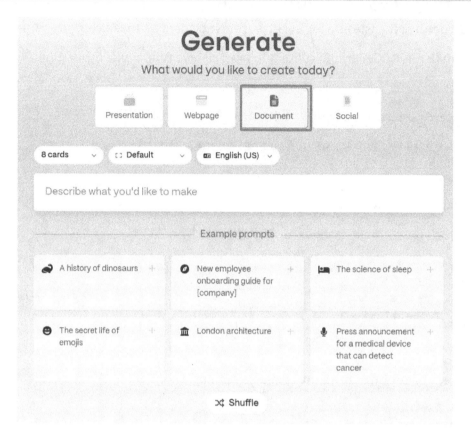

Examples of prompts:

- "The future of renewable energy"
- "How to build a startup from scratch"
- "Introduction to digital marketing"
- "A beginner's guide to investing"

✅ *Tip: Be clear and specific. If you know your audience, mention it (e.g., "Explaining blockchain to high school students").*

Step 2: Letting AI Work Its Magic

Once you submit your prompt:

- Gamma generates a **full outline**, typically with 5–7 main sections.
- Each section contains one or more **prewritten slides**, often including:
  - A title
  - Short introductory paragraph
  - Bullet points or callouts
  - Suggested visuals or layout

The output is editable immediately. You can accept, modify, or delete any part of the AI's proposal.

Step 3: Refining the Structure

Now that you have your AI-generated sections, it's time to refine:

- **Evaluate the flow:** Does the order of sections make sense?
- **Merge or split:** Combine two similar sections or split longer ones.
- **Rename titles:** Make sure each section title aligns with your voice and intent.
- **Add transitions:** Insert connecting slides to maintain narrative flow.

🔍 *Example: If the AI generates a section titled "Benefits of Solar Energy," you might rename it to "Why Solar Energy is the Future" if that fits your tone better.*

Making the Most of AI-Generated Ideas

Generating content is just the start — how you use it matters. Below are strategies to maximize value from AI-generated sections:

1. Use It as a Jumping-Off Point

Sometimes the content generated by AI is spot-on. Other times, it gives you a useful but generic structure. Use these outputs to spark your thinking. Ask yourself:

- What's missing?

- Can I bring in personal experience or original data?
- What would surprise or interest my audience?

2. Combine AI with Manual Research

For deeper topics, especially those that require up-to-date data or industry-specific terms, combine the AI's structure with your own insights. For instance:

- Use the AI to outline a section on "Digital Advertising Channels"
- Then insert fresh data from recent studies or case examples

3. Brainstorm with AI Iteratively

Don't stop at one prompt. Try several versions:

- Prompt 1: "History of social media"
- Prompt 2: "Impact of social media on teenagers"
- Prompt 3: "The psychology behind social media addiction"

Each prompt gives you different angles. Gamma lets you **duplicate and mix** ideas from different outputs into one master presentation.

4. Collaborate Around the Generated Structure

Once AI has produced a starting framework, invite collaborators to refine it. Team members can:

- Add speaker notes
- Modify visual suggestions
- Replace placeholder content with real examples

This is especially powerful in remote teams or class projects.

Tips for Crafting Better Prompts

Garbage in, garbage out — the quality of your AI results heavily depends on the quality of your input. Here are prompt-writing tips to generate stronger content structures:

Weak Prompt	Improved Prompt
"Marketing"	"An overview of digital marketing strategies for small businesses"
"Leadership"	"How first-time managers can develop effective leadership skills"
"Sales techniques"	"Modern sales techniques for B2B tech startups in 2025"

☐ *AI is only as specific as you ask it to be. More context = better slides.*

Real-World Examples: Prompt to Presentation

Let's walk through two full examples.

Example 1: Business Strategy Presentation

Prompt: "Strategic planning for startups"

AI Output:

1. Introduction to Startup Strategy
2. Vision and Mission Clarity
3. Market Analysis Essentials
4. Business Model Design
5. Setting SMART Goals
6. Measuring Success

Each section includes key points, such as how to define a vision, ways to conduct SWOT analysis, and how to track key performance indicators (KPIs). With minor edits, the presentation is ready for investors or internal planning.

Example 2: Educational Content

Prompt: "Photosynthesis explained for middle school students"

AI Output:

1. What is Photosynthesis?

2. Why is it Important?

3. The Key Ingredients: Sunlight, Water, CO_2

4. Inside the Leaf: The Chloroplast

5. Step-by-Step: The Process

6. Fun Facts and Review Quiz

Gamma generates a kid-friendly tone with analogies like "plants eat sunlight for breakfast." You can add visuals, video embeds, or even quizzes using Gamma's interactive tools.

Limitations and How to Overcome Them

AI is powerful — but not perfect. Here are a few common challenges and how to work around them:

Challenge	Solution
Content is too generic	Edit for originality; add your own insights
Misses key details	Supplement with research or custom sections
Doesn't understand niche topics	Be more specific in your prompt, or build on AI's skeleton manually

---

Conclusion: AI as Your Creative Assistant

Gamma's AI-generated sections and content ideas are like working with a smart assistant. It doesn't replace your creativity — it **amplifies** it.

By mastering the art of crafting clear prompts and knowing how to build on AI's suggestions, you'll create high-quality, structured presentations in a fraction of the time it used to take. In the next section, we'll explore how to go beyond ideas and use Gamma's AI to **rewrite, summarize, and expand** your content dynamically.

✅ **Next Up:** *3.1.2 Rewriting and Summarizing Text*

3.1.2 Rewriting and Summarizing Text

Artificial Intelligence (AI) can do more than just generate new ideas—it can also help refine and distill your content for clarity, tone, and brevity. In this section, we'll explore how Gamma's AI rewriting and summarizing features can elevate your presentations, making them sharper, more impactful, and better suited for your audience.

Understanding the Power of Rewriting and Summarization

Before diving into the "how," let's understand the "why." Presentations aren't just about stuffing information onto slides—they're about communicating effectively. Often, the way we initially write something may be:

- **Too long** or filled with unnecessary details
- **Too technical** for a general audience
- **Not engaging** or persuasive
- **Lacking structure** or clarity

Gamma's AI tools are designed to help you **refine your writing** and **optimize content** based on your intent. Whether you're creating a persuasive pitch, a product summary, or an educational presentation, these tools act as a smart editor working alongside you.

Key Benefits of Rewriting and Summarizing in Gamma

1. **Time Efficiency**: You don't need to start from scratch every time. Use Gamma to iterate quickly by refining rough drafts.

2. **Improved Clarity**: Simplify complicated sentences for a broader audience without losing the core message.

3. **Consistency of Tone**: Whether you're aiming for formal, friendly, or professional, Gamma helps align the tone across your content.

4. **Focus and Brevity**: Summarization helps reduce wordiness, keeping your slides concise and visually clean.

How to Rewrite Text with Gamma

Rewriting with Gamma is a simple, intuitive process that involves a few key steps. Here's how you can get started:

Step 1: Select the Text You Want to Rewrite

Start by highlighting or selecting any text block within your slide. You can do this in any text-based element, including paragraph blocks, bullet points, or headers.

Step 2: Open the AI Assistant

When you select text, Gamma's AI toolbar typically appears, giving you options like:

- ✦ Rewrite

- ✂️ Summarize

- 🎯 Shorten

- 🖊️ Expand

- 🎨 Change Tone

Click on **"Rewrite"** to begin the rewriting process.

Step 3: Choose Your Rewrite Style

Once you select "Rewrite," Gamma will often give you options based on your goals. For example:

- Rewrite to be **clearer**

- Rewrite to be **more concise**

- Rewrite to be **more persuasive**

- Rewrite for a **specific tone** (e.g., professional, casual, confident)

You can pick one of the suggested styles or use the custom prompt feature to tell the AI *exactly* how you'd like the text to be rewritten.

Step 4: Review the Suggested Rewrites

Gamma will generate one or more rewritten versions of your original text. Each version maintains the core message but presents it in a different way—perhaps more clearly, more persuasively, or more concisely.

You can:

- **Accept** a suggestion to replace the original text
- **Edit** the suggestion further
- **Regenerate** new suggestions if none of them suit your needs

Step 5: Iterate and Customize

AI rewriting should be seen as a **starting point**, not the final output. Feel free to tweak the rewritten version to match your personal voice or brand style.

Examples of AI-Powered Rewriting in Gamma

Let's look at some before-and-after examples to see how rewriting improves content.

Example 1: Simplifying Complex Language
Original:
"Leveraging cross-functional alignment strategies across departmental verticals can enhance productivity outcomes."
AI Rewrite (Clearer):
"Working together across departments can boost productivity."

Example 2: Making Text More Persuasive
Original:
"Our solution has a range of features that users may find useful."
AI Rewrite (Persuasive):
"Our solution offers powerful features designed to make your workflow faster and more effective."

Example 3: Adjusting Tone to Be More Friendly
Original:

"Submit the form before 5 PM to ensure processing."
AI Rewrite (Friendly):
"Don't forget to send in your form by 5 PM so we can take care of it right away!"

Using the Summarize Feature in Gamma

Now, let's turn to summarization—another powerful tool to help you condense content while retaining key ideas.

Step 1: Select a Large Text Block

Summarization works best with content-rich sections—like long paragraphs, multiple bullet points, or full explanations. Highlight the section you want to summarize.

Step 2: Click "Summarize" in the AI Toolbar

After selecting your text, choose the **"Summarize"** option. Gamma will analyze the content and generate a condensed version that still captures the essence.

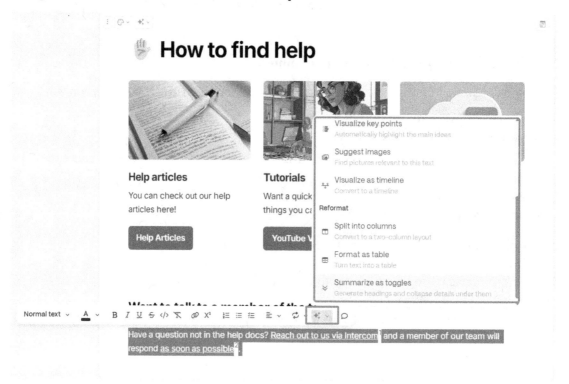

Step 3: Choose the Level of Detail

Gamma may offer several summary options:

- **Brief summary** (1–2 sentences)
- **Mid-length summary** (a short paragraph)
- **Bullet point summary** (highlighting key takeaways)

You can pick the one that works best for your slide or your audience.

Step 4: Edit and Finalize

You may want to tweak the AI-generated summary to better fit the tone or visual layout of your presentation.

Tips for Effective Rewriting and Summarizing

- ☐ **Don't settle for the first result.** Click "regenerate" or refine the prompt for better output.

- ☐ **Know your audience.** Rewriting for an investor pitch is different from a classroom lecture.

- ⛶ **Match the slide format.** Long summaries might be better suited to speaker notes than on-screen text.

- ▬☐ **Use your voice.** Don't be afraid to personalize AI-generated content.

Combining Rewriting and Summarizing for Maximum Impact

Often, you'll need to **rewrite first** to clean up your initial draft, and then **summarize** to fit it into a concise slide. Gamma allows you to use both tools in sequence for best results.

Example Workflow:

1. Draft a paragraph about your company's mission.

2. Use **Rewrite → Make it more compelling**.

3. Use **Summarize → Bullet points** to turn it into a concise slide.

When Not to Use AI Rewriting or Summarization

AI is a helpful assistant, but not a replacement for thoughtful communication. Avoid over-relying on it in cases like:

- **Highly sensitive content** (e.g., legal, financial)

- **Original storytelling or case studies** requiring personal voice

- **Quoting sources** or referencing factual information that must be accurate

Always review AI-generated text with a critical eye.

Future Updates: What to Expect

Gamma is continuously improving. Upcoming versions may include:

- **Tone detection** to suggest rewrites proactively

- **Auto summarization tools** for entire decks

- **Voice-based prompts** to convert speech into refined content

Keep an eye on Gamma's release notes and product updates for new capabilities in this space.

Summary of This Section

Rewriting and summarizing content are two of the most powerful tools in Gamma's AI toolkit. They help you:

- Improve clarity, tone, and impact

- Tailor your message to your audience

- Save time without compromising quality

By learning how to use these tools effectively, you'll elevate your presentations and communicate your ideas with greater precision and professionalism.

Now that you know how to refine your writing with AI, the next section will show you how to make your presentation *look* great—by leveraging Gamma's **Visual Design Assistance**.

3.1.3 Expanding on Bullet Points

When creating presentations, bullet points are a quick and popular way to structure information. They help keep your content concise and digestible. But what happens when you need to turn those bullets into more engaging, detailed content? That's where **Gamma's AI-powered content expansion** tools come in.

In this section, we'll explore how to transform simple bullet points into rich narratives, professional paragraphs, and visually compelling content using Gamma. We'll cover the key steps, best practices, and practical use cases that allow you to get the most from this powerful feature.

Why Expand Bullet Points?

Bullet points are excellent for summarizing, but they're not always suitable for:

- Telling stories

- Explaining processes

- Persuading audiences

- Providing detailed context

Expanded content brings clarity, structure, and flow to your message—making your presentation feel more human, more professional, and more complete.

In Gamma, you can use AI to expand any bullet point into full, readable content that matches the tone and purpose of your presentation. Whether you're crafting a business pitch, educational content, or a team update, this feature can save hours of writing time while improving communication.

How to Expand Bullet Points in Gamma

Step 1: Create Your Bullet List

Start with a short list of ideas you want to expand. For example:

- Launch new product

- Conduct market research

- Prepare social media campaign

You can write these bullets directly into a Gamma slide or block.

Step 2: Highlight the Bullet(s)

Once your bullet list is created, simply click on the bullet or highlight the text you want to expand. Gamma will detect your selection and offer AI-based tools for enhancement.

Step 3: Use the "Expand with AI" Option

A small contextual menu will appear, often with suggestions like:

- Rewrite

- Summarize

- Expand
  Click on **"Expand"**, and Gamma's AI will transform the bullet point into a paragraph or series of sentences that articulate your idea in more detail.

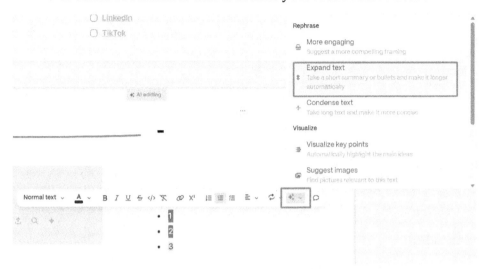

For example:

Original Bullet: Conduct market research

Expanded Text: "Before launching the product, we will carry out comprehensive market research to understand current customer needs, identify competitors, and gather insights into pricing strategies. This will help inform both the product's features and our go-to-market strategy."

Step 4: Edit and Refine (If Needed)

While Gamma's AI does a great job generating content, it's always a good idea to review and tweak it:

- Make sure facts are accurate

- Adjust the tone to fit your audience

- Remove redundancy or add specifics

Remember: AI is a collaborator, not a replacement for your judgment and expertise.

Tips for Effective Expansion

To get better results, consider the following:

1. Use Clear, Descriptive Bullets

The more context you give, the better the AI can generate meaningful output.

Instead of:

- Launch product

Try:

- Launch a new fitness tracking app targeting Gen Z users

2. Group Related Ideas

If your bullets are part of the same topic, keep them close together. This helps the AI understand the theme and maintain consistency across expanded content.

3. Use Hierarchical Bullets

For complex ideas, you can use nested bullets. Gamma understands indents and structure.

Example:

- Launch plan
  - Finalize product design
  - Build launch landing page
  - Reach out to beta users

Gamma can then help expand both high-level and nested points into structured sections.

4. Use Commands and Prompts

If Gamma doesn't give you what you want, use prompts like:

- "Explain this further"
- "Add a real-world example"
- "Write this in a formal tone"

These prompts help refine AI output and direct it toward your desired style.

Use Case Examples

Let's explore how bullet expansion works in real scenarios.

Example 1: Startup Pitch Deck

Bullet Point:

- Secure early adopters

Expanded Content (via Gamma AI): "To validate our solution and gain valuable feedback, we aim to secure a group of early adopters from our target demographic. These users will participate in our beta program, providing insights that help us fine-tune the product before a full-scale launch."

Example 2: Internal Team Presentation

Bullet Point:

- Improve employee retention

Expanded Content: "Improving employee retention is a top priority for our HR team. We plan to conduct regular feedback surveys, offer career development opportunities, and enhance our benefits program to create a more supportive and engaging work environment."

Example 3: Marketing Strategy

Bullet Point:

- Develop influencer partnerships

Expanded Content: "By partnering with relevant social media influencers, we can amplify brand awareness and tap into niche communities. These collaborations will include sponsored content, giveaways, and behind-the-scenes product features."

Working with Expanded Content

Once AI-generated text is inserted into your slide or block, you can:

- Split it across multiple slides or blocks
- Highlight key phrases with bold/italic formatting

- Pair it with images or icons

- Add supporting bullet points, quotes, or examples

This gives you flexibility to go from **raw idea → professional content → visual story** in minutes.

Common Mistakes and How to Avoid Them

Mistake	How to Fix It
Over-expanding simple bullets	Focus on clarity; don't force AI to write too much.
Leaving AI-generated text unedited	Always review for accuracy and tone.
Using vague or unclear bullet points	Provide more detail and context before expanding.

When NOT to Expand

There are cases where keeping bullets is better:

- When presenting executive summaries

- For checklists or timelines

- When the slide is meant to be quick-reference

Use expansion selectively, balancing depth with clarity.

Beyond Expansion: Repurposing Bullets

After expanding, consider turning content into other formats:

- **FAQs** – turn each bullet into a question-answer pair

- **Reports** – build a narrative document using expanded bullets

- **Infographics** – break expanded content into visual highlights

With Gamma's flexible blocks and layout tools, you can mix content types seamlessly.

Final Thoughts

Expanding bullet points with Gamma AI bridges the gap between a **rough outline** and a **polished message**. It's perfect for when you have great ideas but not enough time to write them all out.

The key is to:

- Start with clear, structured bullet points

- Use AI to quickly develop the core message

- Edit and refine the tone and flow

- Present the content in a visually appealing format

With practice, you'll develop an intuition for when and how to use this feature effectively— and your presentations will be better for it.

3.2 Visual Design Assistance

3.2.1 Choosing Visual Themes

Creating an impactful presentation isn't just about having the right words—how your content looks can dramatically affect how it's received. In Gamma, one of the standout features is its ability to elevate visual design using smart, user-friendly tools powered by AI. At the core of this capability is the concept of **visual themes**.

This section will walk you through the purpose and use of visual themes in Gamma, how to choose the right theme for your project, and how AI assists you in making design decisions that align with your content's message and tone.

What Are Visual Themes in Gamma?

In Gamma, a **visual theme** is a combination of typography, color palettes, layout styles, and image treatments that work together to create a cohesive visual identity for your presentation or document. Themes are designed to save you time and eliminate the guesswork of manually styling individual slides.

Gamma's themes are not static like traditional PowerPoint templates. Instead, they're dynamic, meaning they automatically adapt to the content you input—thanks to AI. This ensures that your visuals are always polished and consistent without needing advanced design knowledge.

A theme includes:

- **Typography**: Font pairings and text sizing
- **Color schemes**: Backgrounds, highlights, accent colors
- **Layout structure**: Margins, padding, hierarchy of information
- **Design tone**: Whether it feels professional, playful, minimalist, etc.

Why Choosing the Right Theme Matters

Choosing the right theme is about more than aesthetic appeal—it influences how your audience perceives your message.

For example:

- A **corporate theme** with muted colors and clean fonts suits a financial report or internal company briefing.

- A **bold and colorful theme** might be perfect for a product launch or creative pitch.

- A **minimalist theme** is ideal for educational or data-heavy content, helping reduce visual noise.

Gamma's themes give you a way to **set the tone of communication visually**, helping you connect better with your audience.

How to Choose a Visual Theme in Gamma

Let's walk through the steps to select a visual theme in Gamma.

Step 1: Start or Open Your Gamma Document

When you create a new presentation or open an existing one, Gamma automatically applies a default theme. You can change this at any time, even mid-way through your project.

To access themes:

- Look at the **right-hand sidebar** labeled *Design* (or click on the "Design" icon in the top bar).

- This will open a **theme panel** with multiple pre-built options to choose from.

Step 2: Browse Theme Categories

Gamma currently categorizes themes into different styles. Here are some common categories you might encounter:

- **Professional**: Clean, corporate, neutral palettes

- **Creative**: Bold colors, unique fonts, asymmetrical layouts

- **Minimalist**: Lots of white space, sleek lines

- **Playful**: Bright colors, round fonts, soft visuals

- **Dark Mode**: Sleek backgrounds, ideal for tech-related content

Each theme in the panel comes with a small preview thumbnail. Click on a theme to see how your content adapts instantly.

🔍 *Tip: Hovering over a theme may show a full preview of a sample slide deck styled in that theme, which helps visualize your content before committing.*

Step 3: Apply the Theme

When you find a theme that suits your project:

- Click on it once to **apply it immediately**.
- Gamma's AI will automatically **re-style all elements**—including text, layout blocks, images, and buttons—based on the new theme's visual logic.

There's no need to manually reformat your content. The AI ensures the transition is smooth and keeps readability intact.

Customizing Your Theme

While Gamma's pre-built themes are polished, sometimes you may want to adjust the details. Gamma allows limited—but thoughtful—customization that preserves consistency while giving you creative control.

Adjusting Color Palettes

- Navigate to **Design** → **Color**
- Choose a **preset color palette** or create a **custom palette** by selecting primary and accent colors
- Gamma applies your new palette intelligently across headings, backgrounds, buttons, and highlights

You can also enable **Dark Mode** versions of most themes, which will reverse the contrast for better night-time or tech-forward presentation styles.

Changing Typography

Gamma offers curated font pairings that match each theme's intent. You can:

- Select **Header and Body fonts** separately (within limits)

- Adjust **font sizes** for clarity and emphasis

- Choose between **serif** or **sans-serif** styles

Changing typography across a theme ensures text remains readable while staying visually aligned with your brand or message.

Tweaking Layout Preferences

Gamma's AI engine makes subtle layout decisions like:

- Line spacing

- Content box margins

- Hierarchy of titles, subtitles, and body text

While most of this happens behind the scenes, you can:

- **Drag and drop blocks** to adjust spacing

- Select **alignment options** (centered, left-aligned, justified)

This lets you maintain a consistent structure even as you insert new blocks or media.

AI-Enhanced Theme Recommendations

One of Gamma's biggest strengths is how it leverages AI to make **intelligent theme suggestions**.

For example:

- When you input a **title and brief**, Gamma can suggest 2–3 visual themes that match the **tone of your content**.

- If you're writing about a tech product, it may offer darker, modern themes.

- For educational content, it may recommend lighter, more spacious layouts.

These recommendations reduce the friction of decision-making and help non-designers look like pros.

💡 *Example: You're creating a pitch deck for a SaaS startup. Gamma might suggest the "Neo-Tech" theme with blue gradients and a clean sans-serif typeface to give a futuristic but credible vibe.*

Matching Your Theme to Your Brand

If you're working on behalf of a company, startup, or personal brand, consistency is key.

Gamma allows you to:

- Save **custom themes** (with brand colors and fonts)
- Create a **shared team theme** that teammates can apply across multiple documents
- Upload **brand logos and imagery** to maintain cohesive branding

This makes Gamma a great fit for teams, agencies, or freelancers looking to build client-ready content at speed.

Testing Themes Across Devices

Because Gamma presentations are inherently web-based and mobile-responsive, it's important to **test your theme across different screen sizes**.

Use the **Preview** mode to:

- View your presentation on desktop, tablet, and mobile layouts
- See how color contrasts and font sizes adapt
- Ensure that visuals and text blocks don't overlap or truncate

Gamma optimizes layouts automatically, but it's always smart to double-check for accessibility and usability.

Best Practices for Selecting Visual Themes

Here are a few best practices when working with themes in Gamma:

✅ Match Theme to Purpose

- Use clean, minimal themes for reports or analytics decks
- Choose bold, creative ones for marketing campaigns or portfolios

✅ Keep It Consistent

- Avoid switching themes mid-project unless necessary
- Keep typography and palette steady throughout

✅ Consider Your Audience

- Professional audiences often prefer subtle design
- Younger or creative audiences might engage more with color and playfulness

✅ Don't Overdo It

- Let Gamma handle visual hierarchy
- Too much manual adjustment can create visual clutter

Conclusion: Let AI Be Your Designer

Gamma's visual themes are more than just color and fonts—they're a powerful, AI-enhanced design system that turns your raw ideas into polished, professional content. Whether you're building a report, proposal, or product pitch, choosing the right visual theme sets the foundation for impactful storytelling.

With just a few clicks, you can ensure that your presentation:

- Looks beautiful
- Reads clearly
- Feels consistent
- Reflects your purpose

And the best part? You don't have to be a designer. Gamma's AI takes care of the heavy lifting, so you can focus on the message.

☉ In the next section, we'll explore how Gamma assists with layouts and formatting through auto layout tools—another way AI makes content creation easier than ever.

3.2.2 Auto Layout and Formatting

Creating stunning presentations isn't just about writing compelling content—it's equally about how that content is **visually presented**. Poor formatting and disorganized layouts can easily distract your audience, weaken your message, and reduce the overall impact of your presentation. Gamma's **Auto Layout and Formatting** feature addresses this challenge by using AI to automatically structure and style your content for maximum clarity, flow, and visual appeal.

In this section, we'll explore what Auto Layout is, how it works in Gamma, and how you can use it effectively to enhance your presentation's design while saving time and effort.

What Is Auto Layout in Gamma?

Gamma's Auto Layout system is an AI-driven engine that **intelligently arranges your content**—text, images, embeds, and interactive elements—into visually pleasing and functional layouts. It's like having a professional designer work behind the scenes, interpreting your content and choosing the best layout patterns so that you don't have to fuss with manual design adjustments.

Unlike traditional presentation tools where you must drag, resize, and align every element manually, Gamma uses layout logic that adapts to the type of content you're adding. Whether it's a list of ideas, a block of text, a photo grid, or a data visualization, Gamma auto-selects and applies the optimal layout for that block—instantly and effortlessly.

Key Benefits of Auto Layout in Gamma

- **Speed:** Save hours of formatting time with automatic arrangements.
- **Consistency:** Maintain a cohesive look throughout the presentation.
- **Responsiveness:** Content adapts beautifully across desktop, tablet, and mobile views.
- **Professionalism:** Enjoy designer-level layouts without needing design experience.

Understanding Gamma's Layout Engine

Gamma's layout engine is built on the idea of **"blocks."** Each slide or page you create consists of multiple blocks, and each block can contain various types of content: headings, bullet points, images, call-to-action buttons, and more. The AI evaluates the content within each block and formats it using smart layout presets.

Some examples of layouts that Gamma can apply automatically include:

- **Side-by-side text and image**
- **Three-column grids**
- **Vertical timelines**
- **Checklist or bulleted lists**
- **Quote blocks**
- **Call-to-action (CTA) sections**
- **Header + content pairings**

These layouts are not just visually appealing—they are also context-aware. Gamma can detect the intent of your content (e.g., a comparison, a sequence, a highlight) and recommend or apply formatting accordingly.

How to Use Auto Layout in Your Gamma Presentation

Let's walk through how to take full advantage of this feature.

Step 1: Add or Paste Your Content

Start by creating a new block in Gamma. You can either:

- Use the **"/" slash command** to insert elements like images, text, embeds, etc.

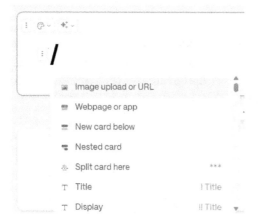

- Paste in a full paragraph or list, and let Gamma auto-detect the type.

- Use the AI prompt to generate initial content blocks with a structured flow.

Example:
Paste in a paragraph describing your product benefits. Gamma may auto-format this into a bullet list or a feature grid, depending on how the information is written.

Step 2: Choose "Auto Layout" Option

Once your content is inserted:

1. **Hover over the block** to reveal formatting tools.

2. Click on the **"Layout" button** or select **"Suggested layouts"** from the right-hand menu.

3. Gamma will suggest or apply a layout style automatically. You can keep it, switch it, or tweak it further.

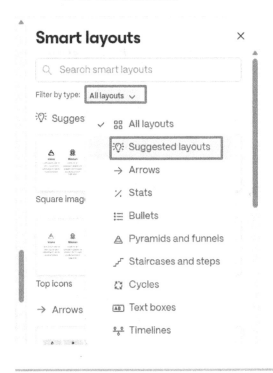

Step 3: Fine-Tune Your Layout (Optional)

Although Gamma does a great job auto-formatting, you can still manually tweak:

- **Alignment:** Change text alignment or image position.

- **Spacing:** Adjust padding or margins between elements.

- **Width and Columns:** Choose between full-width, 2-column, or 3-column layout.

- **Style:** Apply consistent visual themes across all blocks.

To do this:

- Click the block.

- Use the **right sidebar** to adjust layout settings, spacing, and block styles.

- Click **"Apply to all"** if you want the layout style to be consistent across multiple blocks.

Step 4: Maintain Visual Hierarchy

Auto Layout does the heavy lifting, but it's still up to you to **ensure clarity and structure.** As you add more content:

- Use **headings** to separate sections.

- Keep **paragraphs short and scannable**.

- Use **icons or bullets** to break up dense text.

- Highlight important information with **bold text or color accents.**

Gamma's auto-formatting supports all of these stylistic options, and applies them smartly based on what you've written.

Using Themes in Conjunction with Auto Layout

Gamma allows you to apply **visual themes** (covered in Section 3.2.1), and these themes work hand-in-hand with Auto Layout.

When you apply a theme:

- Fonts, colors, and backgrounds are harmonized.

- Layouts are adjusted to match the overall brand tone.

- CTAs, headers, and footers are styled consistently.

Every time you add a new block or section, Gamma's AI references your theme to format the layout in a way that fits your overall presentation design.

Example: If your theme uses bold accent colors and large typography, Auto Layout will reflect that even when adding new bullet points or image cards.

Best Practices for Using Auto Layout Effectively

1. **Start with Structured Text:** Use short paragraphs, headers, and bullets to help Gamma recognize patterns.

2. **Use AI Suggestions:** Don't be afraid to click "Regenerate" or "Reformat" when Gamma suggests layout alternatives.

3. **Combine Layout Blocks Creatively:** Mix text, images, buttons, and embeds within the same layout block to create dynamic slides.

4. **Review Responsiveness:** Always preview your presentation in **mobile view** to ensure the auto-layout adapts well.

5. **Lean on Defaults—Then Refine:** Let Gamma do the layout, but give it your final touch—refining colors, spacing, and style where needed.

Troubleshooting Auto Layout Issues

Even the best AI systems can sometimes miss the mark. Here are some common issues and quick fixes:

Issue	Solution
Content looks cramped	Add space between blocks or switch to a multi-column layout
Misaligned images	Adjust block alignment settings manually
Repetitive styles	Shuffle layout or reapply the theme
Layout doesn't match tone	Change to a more appropriate theme or manually tweak the style

When to Override Auto Layout

Although Gamma's AI is powerful, there are cases where manual layout editing is better:

- For **brand-critical** designs where exact placement is required.

- When creating **infographics or diagrams** with precise alignment needs.

- For **custom storytelling flows** that don't follow standard formats.

To manually override layout:

- Select the block and choose "Custom Layout"

- Use drag-and-drop tools to position each element

- Save it as a custom block style if you plan to reuse it

Conclusion: Let Gamma Do the Heavy Lifting

Auto Layout and Formatting in Gamma is a game-changing feature that allows you to **focus on your ideas**, while the AI ensures that your content looks professional, modern, and cohesive. Whether you're working on a 5-minute pitch deck or a 30-page interactive report, Auto Layout helps you maintain visual consistency, reduce design errors, and enhance the overall readability of your content.

The key is to **trust the AI to get you 80% of the way there**, then use your own judgment and editing skills to polish that final 20%. As Gamma continues to evolve, so will the intelligence and customization of its layout system—meaning your work will only get easier and better over time.

3.2.3 Image Suggestions and Smart Placement

One of Gamma's most powerful and transformative features is its **AI-powered visual intelligence**, particularly when it comes to **suggesting images** and **placing them intelligently** within your content. In traditional presentation software, finding the right image and aligning it in a visually balanced layout can be time-consuming and frustrating. With Gamma, these challenges are drastically minimized, thanks to a combination of curated AI recommendations, smart image placement, and automated formatting that makes your content not only faster to create but also more beautiful and professional.

This section will guide you through everything you need to know to fully leverage **Image Suggestions and Smart Placement** in Gamma, including:

- How Gamma generates image suggestions

- Ways to insert, customize, and replace images

- The principles behind Gamma's smart placement

- Best practices for working with visuals in your content

- Real examples and workflows for polished, image-rich presentations

☐ How Gamma's Image Suggestions Work

When you create or edit a presentation in Gamma, the platform uses AI to **understand the context of your content**—whether it's a slide, a section, or a single block of text. Gamma then recommends **relevant, high-quality images** that match your message and design theme.

These suggestions are powered by large-scale image databases (often royalty-free sources like Unsplash or Pexels) and advanced language models that analyze your copy to extract **keywords, sentiment, tone**, and **visual associations**.

For example: If you write "Building a remote team culture," Gamma might suggest:

- A photo of a Zoom call

- People working from home

- Abstract representations of connection or communication

If you're creating a slide that reads "Increase in revenue by 30%," Gamma might suggest:

- Business growth visuals

- Bar or line charts

- People celebrating success

✨ When and Where Suggestions Appear

You'll typically see image suggestions appear in:

- The **slide editor sidebar** when selecting an image block

- During **AI content generation**, especially when you use a prompt to create an entire page or section

- The **right-click context menu**, if you choose "Suggest Image" for a placeholder

These suggestions save you from manually searching through image libraries or stock sites. They also ensure that visuals are **cohesive** with your design and purpose.

🎨 Adding, Replacing, and Customizing Images

Gamma makes it extremely intuitive to work with images. Whether you're using suggested visuals or uploading your own, the process is simple and responsive.

⬇️ Inserting Suggested Images

1. Click on an image placeholder or add a new **Image Block**.

2. Gamma will automatically provide a carousel of suggestions based on the nearby text or title.

3. Browse through the options, then click **Insert** or **Replace** to add it to your slide.

4. If needed, resize or crop using the contextual tools that appear.

☐ Replacing an Existing Image

1. Click on any existing image in your presentation.

2. Use the **Replace Image** option from the toolbar or right-click menu.

3. Choose from:

   - Gamma's suggestions

   - Search for another image using keywords

   - Upload your own file

   - Use an external image URL

☐ Customizing Image Appearance

Once an image is placed, you can:

- Adjust its size by dragging corners

- Change alignment (center, left, right)

- Apply visual effects (e.g., rounded corners, shadows)

- Set the image to cover the full block or scale proportionally

- Add **alternative text** for accessibility

Gamma automatically ensures your design remains clean and balanced regardless of these edits, thanks to its **smart layout engine**.

☐ What is Smart Placement?

Smart Placement refers to how Gamma uses **AI layout intelligence** to automatically position images within your slides or blocks in the most visually effective way. It considers factors like:

- Text-image balance

- Slide symmetry and hierarchy

- Whitespace optimization

- The overall flow of your visual story

Whether you're working on a single-column layout or a multi-block grid, Gamma dynamically adjusts margins, spacing, and sizing to maintain **a polished, professional appearance**—no manual alignment or nudging required.

☐ Smart Placement in Action

Let's say you add a photo of a team to a testimonial slide:

- Gamma will recognize that the image should sit next to the quote or author's name.

- It will adjust the padding so the text doesn't overlap or sit too close.

- It may automatically crop or resize the image to better fit the layout block.

- If there's a title above, Gamma ensures vertical alignment feels natural.

This removes hours of manual formatting, so you can focus on **storytelling and content—** not design grunt work.

☐ Best Practices for Visual Storytelling in Gamma

To take your visual game even further, consider these practical tips when working with images and smart placement:

1. Use Images to Reinforce, Not Repeat

Your visuals should **enhance** your message, not duplicate it. If your text says "Global outreach," an image of a globe is fine—but a creative depiction of cross-cultural teamwork might resonate more.

2. Stay Thematically Cohesive

Choose a visual style and stick to it throughout the deck. Avoid mixing illustrations with ultra-realistic photos unless intentional. Gamma's image suggestions tend to stay in theme, but it's still good to curate as needed.

3. Avoid Clutter

Don't overload a slide with too many visuals. Let whitespace breathe. One high-quality, well-placed image often has more impact than a busy collage.

4. Use Image Blocks Strategically

In Gamma, image blocks can live beside text, inside galleries, or span full-width. Vary the layout occasionally to keep your audience visually engaged.

5. Use Gamma's Accessibility Features

Always add alt text where appropriate and ensure that any image you use maintains legibility and contrast. Gamma assists with visual balance, but you can take it further with accessible design practices.

☐ Workflow Examples: From AI Text to Visuals

Let's walk through a few examples of how image suggestions and smart placement work in practice:

📖 Example 1: Educational Content

Prompt: "The water cycle explained"
AI-generated Slide:

- Gamma generates 3 sections with headers and bullet points

- Suggests a clean diagram of the water cycle

- Places the image side-by-side with explanation text

- Formats the title in larger font with spacing adjustments

📊 Example 2: Business Pitch Slide

Prompt: "Our user growth in Q1 2025"
AI-generated Slide:

- Gamma inserts a graph block

- Suggests background visuals like upward arrows or user avatars

- Places the image subtly behind transparent text or beside the chart

- Ensures smart alignment with bullet points

💼 Example 3: Team Introduction Page

Prompt: "Meet our leadership team"
User Adds: 3 bios and job titles
Gamma Suggests: Profile-style images based on names or roles
Smart Placement: Side-by-side block grid with consistent image sizes and margins
Final Result: A modern, sleek team slide in under 5 minutes

💡 Pro Tips to Get the Most from Image Suggestions

- **Use meaningful headings**: Gamma uses them to recommend better images. A title like "How We Help Startups" yields better image matches than something generic like "About Us."

- **Use the search bar smartly**: Don't hesitate to override the AI and use keywords to search for a specific visual direction.

- **Save your favorite images**: Gamma may allow you to "star" or "favorite" visuals depending on your plan.

- **Pair text and image with purpose**: Always ask, *what does this image add to the story?*

📌 Summary: Why Visuals in Gamma Just Work

Gamma isn't just another AI content tool—it's a **design-aware platform** that gives non-designers the power to create **aesthetic, polished presentations** quickly and confidently. Its **Image Suggestions and Smart Placement** feature is one of the most underrated gems, streamlining what used to be the most painful part of slide design.

With this feature:

- You **save time**

- Your **presentations look better**

- You **focus on ideas**, not layout

And as Gamma continues to evolve, expect even smarter visual integrations, more intuitive drag-and-drop interactions, and deeper personalization of image suggestions.

3.3 Working with AI Responsibly

3.3.1 Editing for Accuracy and Tone

Artificial Intelligence has revolutionized the way we create content. With tools like **Gamma**, users can now generate entire presentations in minutes using natural language prompts. But as powerful as these tools are, **AI is not infallible**. One of the most important aspects of using AI responsibly is **editing**—specifically for **accuracy** and **tone**.

This section will guide you through the best practices for reviewing and refining AI-generated content in Gamma to ensure that your message is not only correct but also communicated effectively and authentically.

✅ Why Editing Matters in AI-Generated Content

AI tools like Gamma are trained on vast datasets and use probabilistic models to generate content. While this allows for remarkable efficiency and creativity, it also introduces some inherent limitations:

- **Factual Inaccuracy**: The AI might "hallucinate" facts—generate plausible-sounding but incorrect information.

- **Generic Tone**: AI outputs may lack the emotional nuance or personality needed for a specific audience.

- **Contextual Mismatch**: Without full understanding of your audience or goals, the AI may frame ideas in an inappropriate way.

- **Style Inconsistency**: Tone, formality, and formatting may not be uniform across your slides.

The goal of editing is not to replace AI, but to **enhance and humanize** it.

➡️ Step-by-Step Guide to Editing for Accuracy

1. Fact-Check Key Claims

Always validate any statistics, dates, names, or cited facts. AI models do not have live access to the internet and might present outdated or incorrect info.

Checklist:

- Look for numbers and references—search them online to verify.

- For business presentations, ensure company data, figures, and benchmarks are up to date.

- Watch out for invented sources or links (AI can sometimes fabricate them).

Tip: If you're creating a product pitch or client deck, **cross-check terminology** specific to your industry. AI may confuse similar concepts.

2. Check for Logical Flow and Internal Consistency

Sometimes AI may jump between unrelated ideas or contradict itself across slides.

Editing techniques:

- Read through your entire deck once to identify repetition or confusion.

- Rearrange sections where the logic doesn't flow well.

- Ensure your conclusion aligns with your introduction.

Example: If Slide 1 introduces three main goals, make sure those exact goals are addressed consistently in the following content.

3. Ensure Accurate Use of Terminology

Particularly in technical, academic, or business contexts, word choice matters. AI might use broad or imprecise language.

Action Items:

- Replace vague terms with precise, domain-appropriate language.

- Review industry-specific phrases to ensure they are being used correctly.

Example: Instead of "use advanced solutions," specify "implementing machine learning algorithms for demand forecasting."

⊕ Editing for Tone and Voice

Accuracy ensures correctness, but **tone ensures connection**. Tone influences how your audience feels about your message. It includes formality, emotion, word choice, and structure.

1. Determine the Right Tone for Your Audience

Start by asking:

- Is this a professional or casual presentation?
- Should it be persuasive, informative, or inspirational?
- What level of detail does your audience expect?

Once you know your intended tone, you can reshape the AI content accordingly.

Examples:

- For an investor pitch → Tone should be confident, focused, and data-driven.
- For a classroom lesson → Tone can be explanatory, friendly, and structured.
- For a marketing slide → Tone might need to be energetic and benefit-oriented.

2. Adjust Formality

Gamma's AI tends to produce content with neutral formality. You can modify this by adjusting sentence structure and word choice.

Before (AI-generated): "It's a great idea to use this method because it helps a lot."

After (Formalized): "This approach is highly recommended due to its effectiveness in streamlining workflows."

After (Informal): "This method's a game-changer—it really makes things easier."

Be consistent throughout your presentation once you choose a tone.

3. Humanize the Language

AI-generated writing often lacks personality. You can add warmth or character by:

- Using rhetorical questions

- Including brief personal examples or metaphors

- Breaking the fourth wall (e.g., "You might be wondering...")

Example Edits:

- Change "This software automates tasks." to
  "Imagine saving hours of your time—this software makes it happen."

- Change "The team achieved results." to
  "Our team pushed hard—and the results speak for themselves."

This kind of editing increases audience engagement and relatability.

4. Trim the Fluff

AI might pad content with filler or over-explained phrases. Tightening the language improves clarity and professionalism.

Common phrases to cut or tighten:

- "It is important to note that..." → just state the fact.

- "In order to" → "To"

- "Due to the fact that" → "Because"

Exercise: Try removing 10% of the words on a slide and check if the meaning remains. If so, keep the tighter version.

☐ Using Gamma's Tools to Assist Your Editing

Gamma isn't just about generation—it also helps you refine.

AI Rewrite Tool

Highlight any paragraph and choose "Rewrite" to explore different phrasings or tones. You can select from:

- Formal

- Concise

- Friendly

- Persuasive

Use this to experiment with tone before finalizing your version.

Manual Edits + AI Suggestions

Don't be afraid to overwrite AI text completely when needed. Sometimes a clean slate is better than adjusting clunky content.

Pro Tip: Use AI as a collaborator, not a ghostwriter. Let it give you a starting point, then build upon it.

🔍 Real-World Example: Editing a Gamma-Generated Slide

Let's walk through an example from a presentation on **sustainable packaging**.

Original AI Output:

"Sustainable packaging is important because it helps reduce waste and protect the environment. Using eco-friendly materials can be good for business and also for the planet. This presentation talks about some ideas."

Edited Version:

"Sustainable packaging is more than a trend—it's a business imperative. In this presentation, we'll explore practical ways to reduce waste, cut costs, and build a brand that cares about the planet."

Changes Made:

- Shifted from generic tone to confident and persuasive

- Removed filler language ("can be good," "talks about")

- Focused on benefits and clarity

Final Tips for Editing AI-Generated Content

1. **Read Aloud**: Hearing your slides can help you spot awkward phrasing or unintended tone.

2. **Get a Second Opinion**: Share with a colleague to catch inconsistencies.

3. **Edit in Layers**: First for accuracy, then for tone, then for clarity.

4. **Trust Your Instincts**: If something "feels off," it probably is.

5. **Own the Content**: AI gives you a draft, but your personal input makes it resonate.

Summary

Editing for accuracy and tone is not just a final polish—it's an essential phase in using Gamma responsibly. As users of AI-powered tools, we carry the responsibility of ensuring that the content we present is **truthful, thoughtful**, and **tailored** to our audience. By fact-checking diligently and shaping the message with intention, you elevate your AI-generated slides from passable to powerful.

Remember: AI is your assistant. **You are the storyteller.**

3.3.2 Avoiding Over-Reliance

As powerful as Gamma's AI tools are, they should be seen as *assistants*, not *replacements*. While AI can accelerate content creation, structure ideas, and even improve language or design, depending too heavily on it can result in presentations that are impersonal, generic, and even misleading. This section will help you develop a balanced approach—where AI amplifies your creativity rather than replacing it.

Why Avoiding Over-Reliance Matters

AI tools like Gamma are designed to streamline your workflow, but there are several risks to be aware of when relying on them too much:

- **Loss of Authenticity**: Presentations that are entirely AI-generated often lack the unique voice or personality that connects with your audience. When everything is machine-written, your message might feel robotic or overly polished.

- **Generic Content**: AI may provide good starting points, but it tends to offer safe, average responses that may not fully capture your original idea, brand voice, or domain-specific expertise.

- **Potential Inaccuracies**: Gamma's AI, like other large language models, can sometimes "hallucinate" facts—confidently presenting incorrect or outdated information. Blindly trusting AI outputs without fact-checking could damage your credibility.

- **Missed Opportunities for Creativity**: The act of creating forces us to reflect, shape, and evolve ideas. Relying only on automation may rob you of deeper insights and creative breakthroughs.

- **Overdependence Hinders Growth**: The more you let AI do all the thinking and creating, the less likely you are to develop your own presentation and storytelling skills.

A Balanced Workflow: Human First, AI-Assisted

To avoid over-reliance, think of Gamma's AI as a **creative collaborator** rather than an author. The ideal workflow should look like this:

1. **Start with a clear objective.** Know your audience, your message, and the result you want. Don't start with "whatever the AI gives me." Begin with a clear structure or concept in your head.

2. **Use AI for speed, not strategy.** Let AI assist with drafting bullet points, writing sections, or offering design options—but keep the strategic thinking, storytelling, and judgment firmly in your hands.

3. **Review and refine rigorously.** Edit AI-generated text to reflect your tone, correct nuances, and enhance clarity. Replace generic statements with data, stories, or examples that only *you* can provide.

4. **Inject your personality.** Your voice, humor, opinions, and insights are what make the content *yours*. AI can't replicate your personal experience, so always add that layer back in.

5. **Customize design intentionally.** AI can provide default designs and layout suggestions, but ensure they reflect your brand identity and visual intention. Tweak fonts, colors, or image choices for relevance.

Common Signs You're Over-Relying on AI (and How to Fix It)

Here are a few red flags to watch for—plus tips on how to correct course:

⚠️ **Red Flag #1: All your slides sound the same.** If each slide starts with "In today's world…" or contains overly formal, generic phrases, it's likely AI has taken over the tone.

✅ **Fix:** Edit each section with your natural speaking voice. Use contractions, analogies, or storytelling that reflects your style.

⚠️ **Red Flag #2: You don't understand what's on your slide.** If you find yourself presenting AI-written content that you didn't write, didn't check, or don't fully understand—stop.

✅ **Fix:** Rewrite it in your own words. Make sure every slide reflects your understanding of the topic. If you can't explain it, you shouldn't be presenting it.

⚠️ **Red Flag #3: You're skipping research because "AI will fill it in."** AI is a writing tool, not a knowledge engine. It should never replace real research, data, or insights from trusted sources.

✅ **Fix:** Do your homework. Use AI to help shape how you present facts, not to generate the facts themselves.

⚠️ **Red Flag #4: Your audience feels disconnected.** If people find your presentation impressive but uninspiring, chances are it lacks emotional connection or originality.

✅ **Fix:** Add anecdotes, personal stories, or questions that invite your audience to engage. Let your passion show.

Practical Guidelines for Responsible AI Use in Gamma

Let's break down a few **specific ways** you can use Gamma's AI features responsibly.

✅ When Generating Content

- Use the prompt generator to *explore ideas*, not *define conclusions*.
- After receiving suggestions, pick and choose what fits your message. Don't paste everything as-is.
- Rewrite AI-generated headlines to match your brand tone or campaign voice.

✅ When Summarizing or Rewriting

- Use it to simplify jargon or complex text—but double-check if anything important was removed or misrepresented.
- Be wary of overly vague or positive language like "revolutionary," "state-of-the-art," or "next-gen"—replace with real benefits or examples.

✅ When Visualizing with AI

- Accept AI's image suggestions only if they align with your narrative.
- Use your own photos or brand materials when possible.
- Always preview how your layout looks across different devices—what looks "neat" in the AI preview may look cluttered live.

Use AI as a Creative Multiplier, Not a Shortcut

Here's an analogy: **AI is like a GPS for content creation.** It can help you find your way faster, but *you* are still the driver. You know the scenery, the stops you want to make, the detours worth taking. AI might offer directions—but only *you* know the destination.

Instead of replacing your creativity, let Gamma's AI *amplify* it:

- Got writer's block? Use AI to get unstuck with a draft.

- Need a headline fast? Generate five options and fine-tune the best one.

- Unsure how to structure a topic? Ask Gamma to suggest an outline—and then adapt it to your vision.

The goal is not to eliminate effort—it's to reduce the *busywork*, so you can focus on *big thinking* and *meaningful messages*.

Case Study: Balancing AI and Human Insight

Let's look at a real-world example:

Use Case: A marketing team is preparing a pitch deck for a product launch.

- **Step 1: Structure** – The team outlines key topics: pain points, product solution, case study, pricing.

- **Step 2: Generate Content** – They use Gamma's AI to write draft content for each slide.

- **Step 3: Refine** – The team rewrites every section, replacing the AI's placeholder copy with language that fits their brand voice.

- **Step 4: Add Proof** – They insert client quotes, demo screenshots, and unique value propositions.

- **Step 5: Final Polish** – They ask Gamma for a design refresh, apply their color scheme, and check animations.

Result: A deck built faster than usual—but rich in substance, authenticity, and impact.

Final Thoughts

Gamma's AI is a powerful ally, but it's not a substitute for your knowledge, your message, or your creativity. As you grow more skilled in using the platform, strive to develop your **critical eye**, your **editorial voice**, and your **empathy for your audience**.

Use Gamma to do more, faster. But make sure that what you create is still **yours**.

3.3.3 Fact-Checking AI-Generated Content

In today's world, artificial intelligence is revolutionizing how we create and consume content. Gamma, like many other AI-powered tools, can generate stunning visuals, polished writing, and even persuasive arguments with just a few prompts. But with all its power, AI remains fallible. It is not a human, and it does not always understand nuance, accuracy, or the implications of misinformation. That's where **fact-checking** becomes essential.

In this section, you'll learn:

- Why fact-checking AI-generated content is important

- The common pitfalls of relying solely on AI

- Best practices for verifying information

- Tools and resources for efficient fact-checking

- Real-world examples and use cases in Gamma

Why Is Fact-Checking AI-Generated Content Important?

AI is trained on large datasets pulled from across the internet. This includes high-quality academic resources, blogs, news articles—and sometimes incorrect or outdated information. While Gamma's AI is optimized to be helpful, informative, and accurate, it **does not inherently understand truth or falsehood**. It generates content based on **patterns**, not **critical thinking**.

The consequences of unverified content can include:

- **Spreading misinformation** in your presentation

- **Damaging your credibility** with audiences

- **Legal or compliance risks** in regulated industries

- **Misleading data and arguments** that harm decision-making

Whether you're building a business pitch, educational resource, or internal report, fact-checking ensures your message is **responsible, professional, and trustworthy**.

Common Pitfalls of AI-Generated Information

AI tools like Gamma can produce content that **sounds** correct but is **factually inaccurate**. Here are some common issues to watch for:

1. Outdated Information

AI models are trained on past data, and unless connected to real-time sources, they may not include current developments. For example, a presentation about tech trends in 2025 might cite 2022 data if not updated.

2. Hallucinations

AI sometimes "hallucinates" facts—creating names, numbers, or sources that **don't exist**. This could include made-up statistics, fake studies, or incorrect attributions.

3. Misinterpretation of Data

Gamma might present data summaries or conclusions that are **over-simplified**, **misleading**, or **lacking context**—especially for complex topics like science, finance, or law.

4. Bias in Language or Perspective

AI can reflect the biases in the data it was trained on. This might show up in how topics are framed or in skewed representations of sensitive issues.

Best Practices for Fact-Checking AI-Generated Content

To maintain high standards in your Gamma presentations, follow these actionable steps:

✅ Step 1: Identify Factual Claims

After generating content, skim through it and **highlight any statements that contain facts, figures, dates, names, or references**. These could include:

- Statistics

- Historical events

- Scientific terms or theories

- Names of individuals or organizations

- Quotes or attributed ideas

- Legal or financial terminology

Use Gamma's editing tools to annotate or leave notes as reminders for checking each one.

✅ Step 2: Cross-Verify with Trusted Sources

Use **multiple reputable sources** to verify any factual claims. These might include:

- Official government websites (e.g., data.gov, cdc.gov)

- Academic databases (e.g., JSTOR, Google Scholar)

- Reputable news agencies (e.g., BBC, Reuters, AP News)

- Industry reports (e.g., McKinsey, Gartner, Deloitte)

- Corporate websites and official press releases

If a piece of information doesn't appear in at least **two independent and reliable sources**, **don't include it as fact**.

✅ Step 3: Cite Your Sources (When Appropriate)

When creating professional or academic presentations, always **cite the sources** for critical claims. Gamma allows you to insert footnotes, links, or small text references to enhance credibility.

For example:

"According to a 2023 report by McKinsey, 71% of companies are now using AI in some form of operations." *(Source: McKinsey & Company)*

Even if Gamma helped draft the sentence, **you need to trace and confirm the reference** before quoting it.

✅ Step 4: Use Fact-Checking Tools and Plugins

You can speed up your verification process by using some of these tools:

Tool	Use
Google Fact Check Tools	Search for fact-checked claims from around the web
Snopes	Verifies urban legends, internet myths, and fake news
PolitiFact	Validates political statements and statistics
Media Bias/Fact Check	Helps assess the reliability of media sources
AI Detector Plugins	Some browser tools can help detect hallucinated or suspicious text from AI models

Pro Tip: You can copy Gamma-generated content into tools like Grammarly or Quillbot with citation assistance to flag suspicious phrasing or unsupported claims.

✅ Step 5: Update Outdated Information

Even if the original AI content was accurate once, it may no longer be valid. Make a habit of checking:

- Dates of statistics

- Laws or regulations mentioned

- Prices, costs, or rates

- Trends and projections

If you're presenting for business or academia, **data older than 2 years should be reviewed**, unless you're discussing historical analysis.

Case Study: A Real Gamma Use Case

Scenario:
A marketing professional uses Gamma to generate a slide deck on consumer trends for 2025. Gamma writes:

"According to a Nielsen study, Gen Z prefers email marketing over social media by 45%."

Action Taken:

- The user searches Nielsen's 2023-2024 research database.

- No such statistic is found.

- Upon further review, it's discovered the AI invented the number.

- The user updates the slide to say:

"While Gen Z continues to engage with social media marketing, email remains a preferred channel for direct promotions. (Source: HubSpot, 2023)"

Result:
The final slide is now **accurate, cited, and credible**—increasing the presenter's authority and protecting their brand.

What to Do When You Can't Verify the Content

Sometimes, Gamma might generate a compelling idea that seems plausible but **you can't find a clear source**. What should you do?

- Rephrase it as an opinion or general trend.

- Label it clearly as "hypothetical" or "for illustration."

- Consider deleting or replacing it with verifiable data.

Example:

Instead of:

"AI will replace 40% of jobs by 2030."

Say:

"Some experts speculate that AI could automate a significant portion of jobs in the coming decade, though estimates vary widely."

Final Thoughts: Balance AI Creativity with Human Responsibility

Gamma is a powerful ally—but **you are still the editor-in-chief** of your presentation. Think of AI as your research assistant, not your final authority. When used wisely, Gamma can save hours of work, spark new ideas, and generate beautiful presentations. But **fact-checking is your compass**, guiding your content toward truth and trust.

By adopting fact-checking as a natural part of your creation process, you will:

- Earn trust from your audience

- Deliver more professional and accurate work

- Avoid embarrassment, confusion, or even legal risks

- Build a lasting reputation for thoughtful communication

✅ Quick Summary Checklist

Before you hit "Publish" on a Gamma presentation:

- 🔍 Have you checked all statistics and claims against trusted sources?

- 📚 Are sources cited where necessary?

- ✖ Have you removed or edited unverified, misleading, or hallucinated content?

- ☐ Have you updated outdated information?

- 🏴 Have you used tools to assist in your fact-checking workflow?

Let your content be creative, but always let your **commitment to truth** lead the way.

CHAPTER IV
Making Your Presentations Interactive

4.1 Adding Interactive Elements

4.1.1 Buttons and Clickable Links

Interactivity is at the core of modern digital presentations. Gone are the days of linear slideshows with static information. Today's audiences expect more than just a series of bullet points—they crave engagement, dynamic storytelling, and navigable experiences. In Gamma, **buttons and clickable links** are two of the most powerful tools you can use to make your presentations interactive, intuitive, and user-friendly.

In this section, we'll explore **what buttons and links are in Gamma**, **why they matter**, and **how to create and customize them effectively**. By the end, you'll have everything you need to start turning your presentations into fully interactive experiences.

📌 **What Are Buttons and Clickable Links in Gamma?**

Buttons in Gamma are customizable interactive elements that can be embedded directly into your slides or content blocks. They can perform various actions such as:

- Linking to another page within your presentation

- Directing users to an external website

- Jumping to a specific section or anchor point

- Triggering an embedded function (e.g., opening a form)

Clickable links, on the other hand, are **inline hyperlinks** placed inside text. They can direct users to:

- Web pages

- Email addresses (mailto:)

- Internal pages within the Gamma presentation

- Downloadable resources like PDFs or videos

While both buttons and links serve similar functions, they differ in visibility, emphasis, and user experience. Buttons are more **visually prominent**, making them ideal for **calls to action (CTAs)**, while links are more **subtle** and typically embedded within text for supporting information.

Why Use Buttons and Links?

- ✅ **Enhance User Navigation**: Make your content feel more like a website, allowing viewers to jump to the parts that interest them most.

- ✅ **Encourage Engagement**: Guide viewers to take action, such as visiting your website, filling out a form, or accessing a downloadable guide.

- ✅ **Tell Non-Linear Stories**: Let viewers explore your content in the order they choose, especially in interactive portfolios or sales decks.

- ✅ **Create Seamless Multi-Page Experiences**: Links and buttons allow your presentation to feel like a web-based journey rather than a simple slideshow.

How to Add a Button in Gamma

Step 1: Insert a Button Block

To insert a button:

1. Hover over the section where you want to insert the button.

2. Click on the **"+" icon** or type "/button" to bring up the block menu.

3. Select **"Button"** from the list.

Step 2: Customize Button Text

Click on the default text and type your own CTA, such as:

- "Learn More"
- "Start Now"
- "View Portfolio"
- "Download PDF"

Keep it short, clear, and action-oriented.

Step 3: Add a Link to the Button

Once the button text is set:

1. Click the **link icon** in the button's toolbar.
2. Choose one of the following destinations:

- o 🔗 **External link** (e.g., https://yourwebsite.com)

- o ☐ **Internal link** (to another page in the Gamma doc)

- o 📧 **Email link** (e.g., mailto:hello@example.com)

- o 🔍 **Anchor link** (to a specific section within the current page)

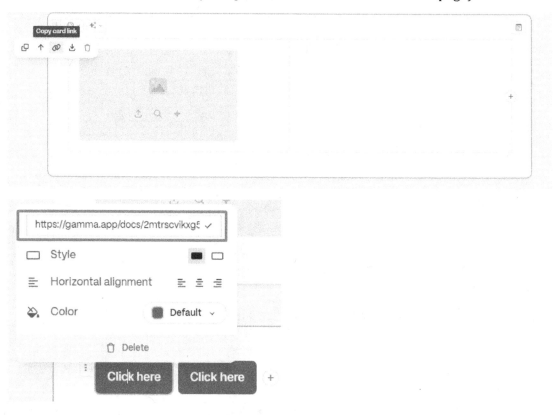

You can also paste the URL directly, and Gamma will automatically convert it into a hyperlink for the button.

Step 4: Style the Button

Gamma allows light customization to match your presentation's branding:

- Change button color to match your theme

- Adjust alignment (left, center, right)

- Add icons or emojis for visual appeal

- Increase padding for a larger clickable area

While Gamma doesn't yet offer full design control like CSS-style customization, it offers enough flexibility to keep your presentation clean and branded.

∞ How to Add a Clickable Link Inside Text

Step 1: Select the Text

Highlight the word or phrase you want to turn into a link.

Step 2: Add a Hyperlink

- Use the **link icon** in the formatting toolbar, or
- Press Cmd + K (Mac) / Ctrl + K (Windows) to open the link input.

Step 3: Enter Your Link Destination

You can link to:

- An external URL
- A section header (internal navigation)
- An email address
- A downloadable file

Gamma even allows smart linking—if you paste a YouTube URL, for example, it may offer to auto-embed the video directly instead of just linking it.

☐ Linking Internally Within the Same Presentation

This feature is crucial for non-linear navigation, such as:

- Table of contents with jump links
- Back-to-top buttons
- FAQ sections with collapsible navigation

To do this:

1. Add a **Header Block** or **Section Title**.

2. Click the "●●●" menu next to it and **Copy Link**.

3. Paste this as the destination in your button or hyperlink.

Gamma creates **anchor links** for all headers automatically, making internal linking incredibly simple.

☐ Practical Use Cases for Buttons & Links

✅ Business Pitch Decks

- "Request a Demo" button linking to a form

- "Meet Our Team" linking to an internal page with bios

- Links to case studies or testimonials

✅ Portfolios

- Buttons to view individual projects

- Inline links to GitHub, Behance, or personal blogs

- Navigation bar at the top of the presentation

✅ Online Courses or Lessons

- Buttons for "Next Lesson" or "Take Quiz"

- Links to downloadable worksheets

- Back buttons to navigate between topics

✅ Event or Product Launch Pages

- "Buy Tickets" button linking to checkout

- "Explore the Features" section jump links

- RSVP form via external link or embedded integration

🎨 Design Tips for Effective Buttons and Links

- **Use Contrasting Colors**: Make sure buttons stand out from the background.

- **Limit to One Primary CTA per Slide**: Too many buttons dilute focus.

- **Use Descriptive Link Text**: Avoid "click here"—opt for meaningful phrases like "Read the full report."

- **Check on Mobile View**: Ensure buttons are large enough to tap on small screens.

- **Avoid Dead Ends**: Always guide users forward or give them a way to return.

⚠️ Common Mistakes to Avoid

- ✗ **Overlinking Everything**: Too many links can confuse users.

- ✗ **Generic Link Text**: "Click here" doesn't tell the user what to expect.

- ✗ **Inconsistent Style**: Make sure all buttons follow the same format and spacing.

- ✗ **Broken Links**: Always test your links before publishing!

✅ Best Practices Recap

Tip	Why It Matters
Use clear button text	Encourages user action
Test every link	Prevents broken navigation
Prioritize mobile usability	Ensures responsive interactivity
Group related links	Organizes user flow logically
Use internal links for structure	Improves navigability

☐ Bonus: Create a Navigation Menu Using Buttons

To simulate a website-style top menu:

1. Add a horizontal stack of buttons at the top of your first slide/page.

2. Label each button (e.g., "About", "Services", "Contact").

3. Link each button to a section or page in your Gamma presentation.

4. Use consistent formatting and spacing.

This gives your Gamma project the look and feel of a **microsite**—ideal for portfolios, proposals, or landing pages.

■ Summary

Buttons and clickable links are foundational to making your Gamma presentations interactive, navigable, and action-driven. Whether you're directing users to external resources or guiding them through a multi-page experience, these tools allow you to turn static content into a journey.

With Gamma's intuitive interface and built-in link management, anyone—from business professionals to students—can implement dynamic interactivity without needing to code. Practice thoughtful placement, test every interaction, and watch your content come to life.

4.1.2 Embedded Media and GIFs

Presentations are no longer just a series of static slides. In today's world of digital communication, audiences expect engaging and immersive experiences. One of the best ways to breathe life into your Gamma presentations is by embedding media such as videos, audio clips, and animated GIFs. These elements not only enhance visual appeal but also communicate information more effectively, keeping your audience attentive and involved.

In this section, we'll explore everything you need to know about working with embedded media and GIFs in Gamma, from basic steps to advanced tips.

Why Embedded Media Matters in Presentations

Before we dive into the "how," it's worth understanding the "why." Embedded media is more than decoration—it's a storytelling tool. Here's why it makes a difference:

- **Visual Engagement**: People process visuals 60,000 times faster than text. A short video or animation can convey emotion, tone, and information far more effectively than a block of text.

- **Audience Retention**: Studies show that presentations with video and interactive content hold audience attention significantly longer.

- **Contextual Reinforcement**: Videos or GIFs that demonstrate a concept or product in action reinforce the message in a powerful way.

- **Accessibility**: Audio or subtitled media can make content more inclusive for diverse learning styles and needs.

Now let's look at how to actually embed this content in Gamma.

How to Embed Media in Gamma

Gamma makes it incredibly simple to embed media. Here's how you can add videos, audio, and animated GIFs to your slides.

Embedding Videos

Step 1: Choose Your Video Source

Gamma supports embedding from popular video platforms such as:

- YouTube

- Vimeo

- Loom

- Wistia

- Vidyard

- Other sources using iframe/embed codes

You can either paste a direct video link or use the embed code provided by the platform.

Step 2: Insert the Video

- Open your presentation in Gamma.
- Click the "+" button where you want to insert content.
- Select **"Embed"** from the content options.
- Paste your video link or iframe embed code into the field.
- Gamma will automatically recognize and render the video player in your slide.

Step 3: Resize and Position

Once added, you can:

- Drag the corners to resize the video box.
- Click and drag to reposition it on the page.
- Use the alignment tools in the toolbar for a cleaner layout.

Step 4: Adjust Settings (Optional)

Some video platforms let you customize playback settings (e.g., autoplay, loop, start time). If you're using embed code, modify it before pasting into Gamma.

Embedding Audio Clips

While Gamma is more focused on visual storytelling, you can still include audio in creative ways:

- **Use Audio Players from External Services**: Upload your audio to platforms like **SoundCloud** or **Anchor**, then embed their player.
- **Use a Clickable Link to Audio Files**: If you host an MP3 or podcast episode, you can add a link or button that opens the audio in a new tab.

Steps:

- Click "+" → **"Embed"** and paste the SoundCloud or external audio link.
- Gamma will display an inline audio player if supported.
- Style the block using design options or pair it with a description.

Inserting Animated GIFs

GIFs are fantastic for:

- Demonstrating a quick process or animation
- Adding personality or humor
- Replacing short videos with a lightweight alternative

Step 1: Find or Create a GIF

- Use platforms like **Giphy**, **Tenor**, or **Imgur**
- Create your own using tools like **EZGIF** or **Canva**

Step 2: Add the GIF to Gamma

You can add a GIF to Gamma in two main ways:

- **Upload as Image**:
  - Click the "+" button.
  - Select **Image**.
  - Upload the .gif file from your computer.
  - The animation will play automatically in the preview and final version.
- **Insert by Link**:
  - If the GIF is hosted online, copy its image URL.
  - Use the image block and paste the URL.
  - Make sure it ends in ".gif" (e.g., https://media.giphy.com/media/xT0GqF3vlQ41CLsV9e/giphy.gif)

Step 3: Position and Resize

- Just like other media blocks, GIFs can be resized and repositioned.
- Use spacing tools to avoid crowding your layout.
- Consider combining a GIF with explanatory text or icons for context.

Best Practices for Using Embedded Media

To ensure that media supports your message rather than distracting from it, follow these tips:

1. Use Media Sparingly and Strategically

- Don't overuse videos or GIFs. One or two per section is usually enough.
- Make sure each media asset has a clear purpose.

2. Optimize for Load Time

- Avoid heavy or high-res media that slows down loading.
- Use compressed video or GIF formats when possible.

3. Add Captions or Labels

- Always accompany videos or GIFs with text explaining their purpose.
- Use captions for accessibility and clarity.

4. Test Your Presentation

- Always preview the full presentation to ensure media loads properly.
- Test on different devices (desktop, mobile) and browsers.

5. Use Loops Wisely

- For GIFs, loop only if the motion enhances understanding or emotion.
- Avoid endlessly looping distractions.

Creative Use Cases for Embedded Media

Product Demos

- Embed a Loom video showing how your app works.
- Use a GIF to demonstrate a UI feature in motion.

Customer Testimonials

- Insert video interviews of satisfied clients.
- Add an audio clip with voiceover feedback.

Educational Explanations

- Embed a YouTube video for further explanation of a concept.
- Use GIFs to visually walk through a process (e.g., math equation animation, coding result).

Interactive Campaigns

- Include audio jingles or promotional video ads.
- Create a slide with multiple GIFs representing different user choices.

Accessibility and Compliance

When using media, make your content inclusive:

- **Always include alt text** for media (Gamma allows you to do this in image settings).
- **Use subtitles or closed captions** for embedded videos whenever possible.
- Ensure color contrast and volume settings meet accessibility guidelines.

Troubleshooting Embedded Media in Gamma

Here are common issues and how to resolve them:

Issue	Solution
Media doesn't display	Double-check URL or embed code format. Use HTTPS links.
GIF doesn't animate	Make sure you uploaded the file as .gif and not as a static image format.
Video is too large	Use a video platform to host, then embed instead of uploading.

Issue	Solution
Slow load times	Compress GIFs/videos using external tools (e.g., EZGIF, Handbrake).
Media autoplay doesn't work	Modify the embed code to include autoplay settings, if supported.

Final Tips: Blending Media Seamlessly into Design

- Don't let media "float" awkwardly—frame it with text, icons, or spacing.

- Align embedded videos and GIFs to your theme colors and visual identity.

- Use transitions and interactive links to create smooth flows from one media item to another.

Conclusion: Bring Your Content to Life

Embedded media and GIFs are not just design elements—they are storytelling superpowers. Gamma's intuitive embed tools make it easy to integrate dynamic content, whether you're pitching a product, educating an audience, or simply adding energy to your message. By combining visual motion, interactivity, and a thoughtful layout, you can transform your static ideas into engaging experiences.

In the next section, we'll explore how to turn your presentations into web-like experiences—think of them as microsites—so you can deliver an even more immersive narrative.

4.1.3 Surveys and Feedback Forms

In the digital age, a one-way presentation is no longer sufficient to engage modern audiences. Whether you're pitching a product, delivering training, or teaching in a virtual classroom, interaction is key to keeping your audience involved, informed, and inspired. One of the most powerful ways Gamma enables interaction is through **surveys and**

feedback forms—built-in or integrated—allowing you to collect real-time data and insights directly within your presentation.

In this section, we'll explore how to incorporate surveys and feedback forms into your Gamma presentations, from simple polls to more detailed multi-question surveys. You'll learn **why** they matter, **how** to create them effectively, and **best practices** to encourage responses that inform and empower your work.

Why Use Surveys and Feedback Forms in Presentations?

Before diving into the technical steps, it's important to understand the strategic reasons behind using surveys and feedback forms in your Gamma content:

- **Engagement Boost**: Interactive elements like surveys demand attention. They break the passive viewing experience and convert your audience into participants.

- **Insight Collection**: Feedback forms allow you to gather useful data—opinions, preferences, or even learning assessments—from viewers in real-time.

- **Audience Validation**: Showing that you value audience input increases trust, which is especially critical in business proposals and educational sessions.

- **Content Adaptation**: Surveys can help you adjust the flow or depth of content during live sessions based on real-time feedback.

- **Performance Tracking**: By collecting responses, you can evaluate how well your message is resonating and adjust future content accordingly.

Survey Options in Gamma

Gamma offers flexible ways to include surveys and feedback forms in your presentation, either:

1. **Using Native Blocks**: Embedding simple interactive blocks directly in the presentation using built-in features.

2. **Embedding External Tools**: Incorporating third-party forms (like Google Forms, Typeform, or SurveyMonkey) using Gamma's embed functionality.

3. **Linking Out to Forms**: Using buttons or hyperlinks to direct users to a survey hosted elsewhere.

Creating Surveys with Native Gamma Features

While Gamma doesn't (yet) offer complex survey logic natively, it provides essential interactivity for quick polls and input collection. Here's how to use them effectively:

Step-by-Step: Creating a Native Poll Block

1. **Open Your Presentation**: Navigate to the slide or section where you want the survey.

2. **Click '+' to Add a Block**: Hover over the desired area and click the + button.

3. **Choose the Poll Block**: From the interactive blocks, select "Poll" or "Multiple Choice".

4. **Edit the Question**: Click into the default question and rephrase it according to your context.

5. **Add Response Options**: Provide two or more answer choices. You can allow multiple selections if needed.

6. **Enable Result Visibility (Optional)**: Let participants see how others have answered.

📋 *Tip: Use this for icebreakers, quick knowledge checks, or audience preference polling.*

Embedding Third-Party Feedback Forms

If you want more advanced features like text input, file uploads, or conditional logic, it's best to use an external survey tool. Gamma supports embedding these tools directly into your presentation.

Popular Tools to Embed:

- **Google Forms** – Free, customizable, integrates well with Google Workspace.

- **Typeform** – Visually engaging and easy to use, perfect for customer feedback.

- **SurveyMonkey** – Feature-rich platform for professional surveys.

- **Tally** – Clean design, no-code logic, free option with high flexibility.

Step-by-Step: Embedding a Google Form (or Similar)

1. **Create Your Form**: In Google Forms (or another platform), design your survey or feedback form as needed.

2. **Get the Embed Code**:

   o For Google Forms: Click the "Send" button > choose the <> (embed HTML) tab > copy the code.

   o For Typeform, Tally, etc.: Look for the "Embed" or "Share" options.

3. **Return to Gamma**:

   o Navigate to the slide where you want the form.

   o Click + > Select "Embed" block.

4. **Paste the Embed Code**: Drop in the iframe or link, and adjust the dimensions if needed.

5. **Preview and Adjust**: Ensure the form displays properly and fits within the flow of your presentation.

✍ *Note: Some platforms may require you to make the form public or accessible via a shared link.*

Using Buttons and Links to Direct to Surveys

If embedding isn't suitable (due to visual layout, mobile limitations, or personal preference), you can simply link to your survey externally:

How to Add a Survey Link or Button:

1. Click into any text block or add a new button.

2. Highlight the text or select the button.

3. Click the link icon or "Add link" option.

4. Paste your survey URL (e.g., from Google Forms or Typeform).

5. Customize the display text like "Give Feedback" or "Take the Survey".

👆 *Use this when your survey is long, requires scrolling, or is intended to be answered after the session.*

Best Practices for Designing Surveys in Presentations

To ensure you're using surveys effectively in Gamma, follow these design and strategic best practices:

1. Keep It Short and Focused

Long surveys lose participants. Stick to 3–5 questions unless absolutely necessary.

2. Use Simple, Clear Language

Avoid jargon. Keep questions concise and easy to understand.

3. Offer Multiple-Choice When Possible

They're faster to complete and easier to analyze later.

4. Time It Right

Place surveys after key sections or at the end of the presentation when the audience is more informed.

5. Incentivize Responses

Even a small thank-you or entry into a raffle can boost participation.

6. Respect Privacy

Clearly state what you'll do with the information if it's not anonymous.

Ideas for Survey and Feedback Use Cases

- ✅ **Event Registration Follow-up**: "How did we do today?"

- ✅ **Training Module Assessment**: "What topic should we dive deeper into next?"

- ✓ **Lead Generation**: "Would you like a demo call after this presentation?"

- ✓ **Product Feedback**: "What features do you want most?"

- ✓ **Team Retrospectives**: "What went well? What could be improved?"

- ✓ **Classroom Exit Tickets**: "What's one thing you learned today?"

Each of these can be tailored to match your Gamma slide content for a seamless experience.

Analyzing Feedback and Making Data-Driven Improvements

Gathering feedback is only valuable if you act on it. Once your survey has been filled out:

- Export the results (if using external tools).

- Look for common themes and pain points.

- Adjust future content or presentations accordingly.

- Share learnings with your team or stakeholders.

🏆 *Pro Tip: Gamma allows you to pair engagement analytics with survey responses for a full picture of audience behavior.*

Conclusion: Turn Passive Viewers into Active Participants

Surveys and feedback forms transform your presentations into two-way conversations. By asking questions, listening to your audience, and showing responsiveness, you elevate your Gamma creations beyond static decks into **living, evolving experiences**.

As you become more comfortable with Gamma's tools, don't be afraid to experiment with interactive content. Try different survey formats, question styles, and placements. Review results regularly, iterate based on what works, and you'll create presentations that not only look great—but work brilliantly.

4.2 Creating Web-Like Experiences

4.2.1 Multi-Page Presentations

In the age of digital experiences, users have grown accustomed to navigating information through clickable paths, like they do on websites. Gamma leverages this modern behavior by allowing you to create **multi-page presentations** that function more like **microsites** or **interactive reports** than traditional linear slideshows. In this section, we will explore what multi-page presentations are, why they matter, and how you can design them effectively using Gamma's intuitive interface.

☐ What is a Multi-Page Presentation?

A **multi-page presentation** in Gamma is more than a simple collection of slides—it's a structured, web-like environment where viewers can **click, explore, and interact** with different sections of your content at their own pace. Unlike linear slide decks where viewers progress slide-by-slide, multi-page presentations offer branching paths, hyperlinks, and modular sections, making it possible to:

- Present content in a **non-linear** fashion
- **Segment topics** into self-contained pages
- Enable **exploratory learning** or storytelling
- Create portfolios, product showcases, interactive guides, or even landing pages

In essence, you are no longer confined to a beginning-middle-end structure. Instead, you're designing an experience that adapts to how your audience wants to consume content.

💡 When to Use Multi-Page Presentations

Gamma's multi-page presentation format shines in a variety of contexts:

- **Business proposals** with separate sections for goals, budget, timeline, and team
- **Marketing decks** that showcase products, case studies, testimonials, and pricing

- **Online portfolios** with distinct pages for projects, background, contact info

- **Internal documentation** that organizes SOPs, onboarding materials, or internal updates

- **E-learning materials** where users can navigate topics by interest or level

If your content can be broken down into discrete themes, use cases, or decision paths—then a multi-page approach is ideal.

□□ How to Build Multi-Page Presentations in Gamma

Let's now walk through how to **design and manage a multi-page presentation** in Gamma. This process consists of five major steps:

Step 1: Start with a Structure in Mind

Before jumping into Gamma, **plan your content layout**. Ask yourself:

- What are the key sections I want to include?

- Will each section need sub-pages or just a single page?

- How will users move between sections—through a menu, links, or call-to-action buttons?

Create a rough **content map** similar to a website sitemap. For example:

Home Page

—— About the Project

—— Case Studies

—— Pricing

—— Contact Information

This mental model (or a quick sketch) will help you structure your Gamma presentation effectively.

Step 2: Add Pages in Gamma

In Gamma, pages are the primary building blocks of your content—just like slides in a slide deck or pages on a website.

To create new pages:

1. **Click the "+ Page" button** in the left sidebar.

2. Name your page appropriately based on the section (e.g., "Case Studies," "Pricing").

3. Repeat the process to add as many pages as needed for your structure.

💡 *Pro Tip: Use clear, consistent naming conventions so that your navigation system is easy to manage later.*

Step 3: Design Each Page Independently

Each page in Gamma is built using **blocks**—including text, images, media, buttons, and embedded components. When designing multi-page presentations:

- Treat each page as its **own mini experience**

- Use **headers and subheadings** for clarity

- Keep a **consistent design theme** across pages

- Use **call-to-action buttons** to guide users to the next logical step

You can use pre-made **templates** or **design from scratch**. Gamma's AI can also assist by suggesting layouts based on your prompt.

Step 4: Create Navigation Between Pages

Now that your pages are ready, you need to **connect them together** using internal navigation.

Here are several ways to add navigation:

A. Link Buttons to Pages

1. Insert a **Button Block**

2. Choose **"Link to Page"** as the link type

3. Select the desired target page from the dropdown

4. Customize button style and label (e.g., "Learn More," "Back to Home")

B. Use Text Links

1. Highlight a section of text (e.g., "See Our Pricing")

2. Click the link icon in the editor

3. Choose a target page in your Gamma presentation

C. Add a Navigation Menu

You can create a simple **horizontal or vertical menu** using a row of buttons or text links:

- Create a block group at the top or side of each page

- Include links to core sections like "Home," "About," "Contact"

💡 *Tip: Add the same menu block to every page to mimic a fixed site menu experience.*

Step 5: Preview and Test Navigation

Once your internal links are set:

- Use **Preview Mode** to simulate user experience

- Test each link and button to ensure proper navigation

- Check for broken links, unclear paths, or missing "Back" buttons

- Ensure mobile responsiveness if your viewers are likely to use smartphones

---

✨ Tips for Designing Great Multi-Page Presentations

Here are best practices to make your interactive, multi-page Gamma presentations truly stand out:

1. Use a Consistent Visual Style

- Stick to a branded color palette and font

- Use the same header styles and spacing between pages
- This creates a seamless, cohesive look and feel

2. Balance Depth and Simplicity

- Avoid over-nesting (e.g., too many sub-pages)
- Group content logically, and keep pages focused on a single topic

3. Use Anchor Links for Long Pages

- On longer pages, insert **anchor links** at the top to allow quick jumps to subsections
- This mimics a Table of Contents on-page

4. Leverage Interactivity Wisely

- Add interactive media (e.g., embedded videos or GIFs)
- Use collapsible blocks or tabs to organize dense content
- Avoid clutter—each interactive element should serve a purpose

5. Optimize for Navigation Flow

- Provide clear **entry and exit paths**
- Use **back buttons**, **breadcrumbs**, or "Return to Home" links where needed
- Never leave the user wondering where to go next

☐ Example: Multi-Page Product Showcase

Let's say you're creating a product presentation for a software company. A multi-page Gamma layout might look like this:

- **Home** – Brief overview and call-to-action
- **Features** – Divided into "Productivity," "Collaboration," and "Security"
- **Customer Stories** – With case study links to separate pages
- **Pricing** – Comparison table and subscription plans
- **FAQ** – Accordions or dropdowns for common questions

- **Contact** – Embedded form and calendar integration

Each of these would be its own page, connected via a top menu and in-page links. Visitors can explore based on their interests without being forced into a single narrative flow.

☐ Updating and Managing Multi-Page Presentations

As your content evolves, Gamma makes it easy to:

- **Reorder pages** by dragging them in the left sidebar

- **Rename or duplicate pages** for versioning or branching

- **Archive or hide** pages not ready for publication

- **Update navigation links** when pages change or get removed

You can also clone entire presentations as templates for future use.

📈 Why Multi-Page Presentations Matter

Modern communication isn't linear. Whether you're delivering a **sales pitch**, designing an **educational resource**, or showcasing a **portfolio**, letting your audience explore content at their own pace leads to:

- Better **engagement**

- Improved **retention**

- Higher **conversion rates**

Gamma's multi-page functionality bridges the gap between slides and web pages—offering the best of both worlds.

✅ Quick Recap

Step Action

1   Plan your content structure

Step Action

2   Add and name pages in Gamma

3   Design each page with clear layout

4   Link pages using buttons or text

5   Test the navigation and refine

🚀 Next Steps

Once you've mastered multi-page presentations, the next logical step is to add **interactive elements** like animations, quizzes, or feedback forms to further engage your audience. You'll learn more about those in the next section of this chapter.

4.2.2 Smooth Navigation with Links

In traditional presentations, users often move through slides linearly—from beginning to end. However, Gamma allows creators to build **web-like experiences** where navigation is fluid, non-linear, and highly customizable. This level of interactivity is powered by internal and external links that guide the audience through your content based on their interest, much like navigating a website.

In this section, we'll explore how to use links in Gamma to create smooth, intuitive navigation flows that enhance engagement, encourage exploration, and give your audience control over their journey.

Why Smooth Navigation Matters

Smooth navigation is more than a design trick—it's a strategic choice. Presentations built with clear, clickable paths can:

- **Improve user engagement** by letting them choose what to explore.

- **Emulate modern web interfaces**, making content feel more familiar and intuitive.

- **Support different user journeys**, especially for clients, students, or stakeholders with different priorities.

- **Reduce cognitive load** by letting viewers consume content in smaller, digestible segments.

- **Create interactive tools** like portfolios, microsites, or reports where navigation is essential.

Let's now break down how you can implement smooth navigation in Gamma.

Types of Links in Gamma

Gamma offers multiple linking options that serve different purposes:

1. Slide-to-Slide Links (Internal Navigation)

These links allow you to move between slides in the same deck.

- **Use case**: Table of contents, "Back to top" buttons, or branching storylines.

- **Behavior**: Clicking a link jumps directly to the linked slide without a reload, offering seamless in-deck navigation.

2. Section-Based Navigation

Slides in Gamma can be grouped into collapsible sections. You can create links that jump to specific sections within your presentation.

- **Use case**: Long-form presentations where users want to jump to specific sections like "Case Studies" or "Pricing."

3. External Links

Gamma also allows hyperlinks that lead to websites, email addresses, documents, or external tools.

- **Use case**: Linking to a client's website, embedding a Calendly link for scheduling, or directing users to Google Drive resources.

How to Add Links in Gamma

Creating smooth navigation with links in Gamma is easy and requires no coding knowledge. Here's how to do it:

Step 1: Select Text, Button, or Image

Links in Gamma can be attached to:

- A **text block** (such as "Read More" or "Back to Top").
- A **button** block (for clear call-to-action functionality).
- An **image** or **icon** (useful for creating clickable visuals).

💡 **Tip**: Use buttons for primary navigation, and text links for inline guidance.

Step 2: Click the "Link" Icon

Once you've selected your content:

- Click the **link icon** from the formatting toolbar.
- A pop-up will appear with options.

Step 3: Choose Your Link Destination

You'll be prompted to select:

- **Another slide** (internal link)
- **A section** of your presentation
- **An external URL**
- **An email address** (mailto:)
- **A phone number** (tel:)

For internal navigation:

- Simply **select the slide name or number** from the list.
- Gamma will automatically apply the link and generate a smooth scroll/jump experience.

Designing Intuitive Navigation Paths

Smooth navigation requires thoughtful structure. Below are several best practices to follow when designing linked pathways in your Gamma presentations.

1. Use a Clear Table of Contents (TOC) Slide

A clickable TOC at the start of your presentation acts as a **hub**:

- Each item in the TOC should link to a corresponding section.

- Include a "Back to TOC" button on each main section slide.

- Bonus: Add icons next to each link for quick visual recognition.

☐ **Example**:

- Slide 2: "Overview" (TOC)

- Slide 5: "Product Features" → backlinked to Slide 2

- Slide 8: "Pricing Plans" → backlinked to Slide 2

2. Use Call-to-Action (CTA) Buttons

Call-to-actions aren't just for websites. In Gamma, buttons like "Learn More," "Next Step," or "Schedule a Demo" can:

- **Guide users through content**

- **Drive conversions** (via external links)

- **Improve content scannability**

✓ Example: "Want to see customer success stories?
→ [View Case Studies]"

3. Include "Back" and "Top" Navigation

For long or branching presentations:

- Add "← Back" or "↑ Back to Top" at the bottom of slides.

- Helps users avoid getting lost.

- Keeps experience user-controlled without needing to scroll linearly.

4. Use Visual Cues for Linked Content

Visual hierarchy is essential to intuitive navigation:

- **Use underlined text** for inline links.

- **Use color-coded buttons** for primary vs. secondary actions.

- **Icons** (∞, 🔗, ↑) enhance understanding without explanation.

5. Consider Mobile and Responsive Design

Although Gamma presentations are often viewed on desktop, many users will view your content on tablets or phones. When linking:

- **Test link size and spacing** for tap-accuracy.

- Avoid placing too many links close together.

- Use larger buttons for CTAs on mobile.

Building Complex Navigation Structures (Advanced)

If you're designing a **microsite**, **portfolio**, or **product walkthrough**, you might want to use more advanced structures.

Branching Paths

Let users choose their own adventure by linking to different content based on their needs.

Example: "What are you here to explore?"

- [For Investors] → leads to Slide 10

- [For Partners] → leads to Slide 15

- [For Media] → leads to Slide 20

Looping Paths

Link back to earlier slides or key information:

- **Great for recurring FAQs**

- **Helps reinforce learning**

"Forgot how our pricing works? [See pricing again]"

Segmented Portfolios

Each project or case study in a portfolio can live on its own slide or section, linked from a gallery-style menu.

Real-World Examples of Smooth Navigation in Gamma

To visualize how this works, here are a few real use cases:

1. Sales Pitch Presentation

- Starts with an interactive table of contents.
- Each product feature links to a detailed section.
- Call-to-action buttons link to demo request form (external).
- "Back to top" links appear on every section slide.

2. Online Portfolio

- Homepage has visual thumbnails that link to different project slides.
- Each project page includes:
  - Description
  - Images
  - "Back to portfolio" link
- External links to GitHub and LinkedIn.

3. Educational Resource Hub

- Main menu offers navigation to:
  - Tutorials
  - Assignments
  - Feedback
- Each section links back to the main menu.
- Embedded forms for feedback submission.

Tips for Smooth Navigation Success

Tip	Why It Matters
Use consistent styling	Helps users recognize clickable elements
Test all links	Prevents dead-ends or broken flow
Map out navigation on paper first	Clarifies structure before building
Avoid overlinking	Too many links can overwhelm users
Add tooltips or hover effects (if possible)	Gives more context to users

Common Mistakes to Avoid

- **Linking to the wrong slide**: Always double-check your internal targets.

- **Using unclear link labels**: "Click here" is less helpful than "View Features".

- **Forgetting mobile users**: Make sure your links are thumb-friendly.

- **Creating dead-end slides**: Always provide a path back or forward.

- **Overcomplicating navigation**: Keep it simple and purposeful.

Conclusion: Turn Viewers into Explorers

Creating smooth navigation with links transforms your Gamma presentations into powerful interactive experiences. Instead of passively flipping through slides, your audience can actively engage with the content, jumping directly to what matters most to them.

By applying intuitive structure, well-placed links, and strong design principles, you're not just delivering a message—you're creating an experience.

In the next section, we'll explore how to use storytelling and content flow to make your presentations even more immersive.

Ready to tell a story your audience can *explore*? Let's go!

4.2.3 Mimicking Microsites and Portfolios

In the world of digital communication, the line between a presentation and a website is increasingly blurred. With Gamma, users can design presentations that *don't just look like traditional slide decks*—they can behave like full-fledged microsites or digital portfolios. This section explores how to leverage Gamma's structure, features, and design capabilities to **mimic the experience of a microsite** or **build a compelling, navigable portfolio**, all without writing a single line of code.

What Are Microsites and Digital Portfolios?

Before diving into the *how*, it's important to understand the *what*.

- **Microsites** are small, standalone web pages or collections of pages that serve a specific purpose—promoting a campaign, product, or event. They often have custom navigation, sleek branding, and a focused goal.

- **Digital Portfolios** are curated showcases of work, commonly used by creatives, freelancers, designers, developers, and marketers to demonstrate expertise or previous projects.

Gamma empowers you to simulate the feel of both using its *multi-page structure*, *interactive linking*, and *clean, modern layouts*.

Why Use Gamma to Mimic Microsites or Portfolios?

Here's why Gamma is an ideal tool for creating these experiences:

- ✅ **AI Assistance**: Quickly generate copy, summaries, or project descriptions with built-in AI support.

- ✅ **Intuitive Navigation**: You can use buttons and links to move between pages like on a real website.

- ✅ **Custom Branding**: Tailor fonts, colors, layouts, and logos to reflect your brand identity.

- ✅ **Mobile-Friendly**: Gamma presentations look great on both desktop and mobile, ensuring accessibility.

- ✅ **No Coding Required**: Everything can be created using simple clicks, drag-and-drop, and prompts.

Designing the Structure of a Microsite in Gamma

The first step in mimicking a microsite is to rethink your "presentation" as a **multi-page experience** rather than a linear slide deck.

1. Plan Your Sections Like Web Pages

A basic microsite structure in Gamma could include:

- **Home (Landing Page)** – Introduction or headline value proposition.

- **About** – Context or background information.

- **Products / Projects / Services** – A gallery or overview.

- **Case Studies / Testimonials** – Social proof or success stories.

- **Contact / Call-to-Action** – Buttons, email links, or embedded forms.

Each of these becomes a separate *page or section* in Gamma.

2. Use Page Breaks or Navigation Separators

To mimic a true site feel, avoid the traditional vertical scrolling of decks. Instead:

- Use **sections** as distinct "pages"

- Enable **navigation menus** via buttons or link cards (e.g., "Go to Projects")

- Keep each section visually consistent and minimal

Building Navigation Like a Real Website

One of the most powerful features in Gamma is the ability to **link between sections**, enabling seamless navigation just like on a microsite.

1. Use Button Blocks with Internal Links

- Insert a **Button Block**

- Set the action to **"Jump to Section"**

- Label the button (e.g., "View My Work" or "Contact Me")

- Place it strategically at the end of each section

2. Create a Persistent Navigation Menu

To create a website-like header or nav bar:

- Design a **Top Section** as your "menu"

- Add **buttons** or **text links** horizontally (e.g., "Home | Work | Contact")

- Use internal anchors to jump to different slides/sections

- Use the "Duplicate Across Slides" feature to place it on all pages

3. Add a Footer with Navigation or Contact Info

At the bottom of each section or slide:

- Include a **footer** with navigation links, copyright info, or social media buttons

- Add a "Back to Top" button for longer experiences

Showcasing Projects in a Portfolio Format

Gamma is especially powerful for portfolios, allowing you to **visually highlight work samples**, case studies, or creative content.

1. Use Grid Layouts for Visual Projects

- Use **Gallery or Card layouts** to display multiple items at once

- Each card can link to a **separate section** with more details

- Great for showing designs, products, illustrations, or website screenshots

2. Create Detailed Case Studies

For each project:

- Dedicate a **full section** or **multi-slide flow**

- Use **large visuals**, concise descriptions, and client outcomes

- Add testimonials, metrics, or before-after comparisons

Example layout:

- Slide 1: Project Overview

- Slide 2: Process or Tools Used

- Slide 3: Outcome and Results

3. Use Tabs or Accordion-Style Layouts

Gamma supports *accordion* and *toggle* sections, perfect for hiding/showing details on demand—just like interactive web portfolios.

Use them to:

- Organize skills or toolsets

- Provide FAQ-style project explanations

- Let readers dive deeper if they want more info

Design Principles for Web-Like Experiences

Here are some important visual and UX guidelines:

1. Keep it Minimal and Consistent

- Stick to a single **font family**, **color palette**, and **button style**

- Use whitespace to guide attention

- Don't overload slides—treat each like a web page, not a PowerPoint slide

2. Use Visual Anchors

- Include consistent **headers**, **logos**, and **iconography**

- Highlight calls to action (CTAs) with bold buttons or contrast

3. Make It Mobile-Friendly

Gamma is responsive, but you can ensure clarity by:

- Avoiding clutter

- Using legible font sizes

- Spacing out interactive elements

Publishing and Sharing Like a Microsite

Once you've created your microsite-style presentation, it's time to make it live.

1. Publish and Share as a Link

Gamma allows publishing presentations as a **public link**, so:

- It's accessible like a normal web page

- You can control view permissions (public, unlisted, or private)

2. Embed in Other Sites

You can **embed your Gamma content** on your personal website, blog, or online portfolio:

- Copy the **embed code**

- Paste into platforms like WordPress, Notion, Wix, or Webflow

3. Use Custom URLs and Branding

If you're using a professional plan:

- Customize your URL slug (e.g., gamma.app/janedoe-portfolio)

- Add your **logo**, **favicon**, and **brand colors**

- Remove Gamma branding for a cleaner, owned experience

Real-World Use Cases

Creative Portfolios

Designers, illustrators, UX researchers, and photographers can build immersive, clickable galleries.

Personal Websites

Job seekers can build resume-style microsites that include About Me, Experience, and Projects.

Startup Product Pages

Founders can pitch their startup idea with a modern, scrollable, CTA-driven flow.

Event or Campaign Microsites

Marketers can build one-pagers to announce events, showcase promotions, or host resources.

Pro Tips & Best Practices

- Use **section background colors** to visually differentiate parts of your microsite

- Always include a **CTA** (contact button, resume download, scheduling link)

- Avoid long text blocks; instead, use concise copy and bold visuals

- Ask a friend or colleague to **test your site** before sharing—check for broken links or typos

Summary

Gamma is more than just a presentation tool—it's a canvas for creating digital experiences. By structuring your content thoughtfully and using Gamma's interactive features, you can build presentations that **mimic websites and portfolios**, impress your audience, and leave a lasting impact. Whether you're a freelancer, a student, or a business professional, this approach opens new creative possibilities—without needing design or coding expertise.

4.3 Storytelling Through Flow

4.3.1 Structuring Sections

Creating a compelling presentation is not just about throwing slides together; it's about **guiding your audience through a clear, engaging narrative**. In Gamma, where interactivity and AI design tools allow you to go beyond static slides, **structuring your content into meaningful sections** becomes even more critical.

This section will help you understand how to **plan and structure your content using sections in Gamma** to create fluid, story-driven presentations that feel natural, interactive, and purposeful.

📌 Why Structure Matters in Interactive Presentations

In traditional presentation software like PowerPoint or Google Slides, a linear slide-by-slide sequence is the norm. But Gamma gives you a canvas that's **modular, responsive, and web-like**, enabling **non-linear navigation and storytelling**. To harness this potential, you must **divide your content into logical, user-friendly sections**.

Well-structured sections:

- Help your audience follow along and stay engaged

- Make your content easier to update or expand later

- Enable non-linear navigation (i.e., users can jump to what interests them)

- Support storytelling techniques like suspense, problem/solution, and progressive reveal

Think of sections as **"chapters" within your presentation**, each with its own theme or message, but contributing to the overall story.

☐ Step 1: Identify the Core Messages

Before opening Gamma, begin with a planning exercise. Ask yourself:

- What is the **main message** of your presentation?

- What are the **supporting ideas or arguments**?

- What does the **audience need to know first**, and what can come later?

- How might the audience want to **navigate** your content?

Based on these reflections, divide your content into **3–5 core sections**. For example, a pitch deck might break down into:

1. Introduction / Problem Statement

2. Solution

3. Market Opportunity

4. Product Demo

5. Team and Call-to-Action

Each of these becomes a **self-contained content block** that can stand on its own or flow naturally into the next.

🔧 Step 2: Creating Sections in Gamma

Gamma structures your presentation as a series of **cards** or **blocks**, and you can group these cards into **sections**.

To create sections:

1. **Start a new Gamma presentation**

2. **Use "+ Section"** to add a new named section between content blocks

3. Assign each section a clear, descriptive title like:

    o "Meet Our Team"

    o "How It Works"

    o "Customer Testimonials"

💡 **Tip:** Don't make the section titles too long; think in headlines. These titles often become part of your navigation UI, so clarity is key.

☐ Step 3: Organize Your Slides Within Sections

Within each section, place **all the relevant blocks**—text, images, videos, buttons, etc.—that support that topic.

Example: If your section is "Our Product Features", inside that section you might have:

- A quick text summary
- A visual feature comparison chart
- Embedded demo video
- Buttons linking to "More Info" or technical documentation

Use **Gamma's layout templates** to ensure content within a section is visually consistent and easy to scan. You can add:

- Columns for comparison
- Carousels for visual walkthroughs
- Expandable content (for hiding complexity at first glance)

∞ Step 4: Enable Smooth Transitions Between Sections

While Gamma allows for non-linear exploration, most presentations still benefit from a **guided flow**.

To connect your sections:

- Use **"Next Section" buttons** at the bottom of each section
- Use **call-to-action links** that guide the user to the next logical step
- Insert **anchor links** to jump to specific sections from anywhere in the deck

💡 **Pro Tip:** Place a **persistent navigation bar** or "jump menu" at the top of your presentation for easier access to all sections.

☌ Step 5: Match Section Structure with Presentation Goals

Your section structure should reflect your **intent**. Consider these examples:

💼 Business Pitch

- Section 1: Introduction / Problem
- Section 2: Solution Overview
- Section 3: Market Analysis
- Section 4: Product Demo
- Section 5: Business Model
- Section 6: Team & CTA

🎓 Educational Module

- Section 1: Learning Objectives
- Section 2: Key Concepts
- Section 3: Case Studies
- Section 4: Exercises
- Section 5: Summary & Quiz

🎨 Portfolio

- Section 1: About Me
- Section 2: Selected Projects
- Section 3: Skills & Tools
- Section 4: Testimonials
- Section 5: Contact Me

With this intentional structure, your audience won't feel lost—they'll feel led.

📱 Step 6: Optimize Section Flow for Mobile and Web

Since Gamma presentations are **responsive** and often viewed on mobile or embedded in websites, your section structure should support **easy scrolling and tapping**.

Best practices:

- Limit each section to **3–6 content blocks**

- Ensure each section starts with a **headline or lead sentence**

- Use **visual breaks** (color backgrounds, dividers, spacing) to signal new sections

- Place **interactive elements like buttons** near the bottom of sections for easy access

⬜ Step 7: Testing Your Structure

Before publishing:

1. **Preview your presentation** in desktop and mobile views

2. Ask a colleague to navigate through it and give feedback

3. Time how long it takes to get from intro to CTA

4. Check that **each section delivers a single, clear message**

If a section feels too long or unfocused, break it into two. If navigation feels confusing, revisit the flow and add guiding buttons or breadcrumbs.

✨ Bonus: Layering Advanced Techniques

Once you're comfortable with basic section structure, consider enhancing it with:

- **Expandable sections** (for FAQs, nested info)

- **Scroll-based animations** (to reveal content progressively)

- **Thematic color changes per section** to guide emotional tone

- **Section intros with auto-generated summaries** (using Gamma AI)

☐ Summary Checklist: Structuring Sections

✓ Identify the core message of your presentation
✓ Break content into 3–5 logical sections
✓ Use Gamma's section tools to group content
✓ Label each section clearly and concisely
✓ Maintain consistent formatting within each section
✓ Add buttons or links to guide flow between sections
✓ Test your section navigation on different devices
✓ Revise based on user feedback and navigation clarity

🖊 Real-World Example: Structuring a Startup Pitch

Startup: GreenLeaf Tech
Goal: Raise investor interest in a sustainable farming solution
Gamma Section Structure:

1. 🌱 *The Problem*: Unsustainable farming practices

2. ☐ *Our Solution*: GreenLeaf's hydroponic system

3. 📊 *Market Opportunity*: Urban agriculture trends

4. 🎬 *Demo*: Embedded product walkthrough video

5. 💰 *Business Model*: Revenue and pricing plans

6. ☐ *Team*: Founders and advisors

7. 🔊 *Call to Action*: "Let's talk—Book a meeting"

Each section is not only clear but also **purposeful**, helping investors digest key facts quickly and dive deeper into areas of interest.

Final Thoughts

Structuring your presentation into sections is **the cornerstone of interactive storytelling in Gamma**. Whether you're building a course, a pitch, or a personal showcase, organizing your content thoughtfully ensures a smooth, engaging experience for your audience.

Remember: A well-structured presentation is not only easier to build, but also more persuasive, professional, and memorable.

4.3.2 Creating Narratives with Design

Introduction: Why Narrative Design Matters

In the world of digital presentations, good design alone is no longer enough. What truly makes a presentation memorable and impactful is the *story it tells*. Whether you're pitching a startup idea, training a team, or delivering a lesson, the most effective presentations guide the audience through a journey. Gamma allows you to do more than just present information—it empowers you to shape *narrative experiences*.

Creating a narrative through design means intentionally structuring your content to engage, educate, and persuade. With Gamma's flexible and interactive features, you can shape the flow, pacing, and visual language of your presentation to tell a compelling story. This section dives into how to do exactly that—with practical steps, strategic tips, and real-world examples.

1. Understanding Narrative Flow in Presentations

At its core, narrative flow refers to how your content unfolds. Just like in a book or a film, your presentation should have a beginning, middle, and end—each one working together to keep the audience engaged and emotionally invested.

Key Elements of Narrative Flow:

- **Hook**: A strong opening that grabs attention
- **Context**: Background information that sets the stage
- **Conflict or Challenge**: What problem needs solving?
- **Solution or Message**: Your key insight or offering

- **Call to Action (CTA)**: What should the audience do next?

This structure can be applied to a wide range of presentations—from business pitches and product demos to educational content and personal portfolios.

2. Choosing a Visual Language for Your Story

Design choices influence how your message is received. Visual elements like color, typography, layout, and imagery are not just decorative—they are tools for reinforcing your message.

A. Use Color to Set the Tone

- **Warm tones (red, orange, yellow)**: Energetic, urgent, friendly
- **Cool tones (blue, green, purple)**: Trustworthy, calm, professional
- **Neutrals (black, white, gray)**: Minimal, clean, modern

Tip: Stick to 2–3 dominant colors for a cohesive look. Gamma provides ready-made themes, or you can create your own based on brand or mood.

B. Typography as a Voice

- Use **bold headlines** to direct attention
- Use **contrasting sizes** to show hierarchy
- Limit yourself to 2 typefaces for consistency

Gamma lets you customize typography easily within each section, block, or page.

C. Imagery and Iconography

- Use photos to humanize your story
- Use icons to simplify complex ideas
- Maintain style consistency (flat, outline, or filled)

You can upload your own visuals or use Gamma's AI-suggested media based on your content.

3. Structuring Slides to Reflect a Journey

In Gamma, content is built using "cards" or modular sections—similar to a microsite or document rather than static slides. This gives you a lot of flexibility in structuring your flow.

A. Use Sequential Sections

Design each card to represent one idea or step in your story. Gamma allows you to reorder them easily to maintain logical progression.

Example:

- Slide 1: "The Problem" (with a bold quote or statistic)

- Slide 2: "Why It Matters" (visual breakdown or testimonial)

- Slide 3: "Our Solution" (highlight product features with icons)

- Slide 4: "The Impact" (before-and-after visuals or data)

B. Anchor Sections with Transitions

Use visual or textual anchors (e.g., "Let's dive deeper" or a colored divider) to show that a new chapter is beginning. Gamma supports smooth scrolling and interactivity that keeps transitions intuitive and engaging.

C. Repetition for Reinforcement

Design recurring visual elements (e.g., a logo corner, or a "key point" box) to build rhythm and familiarity throughout the presentation.

4. Pacing the Story with Design Choices

Good pacing keeps viewers engaged without overwhelming them. Gamma lets you control pacing through:

A. Slide Length

Avoid overloading slides with text. Instead, break complex ideas into multiple short slides.

B. Visual Breathing Room

Use whitespace strategically to guide the eye and prevent visual fatigue. Gamma's default layouts encourage clean spacing, but you can also manually adjust padding and margins.

C. Strategic Emphasis

Use design elements like bold color blocks, highlighted text, or animation (coming soon to Gamma) to direct focus at key narrative moments.

5. Using Interactive Elements for Immersion

Interactivity enhances narrative immersion and can be used to personalize the experience for your audience.

A. Buttons to Control Flow

Rather than linear slide-by-slide navigation, you can use **buttons** in Gamma to allow:

- Branching logic ("Click to explore Product A vs. Product B")
- Jump-to-section features
- CTAs like "Contact Us" or "Start Demo"

B. Embedded Media as Storytelling Tools

- **Videos** can replace long explanations
- **GIFs** can add personality or visual demos
- **Interactive charts** can turn data into narrative insights

Gamma makes it easy to embed links, videos, and even dynamic web content within a card.

C. Tooltips and Hover Effects *(beta/experimental)*

These allow you to provide micro-information in a subtle, non-intrusive way—perfect for footnotes, references, or definitions.

6. Testing and Refining the Flow

Designing your narrative is an iterative process. Gamma allows easy **previewing**, **real-time edits**, and **collaboration** so you can refine your story until it feels just right.

Tips for Testing:

- Share with a colleague and observe their interaction

- Use viewer analytics (covered in Chapter 5.3) to see where drop-off occurs

- Ask for feedback on emotional impact: "Was it engaging?" "Did it feel connected?"

7. Final Thoughts: Design as a Narrative Tool

Design is not just a visual exercise—it's a storytelling tool. When used with intention, it helps guide the viewer through your ideas, emotions, and ultimately, your goals. Gamma gives you the freedom and power to design not just *presentations*, but *experiences*.

So as you build with Gamma, remember:

- Every layout tells a part of your story

- Every color and image creates emotion

- Every interactive element invites engagement

When these are all aligned with a clear and compelling narrative, your presentation will not just *show* information—it will *move* people.

4.3.3 Balancing Text and Visuals

In today's digital communication landscape, your audience expects more than a wall of text or a pretty slideshow—they crave experiences. One of the most powerful ways to deliver that experience is by carefully **balancing text and visuals** in your presentations. Gamma makes this easier than ever with its intuitive, AI-powered tools that allow users to structure and style content dynamically.

This section explores not only *why* the balance between text and visuals matters but also *how* to achieve that balance effectively using Gamma. Whether you're building a pitch deck, a report, or an interactive one-pager, mastering this principle will make your work more compelling and memorable.

Why Balance Matters

Before diving into techniques, let's explore why balance is crucial:

- **Visual overload** confuses or distracts.

- **Text overload** overwhelms and bores.

- **A thoughtful mix** keeps the audience engaged and guides them through your narrative.

Presentations are a **form of storytelling**, and like any great story, pacing is everything. Too many visuals without context, or too much context without engagement, and your story falls flat. Gamma allows you to build visual rhythm into your content while maintaining message clarity.

Principles of Effective Balance

Here are some high-level principles to keep in mind:

1. **Every Visual Should Serve a Purpose** Don't use visuals just for decoration. Every image, chart, or video should reinforce or clarify the message.

2. **Text Should Be Digestible** Break large blocks into bullets, use headers, and keep sentences concise. If you need to explain something in-depth, consider layering it over multiple cards.

3. **Use the Layout as a Narrative Tool** Gamma's card-based format encourages content to be consumed piece by piece. Use this to your advantage to pace your story.

4. **Let the AI Assist You—But Curate It** Gamma's AI can suggest layout and imagery, but you're the storyteller. Treat AI like a co-author: helpful, but not infallible.

Applying Balance in Gamma

Let's get into actionable techniques for balancing text and visuals using Gamma's tools and features.

1. Designing Card Layouts with Flow

Gamma's canvas uses a card system, which naturally encourages segmenting information. Here's how to apply balance:

- **One Idea Per Card:** Limit content to one key concept per card to keep attention focused. Add supporting visuals where needed.

- **Text-to-Visual Ratio:** Aim for about 60% text and 40% visual space for general content. For data-heavy presentations, flip the ratio.

- **Use Section Dividers:** Break your deck into mini-chapters using bold, graphic-based title cards. These give the audience a moment to refocus.

Gamma Tip: Use AI to auto-layout a section and then tweak individual cards to adjust visual emphasis.

2. Choosing the Right Visuals

Different visuals serve different purposes. Here's how to choose:

Type of Visual	Best For	Example Use Case
Images	Evoking emotion, demonstrating people/context	Team introductions, client case studies
Icons/Illustrations	Emphasizing points, replacing bullet symbols	Feature summaries, checklists
Charts & Graphs	Explaining data or trends	Sales performance, market share
GIFs/Animations	Showing product features or transitions	Product demos, onboarding tutorials
Embedded Videos	Adding depth or external voices	Testimonials, explainer videos

Gamma Tip: Gamma suggests visuals based on context—use the AI-generated options to speed up your workflow, but always review for fit and tone.

3. Optimizing Text for Visual Harmony

Great copy enhances the visual appeal of your deck. Here are tips to write for Gamma:

- **Use Headers Thoughtfully** Keep headings short and bold. Think in terms of *headlines*, not *paragraphs*.

- **Embrace the Power of Bullets** Bullet points are easier to scan and digest. Limit each bullet to one key idea.

- **White Space is Your Friend** Don't cram every corner. Gamma layouts often leave space for breathing—trust the design.

- **Tone Matches Design** Keep tone consistent with visual style. Casual decks can use lighter phrasing; formal decks need more polish.

4. Using Gamma's AI to Suggest Visual Enhancements

Gamma's AI assistant is especially useful when you're stuck deciding how to visualize a point. You can:

- **Highlight a block of text**, click the magic wand icon, and choose "Visual Suggestions." Gamma will suggest related images or layouts.

- **Ask AI to expand or reword content** to make it more concise or engaging.

- **Generate new layout options** based on your current content to explore different design directions.

Example Scenario: You write a paragraph explaining a customer journey. Gamma suggests converting it into a horizontal timeline with icons and one-sentence blurbs. This not only improves flow but makes it easier to understand at a glance.

5. Layering Text and Visuals for Engagement

Sometimes the best presentations are the ones that *feel* like a guided experience. Use layered structure:

- **Start with an image** or bold headline to catch attention.

- **Follow up with text** explaining or supporting the visual.

- **End with a visual summary** like a chart or infographic.

You can use "Reveal More" sections in Gamma to layer content in interactive cards—ideal for progressive storytelling without overwhelming users.

6. Avoiding Common Pitfalls

Here are mistakes to watch out for:

- **Too Many Images:** Makes content feel like a collage, not a story.

- **Text Walls:** If it looks like a Word doc, it probably needs a visual.

- **Mixed Styles:** Don't combine cartoony icons with formal charts. Choose a style and stick to it.

- **Ignoring Mobile Views:** Presentations shared via link may be viewed on phones—test responsiveness.

7. Real-Life Examples of Balance Done Well

Case Study 1: Startup Pitch Deck A founder uses a bold image on the title card, brief overview text, and a chart summarizing traction. Every 3-4 cards, there's a section break or graphic stat to re-engage viewers.

Case Study 2: Online Portfolio A creative designer uses large visuals of her work, short quotes from clients, and interactive buttons linking to detailed project pages. Text is kept minimal, but thoughtful.

Case Study 3: Marketing Report A team presents campaign results using graphs, before/after screenshots, and two-sentence summaries per card. Visuals clarify the story, not just decorate it.

8. Building Your Own Design System in Gamma

As you grow familiar with Gamma, create a consistent design system for your presentations:

- **Pick 2-3 core layout styles** that work well together

- **Define a color palette** and stick to it

- **Use consistent typography hierarchy**

- **Save templates or reuse past cards** for speed and cohesion

You can even create a "Theme" inside Gamma to quickly apply this system across decks.

Conclusion: Design is Storytelling

Balancing text and visuals is not just about making your presentation look good—it's about telling your story effectively. With Gamma, you don't need to be a designer or developer to create stunning, interactive experiences. All you need is:

- A clear message

- Smart use of AI tools

- Attention to structure and pacing

Mastering the balance between text and visuals unlocks the true power of Gamma—and gives your ideas the impact they deserve.

CHAPTER V
Sharing and Collaboration

5.1 Sharing Your Presentation

5.1.1 Sharing via Link or Email

Creating a visually stunning presentation in Gamma is only part of the journey. Once your content is polished, it's time to share it with the world—or at least with your team, clients, audience, or collaborators. One of Gamma's standout features is how incredibly easy it is to share your work. In this section, we'll walk through the first and most fundamental method: **sharing your presentation via link or email**.

Whether you're sending a pitch deck to investors, a lesson plan to students, or a product demo to your client, Gamma offers flexible, fast, and user-friendly ways to make your content accessible. This section will help you master this essential step, including best practices for sharing securely and professionally.

✅ Why Share via Link or Email?

Sharing via link or email in Gamma is:

- **Instant** – No need to export and attach files.

- **Interactive** – Viewers experience your full design, animations, and interactions as intended.

- **Collaborative** – You can control permissions and even enable real-time feedback.

- **Cloud-Based** – No downloading needed, just a URL.

This method is perfect for:

- Remote teams collaborating on a live document

- Presenting in meetings without screen-sharing software

- Sending view-only versions of your content

- Embedding access in newsletters or reports

Let's explore how to do it step by step.

🔧 How to Share via Link

Step 1: Open Your Presentation

Start by navigating to the presentation you want to share. If you're in the main dashboard, click on the presentation to open it in edit or preview mode.

💡 **Tip:** Double-check your content before sharing. Use the "Preview" mode to see what your audience will experience.

Step 2: Click the "Share" Button

In the top-right corner of your screen, you'll find the **"Share"** button. Click it to open the sharing settings window.

This is where the magic happens.

Step 3: Choose Your Link Settings

You'll now see a section labeled **"Get Link"** or **"Anyone with the link"**. Here you'll be able to:

- **Copy the link** to your clipboard

- **Set viewing permissions**
  - View only
  - Comment access
  - Edit access (if you're sharing with collaborators)

- **Enable/disable link sharing** altogether

🔒 **Security Tip:** Be cautious when enabling edit access via public link. Only use it for trusted collaborators.

Step 4: Share the Link

Now simply paste the link wherever you want:

- Slack or Microsoft Teams messages

- Emails

- Notion or Confluence pages

- Social media platforms (if it's public-facing)

- QR codes for print materials or presentations

✉ How to Share via Email

Gamma also allows direct email sharing to invite individuals or teams to view or collaborate.

Step 1: Click "Share" and Go to the "Invite People" Section

When you click the "Share" button, you'll see an input box labeled **"Invite people"**. Here's where you can type in email addresses.

You can invite:

- Colleagues

- Clients

- Students

- Reviewers

Step 2: Set Permissions

Next to each invitee's email, you'll see a dropdown menu with permission options:

- **Viewer** – They can only see the presentation.

- **Commenter** – They can leave feedback but not make changes.

- **Editor** – They can edit the content directly.

Choose the permission level based on the role of the recipient.

⊛ **Best Practice:** Use "Viewer" for final delivery, "Commenter" for review rounds, and "Editor" for true co-creation.

Step 3: Add a Message (Optional)

There's a text box for adding a personal note. Use this to:

- Introduce your project

- Provide context

- Set expectations

- Request specific feedback

Example:

"Hi Jenna, here's the draft for our Q2 roadmap presentation. Please leave your comments by Friday. Thanks!"

Step 4: Hit Send

Click **"Send Invite"** and Gamma will email each person a link with their assigned access. Recipients will be able to open it directly from their inbox.

🔲🔲 Controlling Access and Privacy

Gamma offers robust access controls to make sure your presentation is viewed by the right people—and only the right people.

Change Access Settings Anytime

At any time, you can:

- Revoke access

- Change permission levels

- Disable public sharing

- See who currently has access

This gives you **total control**, even after sharing the link.

Set Expiration Dates (Advanced Feature)

In some premium tiers of Gamma, you can also:

- Set expiration dates on links

- Restrict download/export access

- Enable password protection for extra security

🔒 **Pro Tip:** If you're sharing confidential material, always use limited-time access or password protection.

🗂 Sharing for Different Audiences

Internal Teams

For internal communication, sharing via email is often best. Use editor access to allow real-time teamwork and updates.

External Clients

For client-facing decks, prefer "View-only" links. Use branded link previews and clean visuals.

Public Audiences

If you're posting a Gamma presentation publicly (e.g., blog, portfolio, social media):

- Use "View-only" sharing

- Disable editing and commenting

- Use analytics to track engagement (covered in 5.3)

Events and Conferences

Need to share at scale? Consider:

- Creating a QR code from the link

- Embedding in event apps or agendas

- Adding the link to a slide for audience reference

☐ Best Practices for Sharing

Do	Don't
Use descriptive file names	Leave generic titles like "Untitled"
Set correct permissions before sharing	Accidentally give editor access to the public
Preview before sharing	Send without reviewing final layout
Include context in your email	Leave people guessing why they received it
Use Gamma analytics	Share blindly without tracking engagement

📈 Link Performance and Next Steps

After sharing your presentation, your job isn't over. In fact, it's just beginning!

Once your audience starts engaging with your presentation, you can track:

- Who's viewed it

- How long they stayed on each section

- What they clicked on

These insights will be discussed in detail in **Section 5.3: Tracking Engagement**, but it's worth knowing that sharing via link or email enables these features. You'll receive far more valuable feedback than you would from a static PowerPoint deck.

☐ Summary: Sharing via Link or Email

Sharing your Gamma presentation via link or email offers unmatched convenience and interactivity. You've learned how to:

- Generate and control sharing links

- Invite collaborators with specific permissions

- Tailor your sharing strategy based on your audience

- Avoid common pitfalls

- Prepare for next steps like engagement tracking

Sharing is no longer just a "send and forget" task—it's now a dynamic part of your content strategy.

→ ☐ What's Next?

In the next section, we'll dive into **embedding your presentation on websites**—a powerful way to expand your reach, grow your brand, and showcase your work like a pro.

Ready to go beyond the link? Let's embed!

5.1.2 Embedding on Websites

In today's digital world, content needs to live not only in apps or slideshows but also on the web—accessible, shareable, and engaging. Gamma offers a powerful and flexible feature that allows users to **embed their presentations directly into websites**, blogs, or learning management systems (LMS). Whether you're a business professional embedding a pitch deck into your company site, a teacher integrating a lesson into an online course, or a creative showcasing a portfolio—embedding your Gamma presentation helps you deliver content seamlessly and professionally.

This section walks you through **what embedding is**, **why it matters**, **how to do it step by step**, and **best practices** for a polished, interactive presentation experience on your site.

What Does Embedding Mean?

Embedding is the process of inserting content—such as a Gamma presentation—into another web page so that it displays and functions like it's natively part of that site. Instead of just linking to your presentation, embedding allows visitors to interact with it **directly on your page** without having to open a new tab or leave the site.

Think of it like placing a video from YouTube into your blog post. The video plays right there. Similarly, when you embed a Gamma presentation, users can click through slides, interact with elements, or explore a multi-page structure—all within your web interface.

Why Embed Your Gamma Presentations?

Embedding brings a number of advantages to content creators, businesses, and educators alike:

1. Seamless Experience for Viewers

Visitors don't need to leave your website or platform. Everything is presented inline, reducing drop-offs and keeping engagement high.

2. Professional Online Presence

Embedding allows you to create a **visually cohesive and interactive** section of your site. Gamma presentations are sleek, responsive, and adapt well to different screen sizes.

3. Real-Time Updates

When you embed a Gamma presentation, you can **update the original file in Gamma**, and it will automatically reflect on your embedded page—no need to re-upload or change the embed code.

4. Perfect for Content Portability

If you're a marketer, educator, or business developer, you can reuse the same embedded presentation across different landing pages, online courses, or internal tools.

Where Can You Embed Gamma Presentations?

You can embed a Gamma presentation into any platform that supports HTML or iFrame embedding. This includes:

- Personal or company websites (WordPress, Wix, Webflow, etc.)
- Notion pages (with slight workarounds)
- Online course platforms (Teachable, Thinkific, Moodle)
- E-commerce platforms (Shopify product pages or support documentation)

- Internal tools (Confluence, intranet portals)

- Blogs and newsletters (Ghost, Medium via link previews)

Step-by-Step: How to Embed a Gamma Presentation

Now, let's dive into the process of embedding a presentation from Gamma onto your website or platform.

✅ **Step 1: Finalize Your Presentation**

Before embedding, review your presentation to ensure it's polished and ready for public viewing:

- Review text for grammar and tone

- Check that all links and buttons work

- Confirm visual consistency

- Test navigation between slides or sections

If you're embedding into a high-traffic site, ensure the flow is easy for first-time viewers to understand.

✅ **Step 2: Open the Presentation in Gamma**

1. Log in to your Gamma workspace

2. Navigate to the presentation you want to embed

3. Open it in full editor or preview mode

✅ **Step 3: Publish Your Presentation**

To embed a presentation, it must be published:

1. Click the **"Share"** button at the top right corner of your screen

2. Choose **"Publish to Web"**

3. Select your **visibility settings**:

   ○ *Public*: Anyone with the link or the embed can view

o *Unlisted*: Only accessible through the link or embed (not discoverable via search)

o *Restricted*: Only visible to specific users (embedding in this case may not work unless viewers are authenticated)

4. Click **"Publish"** to generate the shareable version

✅ Step 4: Copy the Embed Code

After publishing:

1. Click the **"Embed"** tab in the sharing window

2. You'll see an HTML iframe embed code generated automatically

3. Click **"Copy Embed Code"** — this code includes width, height, and presentation link attributes

The code will look something like:

```
<iframe src="https://gamma.app/presentation-link" width="100%" height="600px" frameborder="0" allowfullscreen></iframe>
```

You can **customize the width and height** as needed. Using width="100%" makes the embedded presentation responsive across screen sizes.

✅ Step 5: Paste the Embed Code into Your Website

Depending on your platform, the way you insert code varies:

- **WordPress (Classic Editor)**: Switch to HTML view and paste the code

- **WordPress (Block Editor - Gutenberg)**: Use the **"Custom HTML"** block and paste the embed code

- **Wix or Webflow**: Use the Embed HTML widget and paste the code

- **Notion** (with workaround): Paste the link, then use a third-party embed widget (like Apption or Indify)

- **Teachable / LMS**: Use the HTML content block in lesson builder

- **Shopify**: Add to product description or page section in HTML editor

Once embedded, save and **preview your page** to test interaction and responsiveness.

Tips for Optimizing Embedded Presentations

Embedding is easy, but **making it effective** requires attention to detail. Here are some expert tips:

◆ Choose the Right Size

While width="100%" is flexible, you might want to control the height based on your presentation length or web layout. Try:

- 600–800px for standard decks

- 1000px+ for scroll-based or portfolio-style pages

◆ Make It Mobile-Responsive

If you're using custom CSS or advanced page builders, wrap your iframe in a responsive container or use media queries to ensure readability on mobile devices.

◆ Use a Strong Call-to-Action

If your embedded Gamma content serves a purpose (e.g., a product demo), include clear CTAs around it:

- "Explore our solution below"

- "Click through the deck to learn more"

- "Contact us after reviewing the details"

◆ Monitor Engagement

Use **Gamma's analytics** (covered in section 5.3) to track who is viewing your embedded presentations and how they're interacting. Use this insight to improve design and messaging.

Troubleshooting Common Embedding Issues

Even though embedding is straightforward, here are some issues you might encounter and how to fix them:

Issue	Cause	Solution
Presentation doesn't load	Not published or link is private	Ensure presentation is set to "Public" or "Unlisted"
Frame is cut off	Height too small	Increase height in embed code (e.g., 800px)
Doesn't appear on mobile	Not responsive	Use width="100%" and test layout
Can't paste code	Platform doesn't support raw HTML	Use third-party embed tools (e.g., Embedly) or contact platform support
Broken links inside	URLs are incorrect or relative	Use full absolute links when embedding inside Gamma

Embedding Use Cases: Real-World Examples

Here are a few examples to inspire how you might use embedding in practice:

- **Startup Pitch on Landing Page:** A startup uses Gamma to create a sleek investor pitch and embeds it directly on their homepage.

- **Online Course Slide Deck:** An educator embeds interactive slide decks into each module of an online course.

- **Freelance Portfolio:** A designer showcases recent work in a scroll-based Gamma page, embedded into their personal portfolio site.

- **Product Overview in Documentation:** A SaaS company embeds feature tours inside their product docs to help users visualize workflows.

Final Thoughts

Embedding Gamma presentations on your website is a powerful way to **extend the life and reach of your content**. It bridges the gap between creation and distribution, letting you deliver interactive, engaging, and dynamic experiences right where your audience already is. With just a few clicks, your ideas go from slide deck to polished web component—no coding required.

In the next sections, we'll dive into how to **collaborate with others in Gamma (5.2)** and how to **track viewer engagement (5.3)**, both crucial for teams and professionals aiming to grow their impact through presentation content.

Let Gamma do the heavy lifting—**you just bring the ideas**.

5.1.3 Downloading as PDF or PPT

One of Gamma's most powerful features lies in its flexibility—not only can you create stunning, web-based presentations directly on the platform, but you can also export your work into widely used offline formats like **PDF** and **PowerPoint (.PPTX)**. This gives you the freedom to present your content in a variety of environments, from boardroom meetings with no internet connection to traditional classroom setups that require offline access.

In this section, we'll walk through the process of downloading your Gamma presentation, explore the differences between PDF and PPT export options, and offer best practices for preserving interactivity and visual integrity.

◆ Why Download a Gamma Presentation?

Even though Gamma is designed as a modern, AI-powered, cloud-first presentation tool, there are many scenarios where exporting your work is not just helpful—but necessary:

- **Offline access:** Ideal for presenting in places with unreliable or no internet connectivity.

- **Archiving:** Save static copies of presentations for compliance, reference, or long-term documentation.

- **Collaboration:** Share with stakeholders who prefer to view slides in PowerPoint or PDF format.

- **Printing:** Prepare physical handouts or printed materials from your Gamma slides.

- **Customization:** Allow team members to edit content in PowerPoint if they are not using Gamma.

Gamma allows you to export in two primary formats: **PDF** (for static documents) and **PPTX** (for editable slides).

✍ Step-by-Step: Downloading as PDF

PDFs are great for static sharing. Once exported, your design remains consistent across devices and platforms. Here's how to do it in Gamma:

Step 1: Finalize Your Presentation

Before you export, go through a quick checklist:

- Proofread your content.

- Ensure images are rendering correctly.

- Remove any placeholder content.

- Test links if you plan to share both the online and offline versions.

🔍 *Note: PDF exports will not support clickable interactivity (buttons, links, embedded media). It captures only a visual snapshot of the slides.*

Step 2: Access the Download Options

1. Open your Gamma presentation.

2. Click the **"Share"** button on the top-right corner of the screen.

3. In the dropdown, click **"Download"**.

4. Choose **"Download as PDF"**.

You will typically see a few configuration options here:

- **Include All Pages or Select Pages:** Decide if you want the entire presentation or only a portion.

- **Page Format Options (Portrait vs. Landscape):** Choose your desired layout.

- **Include Notes or Not:** For speaker handouts or internal use.

Step 3: Customize Your Settings

Depending on the complexity of your presentation, you may want to:

- **Enable high-resolution download** for image clarity.

- **Exclude backgrounds** to save on ink for printing.

- **Compress file size** for faster sharing via email.

After confirming the settings, click **"Download"**, and Gamma will generate the PDF. This might take a few seconds depending on the size of your file.

📲 Step-by-Step: Downloading as PowerPoint (PPTX)

If your audience prefers traditional formats or your team uses Microsoft Office or Google Slides, exporting as a .PPTX file is ideal. It allows editing after export, making it especially useful for collaborative projects or further customizations.

Step 1: Prepare Your File for Export

Because Gamma's design elements are often more flexible and responsive than traditional slide decks, you'll want to:

- Double-check element alignment.

- Avoid overly complex animations or transitions that may not translate well.

- Replace any AI-enhanced visuals or embedded content that won't transfer.

Step 2: Navigate to Export Settings

1. With your presentation open, click **"Share"** at the top-right.

2. Choose **"Download"** from the menu.

3. Select **"Download as PowerPoint (.pptx)"**.

Step 3: Choose Your Export Preferences

Gamma allows the following:

- Full presentation vs. specific slides

- Include/Exclude speaker notes

- Embed fonts and images

Once selected, click **"Download"**. Gamma will process and generate a .PPTX file that you can open in:

- **Microsoft PowerPoint**

- **Google Slides** (with some formatting adjustments)
- **Apple Keynote** (with conversion)

Important Notes on Compatibility

- **Fonts:** If you used custom fonts in Gamma, they might be replaced by system defaults unless embedded.
- **Layouts:** Complex page layouts may flatten or be adjusted.
- **Animations/Transitions:** These are often lost in translation; recreate them manually if needed.
- **Interactive Elements:** Hyperlinks may transfer, but buttons and embedded forms typically won't work.

☐ Understanding the Differences: PDF vs. PPTX

Feature	PDF	PowerPoint (.PPTX)
Editable	✘ No	✅ Yes
Interactive	✘ No	⚠☐ Limited
Visual Consistency	✅ High	⚠☐ May vary
File Size	✅ Small	⚠☐ Larger
Compatible with	All Devices	Office Tools
Best Use	Viewing/Printing	Editing/Collaborating

✅ Best Practices for Exporting Gamma Presentations

Here are some expert tips to ensure your exported presentations remain high-quality and useful:

1. Keep a Copy in Gamma

Always retain the editable Gamma version of your deck. This allows you to return, update, and iterate with AI-powered tools in the future.

2. Check After Export

Open the PDF or PPTX file immediately after downloading to ensure everything looks correct. Common issues include:

- Misaligned text
- Missing background images
- Font substitutions

3. Maintain a Backup

Save copies of the exported file in cloud services like Google Drive, Dropbox, or OneDrive to avoid data loss.

4. Use Export Versions Strategically

- Use **PDFs** when sharing with clients, printing, or submitting final work.
- Use **PPTX** when collaborating, editing, or combining with other slide decks.

🔲🔲 Troubleshooting Export Issues

Issue 1: Images Not Rendering Correctly

- Try downloading in high resolution.
- Reinsert any images and try again.

Issue 2: Fonts Look Different in PowerPoint

- Use common fonts that exist in most systems (e.g., Arial, Calibri).
- Embed fonts if your version of PowerPoint supports it.

Issue 3: Broken Layouts in PPTX

- Simplify slide layouts before export.
- Adjust manually in PowerPoint after downloading.

Issue 4: Missing Speaker Notes

- Ensure "Include speaker notes" is selected before download.

💡 Pro Tips for Gamma Exports

- Create a **"Print Version"** of your presentation within Gamma by duplicating the original and simplifying the design for PDF export.

- Include **contact information or QR codes** on exported materials to direct people back to your live Gamma link.

- Save export presets if you find yourself downloading regularly (currently, Gamma may or may not support this depending on version—check updates).

🎁 Summary: Export with Confidence

Gamma gives you the best of both worlds: modern, cloud-native presentations with the ability to export to traditional formats. Whether you're preparing offline handouts for a workshop, sending a pitch deck to investors, or collaborating with a teammate who prefers PowerPoint, Gamma's export options ensure your work is always accessible, flexible, and shareable.

As you become more familiar with the exporting process, you'll learn how to design your content with **multi-platform flexibility in mind**—leveraging Gamma's design power while maintaining compatibility across PDF and PPTX formats.

In the next section, we'll explore **real-time collaboration**, including how to co-edit presentations and leave feedback efficiently with your team or clients.

5.2 Collaborating with Others

5.2.1 Inviting Collaborators

Collaboration is at the heart of effective content creation—especially in today's fast-paced, interconnected world. Whether you're working on a team project, preparing a business pitch, or developing an educational module, the ability to collaborate with others in real time can significantly streamline your workflow. Gamma has embraced this need by building intuitive, flexible collaboration tools that are baked right into the platform.

In this section, we will explore how to **invite collaborators** to your Gamma project, discuss **permissions and user roles**, and walk you through **real-world use cases** for effective collaboration.

◆ Why Collaboration Matters in Gamma

Before we dive into the how-to, it's important to understand **why** collaboration is a key feature in Gamma:

- **Efficiency**: Real-time editing reduces the back-and-forth of sending files or slides via email.

- **Creativity**: Different minds contribute diverse ideas, improving the quality of your final output.

- **Feedback**: Colleagues can suggest edits, comment, and refine your message on the fly.

- **Consistency**: Shared content standards and messaging can be more easily enforced when working together.

Gamma is designed with **Google Docs-style collaboration** in mind—but tailored to the world of AI-powered presentations.

◆ Getting Started: How to Invite Collaborators

Inviting collaborators to your Gamma presentation or document is easy and seamless. Follow these steps:

Step 1: Open Your Gamma Project

- Log into your Gamma account.

- From your **Dashboard**, click on the presentation or document you'd like to share.

- Once inside the project, look to the **top right corner** of the interface for the "Share" button. It often appears as an icon with a "+" or a small figure.

Step 2: Click on "Share"

When you click the **"Share"** button, a modal (pop-up window) will appear. This is your central hub for managing access and inviting collaborators.

Here's what you'll see:

- **Invite via Email**: A text box to input email addresses of people you'd like to collaborate with.

- **Permission Settings**: Options to control what each person can do (more on this shortly).

- **Copy Shareable Link**: You can also generate a link with permissions and send it manually.

Step 3: Enter Email Addresses

In the email input field:

- Type in one or multiple email addresses separated by commas.

- You can invite collaborators who **do or do not** have a Gamma account yet.

  - If someone doesn't have a Gamma account, they'll be prompted to create one before they can access the project.

Tip: Consider adding a short message when sending an invite—especially if the recipient might not recognize the project name.

Step 4: Set Access Permissions

Next to each collaborator's name or email, you'll see a **dropdown menu** to assign roles. These roles define how much control each person has.

There are typically three options:

1. **Can View**

    o   The user can see the content but **cannot** make any changes.

    o   Ideal for stakeholders or reviewers who only need to read or comment.

2. **Can Comment**

    o   The user can leave **comments** or suggestions, but **cannot directly edit** content.

    o   Perfect for peer reviews or external partners giving feedback.

3. **Can Edit**

    o   Full editing privileges.

    o   The user can change text, layout, media, add new slides, delete content, etc.

    o   Recommended for team members actively building the presentation.

Choose the appropriate role depending on the person's involvement.

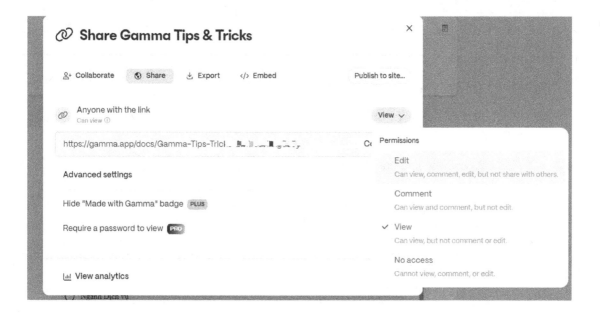

Step 5: Send the Invitation

Once everything looks good:

- Click **Send Invite** (or "Share") to send email invitations directly.
- If you've generated a shareable link, copy it and send it via email, messaging apps, or internal chat platforms like Slack.

The invited collaborators will now have access based on the permissions you've set.

◆ Best Practices When Inviting Collaborators

Collaboration works best when there are clear expectations and respectful digital etiquette. Here are some best practices to follow:

✓ Use Descriptive File Names

- Instead of "Presentation Final V2.5," name your project something that indicates the topic or purpose.
  Example: "Q3 Sales Pitch – North America Team"

✅ Limit Edit Access Strategically

- Give **"Can Edit"** access only to those who truly need to modify content.

- For those reviewing or providing feedback, **"Can Comment"** or **"Can View"** is often sufficient.

- This reduces the chance of accidental edits or formatting changes.

✅ Notify Collaborators of Their Role

- Let them know what's expected: Are they supposed to write, revise, comment, or just read?

- Clear communication ensures no one oversteps or underdelivers.

✅ Use Comments to Avoid Overwriting

- Encourage team members to **leave comments** instead of editing directly, especially for sensitive content.

- Gamma's comment system allows for threaded discussion, keeping the conversation in context.

✅ Schedule Collaboration Times (for Live Editing)

- If you're working on a tight deadline, consider setting specific time slots for **real-time collaboration**.

- This avoids conflicting edits and makes the experience feel more like a virtual team meeting.

◆ Real-World Collaboration Scenarios

To help solidify your understanding, let's look at a few **use cases** where inviting collaborators is especially helpful.

🏦 Business Teams – Sales Pitch Decks

A sales manager creates a Gamma presentation and invites:

- The **marketing lead** to ensure branding is consistent.

- The **data analyst** to verify graphs and metrics.

- The **product manager** to add technical content. Each collaborator has "Can Edit" access so they can update their respective sections.

🎓 Educators – Student Group Projects

A teacher asks students to create a Gamma presentation in groups of 3.

- One student creates the presentation and invites teammates as "Can Edit."

- The teacher is invited with "Can Comment" to review and give suggestions before the final submission.

- This setup encourages peer-to-peer collaboration while still allowing instructor oversight.

💼 Consultants – Client Deliverables

A freelance consultant creates a client report in Gamma.

- They invite the client with "Can View" access for a preview.

- After approval, the client is granted "Can Comment" to provide final feedback.

- The consultant retains editing rights to make changes before publishing the final version.

◆ Security and Access Control Tips

Gamma provides robust controls to ensure your data stays secure while collaborating.

- **You can revoke access** to any collaborator at any time.

- You can **change permissions** from "Edit" to "View" or "Comment" as needed.

- Gamma also allows for **project ownership transfers**—ideal if you're handing off work to another team member.

Always review your collaborator list before sharing externally, especially with sensitive or confidential content.

◆ Troubleshooting Invitation Issues

Sometimes, things don't go as smoothly as planned. Here are common issues and how to fix them:

⊘ The collaborator didn't receive the invite email

- Ask them to check their spam or promotions folder.

- If needed, **copy and send the shareable link** manually.

🔒 Collaborator can't access the file

- Double-check if the correct **email address** was used.

- Review the **permissions**—they may have only "View" access when they need to edit.

☐ Changes aren't showing up

- Remind collaborators to **refresh the page** or ensure they're not in "View" mode.

- Gamma saves automatically, but viewing an old tab might show cached content.

⇐ Summary: Inviting Collaborators Effectively

Collaboration in Gamma is built to be **flexible**, **secure**, and **intuitive**. When inviting collaborators, remember to:

- Choose the right permissions for each person.

- Communicate expectations clearly.

- Use comments and feedback tools to enhance teamwork.

- Revisit your sharing settings regularly to stay in control.

By mastering Gamma's collaboration features, you open the door to smoother teamwork, richer content, and faster iteration cycles—exactly what modern creators and professionals need.

✅ **Next Up:** In the following section (5.2.2), we'll explore **Real-Time Editing and Comments**, and how to harness Gamma's built-in tools for seamless team collaboration.

5.2.2 Real-Time Editing and Comments

Collaboration is one of the defining features of Gamma, making it a powerful tool not only for individual creators but also for teams, educators, consultants, marketers, and anyone who works with others to build presentations or dynamic documents. One of the most crucial aspects of collaboration is the ability to **edit in real time** and **leave comments**, enabling seamless teamwork regardless of physical location or time zone.

In this section, we will explore how Gamma enables real-time collaboration, what features are available, how to use them effectively, and best practices to keep your team aligned and productive.

Understanding Real-Time Collaboration in Gamma

Gamma is a cloud-based platform, meaning your work is automatically saved and synced across all devices and users who have access. When you collaborate with teammates or clients, they can make changes, leave comments, or suggest edits—**all in real time**, just like in Google Docs or Notion.

This ensures that:

- Everyone is working on the **latest version**.

- There is no need to send files back and forth.

- Feedback is **instant**, and edits are **immediately visible**.

Inviting Collaborators

Before anyone can edit or comment on your presentation or document, you need to invite them. Here's how:

1. **Click "Share" in the upper-right corner** of your workspace.

2. You'll be prompted to **add email addresses** of the people you'd like to collaborate with.

3. Set **permissions**:

   o **Can edit**: Allows the collaborator to make changes directly.

   o **Can comment**: Limits the collaborator to only adding comments.

   o **Can view**: Viewer only—no editing or comments allowed.

4. Optionally, you can generate a **sharable link** with specific access levels.

Gamma supports team workspaces as well, where you can organize shared projects by folder and easily manage who has access to what.

Real-Time Editing: How It Works

Once a user with "edit" permission opens the document, you'll notice:

- Their **cursor appears** on the screen with their name.

- Changes they make appear **immediately** on your end.

- You can edit **simultaneously**, with multiple users typing or designing at the same time.

This functionality makes Gamma an excellent tool for:

- **Brainstorming sessions**

- **Group content development**

- **Design reviews**

- **Last-minute pitch preparations**

Supported Collaborative Edits

- **Text editing**: All users can write, delete, and format text at the same time.

- **Layout adjustments**: Users can move blocks, images, buttons, and other elements live.

- **Media uploads**: Collaborators can add and adjust images, videos, and embeds.

- **Style changes**: Themes, colors, and fonts can be changed by any editor.

- **Page creation**: New pages/sections can be added, allowing users to divide and conquer parts of the document.

Adding and Managing Comments

If you don't want to edit directly—or need feedback from stakeholders or clients—Gamma allows for **contextual commenting**, where users can leave notes or suggestions on specific parts of the page.

How to Add a Comment

1. **Highlight** the text, block, or media element where you want to leave a comment.

2. Click the **comment icon** (usually a small speech bubble) or use a shortcut like Ctrl + Shift + M.

3. **Type your comment**, then hit **Enter** to post it.

4. Others will be notified (via email or in-app notifications) and can reply to your comment thread.

Comment Features

- **Replying**: Collaborators can respond directly to a comment thread, facilitating discussions.

- **Tagging teammates**: Use @name to tag specific collaborators.

- **Resolving**: Once an issue has been addressed, click "Resolve" to archive the thread.

- **Comment history**: Comments stay visible in the comment panel until resolved, so there's a record of decisions made.

This system helps avoid back-and-forth emails or meetings and keeps the feedback in the context of the document itself.

Using Comments to Drive Feedback Loops

Teams that use comments effectively often benefit from faster iteration and stronger results. Here's how to incorporate comments into your workflow:

1. **Draft Phase**: Collaborators review the initial draft and leave high-level suggestions.

2. **Refinement Phase**: Comments become more granular, focusing on specific content, visuals, or structure.

3. **Finalization Phase**: Comments are used for final proofing—grammar checks, link validation, and formatting.

This process ensures:

- Clear ownership of revisions

- Improved accountability

- Faster alignment and approvals

Real-Time Notifications and Change Awareness

Whenever a collaborator:

- Edits content

- Comments on an element

- Mentions you (@yourname)

You will receive **real-time notifications**, either:

- In the Gamma interface

- Or via **email**, depending on your settings

This keeps you informed and ensures that tasks don't get missed.

Gamma also includes a **"last edited" timestamp** and, in many cases, a **version history** or activity feed—so you can see what changes were made and when.

Best Practices for Collaborative Editing

Here are a few tips to ensure smooth collaboration using Gamma:

✓ Define Roles Early

Assign roles such as content lead, designer, editor, etc., so everyone knows what they're responsible for.

✓ Set Ground Rules

For example: "Please use comments instead of direct edits on version 1" or "Only change design elements after content is finalized."

✓ Use Comments Strategically

Avoid vague comments. Instead of "Fix this," say, "Consider simplifying this sentence to make it clearer for a general audience."

✓ Communicate Frequently

Use comments, chat tools, or meetings to clarify decisions. Combine Gamma with communication platforms like Slack or Teams if needed.

☑️ Review Permissions Regularly

Especially if the project involves external partners. Double-check who has edit or view access.

Handling Conflict or Simultaneous Changes

Real-time editing can occasionally lead to overlaps or conflicting edits. To avoid this:

- Work on **separate sections** at the same time.

- Communicate **who is editing what**.

- Use the **comment feature** to flag areas you're unsure about instead of guessing.

- If needed, **duplicate the presentation** to explore alternative versions.

Gamma's intuitive design minimizes conflicts by syncing changes live and showing who is working where—but human collaboration always benefits from clarity and courtesy.

Use Case: Real-Time Editing in Action

Let's walk through a quick use case of a remote marketing team working on a product launch presentation.

Team Members:

- **Alice**: Content writer

- **Ben**: Visual designer

- **Chloe**: Project manager

- **Daniel**: Product manager

Workflow:

1. **Alice** starts by generating the first draft using AI and adding bullet points for talking topics.

2. **Ben** jumps in to add branded visuals and layouts simultaneously.

3. **Chloe** leaves comments with suggested edits and copy tweaks.

4. **Daniel** reviews product features and adds links to demo videos, tagging Ben for layout adjustments.

5. All collaborate in real time—resolving comments, adjusting copy, and building slides together.

6. Within a few hours, a polished, branded deck is ready for executive review.

Summary: Why Real-Time Collaboration Matters

Real-time editing and comments are not just convenient—they're transformative for teams working at the pace of modern business. Gamma makes it intuitive and powerful to work together, in sync, wherever you are in the world.

With these tools, you can:

- Cut down revision cycles

- Speed up decision-making

- Reduce misunderstandings

- Empower your team to co-create, not just contribute

Whether you're preparing a sales pitch, designing a learning module, or refining a company update, **Gamma's collaborative tools turn presentations into shared experiences—** built faster, with more voices, and greater impact.

5.2.3 Permissions and Roles

Collaboration is at the heart of modern content creation. Whether you're working with colleagues, classmates, clients, or creative partners, understanding how to manage permissions and roles effectively in Gamma is essential. It allows you to maintain control over your content, prevent accidental changes, and create an organized and secure workflow. In this section, we'll take a deep dive into how permissions and roles work in Gamma, when to use different permission levels, and best practices for managing collaborative environments efficiently.

Understanding the Basics of Permissions and Roles

In Gamma, when you share a project with others, you have the ability to define what each person can do with your content. This is achieved through **roles** and **permission settings**.

Roles are predefined sets of permissions that determine what actions a user can perform on a specific project. These typically include:

- Owner
- Editor
- Commenter
- Viewer

Each role is designed to fulfill a specific function in a collaborative setting. By assigning the right role to the right person, you can enhance productivity while minimizing the risks of accidental changes or misuse.

Roles Explained in Detail

1. Owner

Who they are: The Owner is usually the creator of the project or someone assigned administrative control.

Capabilities:

- Full editing rights.
- Can change or revoke access.
- Can delete the project.
- Can transfer ownership to someone else.
- Can manage sharing settings and integrations.

Use Case: This role should be limited to key team members who need full administrative control, such as project leads or content managers.

Tips:

- Avoid assigning Owner rights to too many people.

- If someone leaves the organization or project, transfer ownership appropriately.

2. Editor

Who they are: Editors are team members responsible for modifying content directly.

Capabilities:

- Can add, edit, or delete content.
- Can rearrange sections or pages.
- Can insert images, buttons, and other interactive elements.
- Can comment and reply to others.
- Cannot delete the entire presentation or change access for others.

Use Case: Designers, marketers, educators, or teammates who are actively contributing to the content development.

Tips:

- Use this role when collaborative content building is required.
- Be clear on editing responsibilities to avoid content conflicts.

3. Commenter

Who they are: Commenters provide feedback without making direct edits to the content.

Capabilities:

- Can view all content.
- Can add comments on slides or blocks.
- Can reply to comments.
- Cannot change or delete any actual content.

Use Case: Reviewers, clients giving feedback, or team members involved in approval processes.

Tips:

- Enable comment-only access for stakeholders during review cycles.

- Encourage specific, actionable comments to improve collaboration.

4. Viewer

Who they are: Viewers are recipients of the final content but are not involved in the creation process.

Capabilities:

- Can only view the presentation or page.

- Cannot make changes, leave comments, or interact with elements beyond what's designed (e.g., buttons or links).

Use Case: External clients, partners, students, or a broader audience accessing the published version.

Tips:

- Use viewer access when you want to present information without risk of modification.

- Confirm that sensitive information is appropriately locked before sharing broadly.

How to Assign and Manage Roles in Gamma

Assigning roles in Gamma is simple and intuitive. Here's a step-by-step guide:

Step 1: Open Sharing Settings

- Click the **"Share"** button at the top-right corner of your workspace.

- A pop-up modal will appear with sharing options.

Step 2: Add Collaborators

- Enter the email addresses of the people you want to collaborate with.

- Gamma will recognize users within your organization or those who have Gamma accounts.

- You can also share via a link if you prefer not to add individuals manually.

Step 3: Set Permission Levels

- For each user or group added, click the dropdown menu beside their name.

- Choose from: **Editor**, **Commenter**, or **Viewer**.

- To assign **Owner** role, you'll need to transfer ownership manually via the "More Options" menu.

Step 4: Share and Notify

- Optionally, write a message that will be included in the email invitation.

- Click **"Send"** to notify collaborators and give them access.

Link Sharing Options and Access Control

In addition to individual sharing, Gamma allows link-based sharing. This is useful when sharing with large audiences or publishing content externally.

Link Sharing Settings Include:

- **Restricted** – Only invited people can access.

- **Anyone with the link (View only)** – Publicly shareable, but no edit or comment rights.

- **Anyone with the link (Comment or Edit)** – Rarely used; use with caution.

Best Practices:

- For internal team projects, keep access **restricted**.

- For public presentations, enable **view-only** sharing.

- Be cautious about enabling editing via public links, as it poses security and version control risks.

Transferring Ownership

Sometimes you'll need to hand off a project to someone else — for example, when changing teams or finalizing a client project. Here's how:

- Open the sharing settings.

- Click the three dots next to the person's name.

- Choose **"Make Owner."**

- Confirm your action. Ownership is transferred immediately.

Important: After transferring ownership, you will become an Editor (unless the new Owner reassigns your role).

Managing Teams and Folders

Gamma also allows managing roles at a higher level — by **teams** and **folders**.

Team-Level Roles:

When working in a team workspace:

- You can define default access for all members.

- Assign roles like Viewer, Commenter, or Editor to the entire team.

- Helps streamline access when onboarding new members.

Folder-Level Roles:

- You can share entire folders with specific people or groups.

- All documents in the folder inherit those permissions.

- Great for organizing collaborative projects like campaigns, course content, or client work.

Tips for Effective Role Management

1. **Start with Least Privilege**: Always begin by assigning the lowest necessary role. You can always upgrade later.

2. **Use Commenter for Reviews**: When asking for feedback, avoid giving editing rights unless absolutely needed.

3. **Audit Roles Regularly**: Periodically review who has access to what — especially in large teams.

4. **Label Folders Clearly**: Use naming conventions like *"Drafts"*, *"Final"*, or *"For Review"* to indicate purpose.

5. **Avoid Role Overlap**: Clearly define responsibilities to avoid stepping on toes or duplicating work.

6. **Educate Your Team**: Make sure everyone understands their role and what they are expected to do (and not do).

Troubleshooting Permission Issues

Even in well-managed environments, permission issues can arise. Here are a few common scenarios and how to solve them:

Problem: A collaborator can't edit the presentation.

Solution: Check that they're not assigned as a Viewer or Commenter. Upgrade their access to Editor.

Problem: Someone accidentally deleted content.

Solution: Use Gamma's version history to restore a previous version. Make sure editors are briefed on best practices.

Problem: A stakeholder forwarded the share link and now others can see it.

Solution: Change link settings to "Restricted" and re-share manually.

Problem: You've lost access to your own project after transferring ownership.

Solution: Contact the new owner or Gamma support to request access restoration.

Conclusion: Collaborate Smarter, Not Harder

Managing permissions and roles may seem like a small technical detail, but it can make or break your collaborative experience. By understanding Gamma's role structure and thoughtfully assigning access levels, you can:

- Protect your content

- Streamline your workflow

- Empower the right people at the right time

As your projects grow in scale and scope, this level of control will become even more valuable. With just a few clicks, Gamma allows you to manage a full creative team — securely, efficiently, and effortlessly.

So take a moment to review your access settings, invite your collaborators, and build something great — together.

5.3 Tracking Engagement

5.3.1 Viewer Analytics

One of the most powerful aspects of creating digital content with Gamma is the ability to track how your audience interacts with it. While traditional slide decks offer little to no feedback once they're emailed or presented live, Gamma's web-based format allows you to gain deep insights into viewer behavior through **Viewer Analytics**.

This section will guide you through how to access, understand, and leverage analytics data to improve your presentations and communication strategies.

What is Viewer Analytics in Gamma?

Viewer Analytics in Gamma refers to the set of tools that help you monitor and analyze how people engage with your presentation after it's been shared. Rather than sending a static file like a PDF or PowerPoint deck and hoping it's viewed, Gamma allows you to:

- See **who viewed your content**,
- Understand **how much time they spent** on each section,
- Know **which slides they interacted with the most**, and
- Determine **where users dropped off**.

This type of feedback is essential for **iterating** on your content, optimizing message clarity, and improving your overall storytelling approach.

How to Access Viewer Analytics

Accessing analytics in Gamma is straightforward and integrated into the platform. Here's how to find it:

1. **Navigate to Your Project Dashboard** From your Gamma homepage or workspace, locate the project or presentation you've shared.

2. **Click the "Share" Button** If you've already shared your presentation, clicking this will show you past links and permissions.

3. **Open the Analytics Panel** Look for the **Analytics** tab or icon associated with the shared link. Gamma typically shows it under a tab named **"Insights"**, **"View Analytics"**, or within the **link management settings**.

4. **Review the Data** Once opened, you'll see a variety of charts, graphs, and tables summarizing user interaction.

Note: Analytics is available for content that's been shared via **public link** or **tracked viewer-specific links**. Anonymous viewers may be logged without names, but interactions will still be captured.

Key Metrics Explained

Gamma provides several key metrics to help you understand engagement:

1. Total Views

- Represents how many times your presentation has been opened.

- Repeated views from the same person may be counted more than once depending on privacy settings.

2. Unique Viewers

- Tracks the number of individual users who accessed the presentation.

- Helps you distinguish between true audience reach and repeat visitors.

3. Average Time Spent

- Measures the average duration a viewer spent navigating your content.

- Low average time might suggest the presentation didn't hold attention or was skimmed.

4. Slide-by-Slide Engagement

- Visual heatmaps or graphs show you how much time users spent on each slide.

- High engagement on a slide might mean the content was compelling or required more thought.

- A slide that many viewers skipped might need to be redesigned or clarified.

5. Click Interactions

- Shows where viewers clicked, including navigation buttons, links, or embedded media.

- Useful for measuring the effectiveness of **call-to-action (CTA)** buttons.

6. Exit Rate and Drop-off Points

- Indicates which slide viewers were on when they exited the presentation.

- A high drop-off at a certain slide may suggest content fatigue, confusion, or lack of relevance.

Advanced Insights with Viewer-Specific Tracking

Gamma allows you to generate **viewer-specific links** to track engagement per individual. This is especially powerful when sharing with:

- Clients or investors,

- Students or trainees,

- Collaborators or reviewers.

Each personalized link enables you to see:

- Exactly how *that specific person* interacted with your content,

- What they viewed multiple times,

- Which sections they ignored, and

- Whether they clicked any embedded buttons or CTAs.

This is invaluable for **follow-up communication**. For example:

"Hi Jordan, I noticed you spent time on our pricing model but didn't finish the ROI section. Happy to walk you through it live if you'd like."

How to Use Viewer Analytics to Improve Your Content

Having data is only powerful if you act on it. Here's how to use insights from analytics effectively:

1. Refine Your Message

- If viewers spend too little time on your value proposition slide, perhaps it's too vague or text-heavy.

- Consider breaking long paragraphs into bullet points or adding a compelling visual.

2. Reorder Content Based on Drop-off Points

- If most people drop off before your main pitch, try **reordering** slides to lead with impact.

3. A/B Test Your Slides

- Create two versions of your presentation (Gamma allows easy duplication).

- Share each with different audiences and compare engagement.

4. Improve Interactive Elements

- If buttons or links aren't being clicked, maybe they're not noticeable or compelling.

- Experiment with placement, color, and text ("Learn More" vs. "Get a Demo").

5. Follow Up Intelligently

- Use viewer-specific data to personalize outreach.

- For instance, if someone viewed a particular product slide three times, they may be a high-interest lead.

Privacy Considerations and Transparency

While analytics is powerful, always be transparent with your audience when tracking their behavior—especially in **client, academic, or team settings**. Consider adding a note at the beginning of your presentation like:

"This link includes engagement tracking to help us better understand your interest and improve future materials."

Gamma also allows you to **disable tracking** if privacy is a concern or if your organization has strict compliance standards.

Using Analytics for Different Scenarios

Let's explore how viewer analytics can be applied in various real-world situations:

Sales and Marketing

- Understand which parts of your pitch resonate most.

- Focus sales calls on areas that got the most attention.

Education and Training

- See which students are engaging with the content.

- Identify parts of the lesson that may need clarification.

Internal Communication

- Track how internal teams interact with onboarding materials, updates, or reports.

- Adjust internal messaging based on how much time employees spend engaging.

Integrating with Other Tools

Some organizations use Gamma alongside tools like:

- **CRM platforms** (e.g., HubSpot, Salesforce),

- **Email tools** (e.g., Mailchimp, ConvertKit),

- **Learning management systems (LMS)**.

While Gamma may not directly integrate with every platform, you can **export viewer reports** or connect through **Zapier** or **manual exports** to consolidate engagement data into your broader strategy.

Best Practices for Maximizing Engagement Metrics

1. **Keep Presentations Concise**: Viewers often skim—optimize for clarity and brevity.

2. **Use Visual Cues to Guide Flow**: Interactive arrows, progress bars, and animated elements keep attention high.

3. **Add Strong Call-to-Actions**: Don't leave your audience guessing what to do next.

4. **Encourage Engagement with Prompts**: Pose questions, offer downloadable extras, or embed short quizzes.

5. **Review Analytics Regularly**: Make it part of your workflow—not a one-time activity.

Summary and Next Steps

Gamma's Viewer Analytics feature provides powerful, real-time insights into how your content performs. Whether you're a sales rep pitching to clients, an educator delivering lessons, or a marketer analyzing engagement, these analytics tools can dramatically boost your ability to iterate and improve.

By paying close attention to how users engage with your content, you can:

- Craft more effective narratives,
- Identify high-performing sections,
- Build trust through intelligent follow-up, and
- Continuously refine your presentations for better outcomes.

In the next section, we'll look at **Heatmaps and Click Tracking**, which offer a visual approach to understanding your viewers' behaviors—an excellent complement to the metrics you've just learned.

5.3.2 Heatmaps and Click Tracking

Creating a visually stunning and content-rich presentation is only half the battle. Once your presentation is published and shared, how do you know whether your audience is engaging with it? Are viewers clicking on the interactive buttons you carefully placed? Do they stop reading after the second slide? What parts of your presentation are working—and which ones aren't?

This is where **heatmaps and click tracking** come in. In Gamma, these tools offer a powerful way to **analyze viewer behavior**, allowing you to make data-informed decisions that improve the effectiveness of your content. Whether you're pitching a business idea, building an online portfolio, or delivering a class presentation, **understanding audience engagement is essential** to refining your message.

In this section, we'll break down how to use Gamma's heatmaps and click tracking features, what kind of insights you can expect to gather, and how to interpret that data to improve your presentations.

What Are Heatmaps and Click Tracking?

Heatmaps are graphical representations of user activity. In the context of Gamma, they show you **where users are clicking, scrolling, or spending the most time** on your presentation. Hotter colors (like red and orange) indicate higher levels of activity, while cooler colors (like blue or green) show lower levels.

Click tracking is a related concept that specifically logs **which interactive elements your viewers are clicking on**. Whether it's a button that leads to another slide, a hyperlink to an external site, or a call-to-action in your final slide, click tracking tells you what content drives action.

Combined, these tools provide **real-time insights into your audience's behavior**, which you can use to optimize everything from slide order to design layout.

How to Enable Engagement Tracking in Gamma

By default, Gamma automatically collects engagement metrics once your presentation is **published and shared using a trackable link**. Here's how to ensure your presentation is set up to collect click and heatmap data:

1. **Publish Your Presentation**: Click the "Share" button in the top right corner and select **"Publish to web."** This ensures your content is hosted and ready to track visits.

2. **Enable Analytics**: Make sure the **"Engagement tracking" toggle** is turned on under the Share settings. This will activate both **click logging** and **heatmap generation**.

3. **Use a Trackable Link**: Gamma generates a unique URL for your presentation. Any viewer accessing the content through this link will automatically be included in analytics tracking.

4. **Optional: Require Email Identification**: If you'd like to track viewer behavior on an individual level (e.g., to see how specific clients interact with your pitch deck), you can **require viewers to input their email** before accessing the content. This is especially useful for lead generation or follow-up.

Accessing Heatmap and Click Tracking Data

To view the data:

1. Open your Gamma dashboard and navigate to your published presentation.

2. Click the **"Analytics" tab** located near the top menu bar.

3. Under this tab, you will find:

   o Viewer Heatmaps

   o Click Events

   o Time-on-Slide Statistics

   o Drop-Off Points

Each of these data types offers unique insights. Let's break them down further.

Understanding Heatmap Data

A **heatmap** in Gamma is typically overlaid on your slides and updated dynamically based on real-time interaction data. It allows you to:

- **See where viewers click most** on each slide.

- **Understand which sections of a slide draw attention** (titles, images, buttons, etc.).

- **Identify which parts are being ignored**, suggesting where you might want to cut or improve content.

Key Metrics in Heatmaps:

- **Click Density**: How many clicks an area receives.

- **Scroll Depth (on long slides)**: How far down viewers go if you've built longer, scrolling presentations.

- **Attention Zones**: Heat-based coloration indicating the "hottest" (most interacted-with) areas.

Practical Use Case Examples:

Use Case	How Heatmap Helps
Marketing Pitch	See if viewers are engaging with your call-to-action buttons.
Education	Identify which concepts or examples draw student clicks or interest.
Portfolio	Learn what projects or samples attract the most attention.

Understanding Click Tracking

Where heatmaps show *where* users are interacting, **click tracking shows *what* they are interacting with.**

Gamma logs interactions like:

- Button clicks (internal navigation or external links)

- Hyperlinks embedded in text

- Interactive elements such as collapsible sections

- File or media opens

Click tracking is valuable for:

- **Testing Calls-to-Action (CTAs)**: Did your viewers click "Book a Call" or "Download PDF"?

- **Measuring Conversion Intent**: Did they follow the link to your website or LinkedIn?

- **Optimizing Internal Navigation**: Are viewers using embedded navigation buttons to explore your content?

Visualizing Click Tracking

Click tracking in Gamma can be viewed in both **tabular format** (logs of interactions) and **overlay format** (dots on slides showing where interaction occurred).

Gamma may provide metrics like:

- **Total Clicks per Element**

- **Unique Clickers**

- **Click-Through Rate (CTR)** per slide or element

- **Time to First Click** (How long it took users to click on an element)

Analyzing Drop-Off and Attention Curves

Another valuable aspect of Gamma's engagement analytics is understanding **viewer drop-off**:

- **Slide-by-slide engagement charts** show how many viewers drop off at each stage.

- These are often visualized as line graphs with declining viewer count across the presentation timeline.

How to Use This Insight:

- **Early Drop-Off**: Might suggest the introduction is too long or unclear.

- **Middle Drop-Off**: Often a sign that the presentation lacks momentum or clarity.

- **Final Slide Drop-Off**: Indicates low interest in the conclusion or CTA—consider making it more compelling.

Interpreting the Data: From Insight to Action

Raw data is just the beginning. The goal is to turn these insights into improvements. Here's a framework:

1. **Identify High and Low Engagement Slides**: Revisit the most and least clicked slides to ask: What's different? Layout? Text? Visuals?

2. **Revise Underperforming CTAs**: If nobody clicks your CTA, test different phrasing or placement.

3. **Reorganize Slide Order**: If drop-off happens early, consider starting with a more compelling hook.

4. **A/B Test Slide Designs**: Create different versions of your presentation to compare click and heatmap performance.

5. **Double Down on High-Interest Areas**: If a particular product or idea gets lots of clicks, consider giving it more space or featuring it earlier.

Tips for Improving Engagement Using Click and Heatmap Data

- **Keep slides concise and focused.** The more cluttered the content, the more distracted the viewer.

- **Use strong visual cues** (arrows, color contrast, size hierarchy) to guide attention to CTAs.

- **Test different designs and wording** for key slides to see what drives interaction.

- **Limit the number of clickable elements per slide** to avoid overwhelming your audience.

- **Consider mobile vs. desktop interaction**—ensure key buttons are thumb-friendly.

Limitations of Engagement Tracking

While heatmaps and click tracking are powerful tools, they have some limitations:

- **Not all clicks mean interest.** Some may be accidental.

- **Heatmaps are anonymized by default** unless you require email sign-in.

- **Engagement doesn't equal comprehension.** A viewer might click without truly understanding the content.

- **Bias in data volume.** If only a small number of users view your presentation, it may be too early to draw conclusions.

Real-World Example: Optimizing a Product Demo Presentation

Let's say you shared a Gamma presentation pitching your new product. You noticed:

- High drop-off after Slide 3

- Most clicks are on Slide 2's "See Pricing" button

- Almost no one clicks the "Contact Us" button on the last slide

Action Plan:

- Move the pricing information earlier (Slide 2 → Slide 1)

- Shorten the intro on Slide 1

- Make the "Contact Us" button more visible, perhaps with a contrasting color

- A/B test two versions of the ending slide: one with a contact form, one with a CTA button

After a week, you see the contact button CTR increased by 40%. Success!

Conclusion: Empower Your Story with Data

In a world where attention spans are short and competition for eyeballs is fierce, **data-driven presentations are the way forward**. Gamma's heatmaps and click tracking features allow you to go beyond just *presenting*—they help you **listen**, **respond**, and **optimize** in real time.

By analyzing how your audience engages with your content, you gain the power to fine-tune every element for maximum clarity, impact, and persuasion.

So don't just share your ideas—**track how they land**, and let the data shape your next brilliant creation.

5.3.3 Improving Based on Feedback

When you've shared your Gamma presentation with the world—whether with teammates, clients, or a broader audience—your job isn't quite done. Effective communication is a two-way street, and one of the most powerful aspects of using Gamma is its built-in feedback loop. By analyzing how viewers engage with your content and using that feedback to refine and enhance your presentation, you ensure that your message not only reaches your audience, but *resonates* with them.

In this section, we'll explore how to collect feedback in Gamma, interpret the data, and use these insights to make strategic improvements to your presentation. We'll also touch on the psychology of user engagement, practical revision strategies, and ways to optimize both content and design for better outcomes.

1. Why Feedback Matters in Presentations

In traditional slide decks, once your presentation is shared or delivered, the only feedback you may receive is a comment from a colleague or a glance from your boss. Gamma, however, brings presentations into the digital, interactive age—where engagement can be measured and feedback can be *actionable*.

Key Benefits of Feedback:

- **Clarifies what works**: Identify which sections your audience spends the most time on.

- **Reveals friction points**: Detect parts of your presentation where viewers drop off or become disengaged.

- **Supports iterative improvement**: Make small, data-driven changes that improve effectiveness over time.

- **Encourages active collaboration**: Empower your team or audience to contribute ideas and improve communication clarity.

2. Collecting Feedback in Gamma

Gamma offers several tools and integrations to help you gather both **quantitative** and **qualitative** feedback. These include:

2.1 In-App Comments and Suggestions

When sharing a Gamma presentation with collaborators, you can allow them to leave comments or suggestions directly on the slides or blocks. These are visible in real time and can be tracked over time.

How to enable it:

- Click the "Share" button.
- Choose to invite people via email or link.
- Under permissions, ensure "Can Comment" is enabled.

2.2 Viewer Analytics

Gamma tracks metrics such as:

- **Views per page**
- **Average time spent on each section**
- **Drop-off rate** (where users stopped engaging)
- **Clicks on interactive elements** (buttons, links, etc.)

You can access these insights via the **"Analytics"** tab once your presentation is shared.

2.3 Feedback Forms

If you want direct, structured feedback from users, you can embed:

- Google Forms
- Typeform
- Microsoft Forms: This is especially helpful for presentations shared publicly or sent out to a broader audience.

Tip: Embed a feedback form at the end of the presentation to capture reactions while the experience is still fresh.

3. Interpreting Engagement Metrics

Once feedback data is flowing in, the next step is understanding what it all means. Let's break it down:

3.1 Time on Slide

- High time spent on a slide may indicate deep interest—or confusion.
- Cross-reference with comments to determine which it is.
- If a short section takes too long to consume, consider simplifying or clarifying the content.

3.2 Click Interactions

- Are viewers clicking on your call-to-action buttons?
- Which links are being clicked more?
- Are users interacting with embedded media?

If your CTAs are being ignored, try:

- Rewording for clarity ("Learn More" → "Get Started in 30 Seconds")
- Changing placement or color
- Reducing surrounding distractions

3.3 Drop-off Points

- Determine where most viewers stop interacting.
- Is it after a long block of text?
- Is the presentation too long without enough visual breaks?

Drop-off typically suggests the need to:

- Break long sections into shorter, skimmable blocks
- Insert visual elements (images, charts, videos)
- Add interactive moments (polls, links)

3.4 Feedback Themes from Comments

- Are there recurring comments like "Too much text" or "Not sure what this means"?

- Highlight repeated language that suggests confusion or dissatisfaction.

- Don't ignore small comments—sometimes one word ("overwhelming", "unclear", "beautiful") can point to deeper trends.

4. Improving Your Presentation: Strategies for Enhancement

After interpreting feedback, it's time to act. Below are some strategic areas where you can revise and refine:

4.1 Content Adjustments

Simplify Language

- Use bullet points or numbered lists instead of long paragraphs.

- Replace complex phrases with plain language.

- Include examples or analogies to clarify abstract ideas.

Reorganize for Flow

- Move high-interest content closer to the beginning.

- Group related ideas under common themes or headers.

- Use section breaks or visual dividers to avoid overwhelming the viewer.

Highlight Key Messages

- Bold important points.

- Add summary boxes at the end of each section.

- Use contrast to make callouts stand out (e.g., colored background blocks).

4.2 Visual Enhancements

Use More Visuals

- Add icons or illustrations for complex ideas.

- Include charts or graphs where applicable.

- Use GIFs or videos for dynamic storytelling.

Improve Layout Balance

- Break up text-heavy slides with whitespace.

- Align content properly to maintain structure and hierarchy.

- Limit the number of colors and fonts for visual consistency.

4.3 Technical Improvements

Optimize Interactive Elements

- Make sure links open in new tabs (if external).

- Ensure buttons are clearly labeled and visible across devices.

- Test all embedded media for proper loading.

Test on Multiple Devices

- Use preview mode to see how your presentation looks on:

  o Desktop

  o Tablet

  o Mobile

- Make layout adjustments for responsive design.

4.4 Personalization and Relevance

- Tailor content to your audience's background and interests.

- Use the viewer data to segment your audience (e.g., clients vs. students).

- Adapt tone: Is it too formal or too casual?

If necessary, create **different versions** of the same presentation for different audiences, each with relevant examples, tone, and calls to action.

---

5. Turning Feedback into a Habit

Improving based on feedback shouldn't be a one-time event—it's an ongoing process. Here's how to build a **feedback-driven mindset** into your workflow:

5.1 Establish a Feedback Loop

- Schedule regular review sessions with collaborators.
- Ask for feedback before every major presentation.
- Update your presentations regularly—even if only minor tweaks.

5.2 Encourage Ongoing Input

- Add a "Give Us Feedback" button in your presentations.
- Show appreciation for comments and act on them.
- Reward contributions from your team (e.g., shoutouts, badges).

5.3 Track Changes Over Time

- Keep a version history of your edits.
- Review analytics before and after major changes.
- Set measurable goals: "Increase button clicks by 15%," "Reduce bounce rate by 20%," etc.

---

6. Case Study: How Feedback Improved a Real Presentation

Let's look at an example:

Initial Version: A startup pitch included:

- A wall of text on Slide 3
- A single CTA button at the end

- No visual summary of the business model

Viewer Analytics:

- 70% of viewers dropped off after Slide 3
- 15% clicked the CTA
- Comments: "Hard to understand," "Too long," "Needs visuals"

Improvements Made:

- Split Slide 3 into three concise slides
- Added a one-minute explainer video
- Moved the CTA button up front with a value proposition

Results:

- Drop-off rate dropped to 30%
- CTA click-through doubled
- Comments turned positive: "Clearer," "Impressive," "Nice layout"

---

7. Conclusion: Feedback as Fuel for Excellence

In Gamma, your presentation is not a static document—it's a living, evolving communication tool. Learning to listen to your audience through engagement analytics and thoughtful feedback allows you to *design better, communicate clearer, and connect deeper.*

Always remember:

- **Track what matters** (time, clicks, drop-off)
- **Listen to what's said** (and unsaid) in comments
- **Adapt and evolve** your content with intention

Your audience is giving you the roadmap. All you have to do is follow it.

CHAPTER VI
Use Cases and Best Practices

6.1 Presentations for Different Needs

6.1.1 Business Pitches

In the world of business, the ability to communicate your vision clearly and persuasively can be the difference between gaining a new investor or walking away empty-handed. A business pitch isn't just a presentation—it's a story, a strategy, and a sales tool all in one. With **Gamma**, you have a modern, AI-powered tool that helps you craft professional, visually engaging, and interactive pitch presentations without needing to be a designer or coder.

This section walks you through how to create effective business pitch decks using Gamma, from structuring your content to enhancing delivery with smart visuals and interactivity.

Understanding the Purpose of a Business Pitch

Before you even open Gamma, you need to understand what a business pitch is for. Whether you're pitching to investors, potential partners, or internal stakeholders, the objective is the same: **to persuade**. A successful pitch must communicate the problem, your solution, why your team is capable, and how you plan to grow and scale.

Gamma can help by allowing you to:

- Generate slide content quickly using AI prompts.

- Maintain a professional visual consistency.

- Embed rich media to showcase your product or service.

- Enable interactive elements for deeper audience engagement.

Structuring Your Pitch Deck in Gamma

An effective business pitch follows a narrative arc. You can use Gamma to build your slides either from a blank canvas or by prompting the AI with a phrase like:

"Create a pitch deck for a startup that provides AI-powered financial planning tools."

Here is a commonly recommended pitch structure and how to build each part in Gamma:

1. Title Slide

Use Gamma's layout blocks to feature your **company name**, **logo**, and a **tagline**. Keep it clean and impactful. You can customize the color scheme to match your brand.

2. Problem

Describe the market gap or pain point. Use Gamma's visual blocks to:

- Insert statistics or graphs to support your argument.

- Highlight a quote from a real customer (using a testimonial-style block).

- Embed a short video of a customer interview (optional).

3. Solution

Show how your product solves the problem. Use:

- AI-generated summaries for clear messaging.

- Image + text blocks to visually explain how your product works.

- Embedded GIF or demo video to illustrate functionality.

4. Market Opportunity

Highlight the size of the market with:

- Charts created directly in Gamma.

- External links to research embedded for transparency.

- A visual timeline or infographic to show growth trends.

5. Product

Dive deeper into your solution. Use:

- Interactive product mockups or animations.

- Slide carousel to show different product views.

- CTA (call-to-action) buttons that simulate feature selection.

6. Business Model

Explain how you make money. In Gamma:

- Use a pricing table layout to show different plans.

- Add icons to illustrate value drivers (e.g., subscription, licensing).

- Use bullets generated by AI to explain revenue streams clearly.

7. Competitive Advantage

Use a side-by-side comparison grid in Gamma to compare yourself to competitors. You can:

- Create visual tables quickly using pre-built blocks.

- Emphasize your "secret sauce" or proprietary tech.

8. Go-to-Market Strategy

Describe how you'll reach customers:

- Add a timeline block for rollout plans.

- Use AI to generate copy for marketing channels and sales tactics.

- Highlight partnerships with embedded logos or testimonials.

9. Traction

Use this slide to demonstrate results:

- Embed charts, metrics, and growth rates.

- Highlight key wins (user growth, revenue milestones, awards).

- Embed a testimonial video or success story.

10. Team

Introduce your founding team:

- Use profile cards with photos, bios, and LinkedIn links.
- Embed mini videos of the team giving quick intros (if available).
- Highlight relevant experience using bullet lists and icons.

11. Financial Projections

Present your 3–5-year financial forecast:

- Insert charts or tables using Gamma's finance templates.
- Use AI to summarize key financial assumptions.
- Embed downloadable spreadsheets if needed.

12. Ask

Clarify what you're asking for:

- Investment amount.
- What the funding will be used for.
- Expected outcomes over the next 12–24 months.

13. Q&A

Create a clean final slide with:

- A CTA button to "Schedule a Call" (link to Calendly or similar).
- Your contact information.
- A thank-you message and embedded logo.

Design Tips for Pitch Decks in Gamma

Gamma excels at helping you keep things **clear, modern, and focused**. Here are some design best practices specific to business pitches:

- **Less is more**: Don't overload slides. Use AI-generated summaries to keep text tight.

- **Consistent styling**: Choose a theme and stick to it. Gamma lets you define global fonts, colors, and spacing.

- **Visual hierarchy**: Use Gamma's text formatting tools to guide attention—large headings, medium subheadings, smaller body text.

- **Brand elements**: Upload your brand kit (colors, logos, fonts) once, and Gamma applies it consistently across all slides.

Using Gamma's AI to Polish Your Pitch

You don't need to be a copywriter to create a compelling narrative. Gamma's AI tools can:

- **Rewrite text**: Select any block and ask AI to make it more persuasive or formal.

- **Summarize content**: Condense longer paragraphs into pitch-friendly bullet points.

- **Brainstorm**: Ask Gamma to suggest ways to frame your competitive edge or business model.

Example prompt:

"Make this slide more investor-friendly with clearer financial assumptions."

Adding Interactive and Multimedia Elements

A good pitch isn't just static—it responds to the audience. Gamma allows you to:

- **Embed product demos** (from YouTube, Loom, or Vimeo).

- **Add buttons** to guide through optional deep-dive sections (like "See Full Financials").

- **Include pop-up footnotes** to keep the main slides clean while offering details.

This creates a microsite-style experience that feels more dynamic than a traditional slide deck.

Presenting Your Pitch

Gamma allows multiple options for sharing and presenting:

- **Live Presentation Mode**: Present in real time with a clean interface.

- **Shareable Link**: Send a dynamic, scrollable pitch to investors.

- **Embed**: Add your deck to your website or landing page.

- **Download**: Export to PDF or PowerPoint for offline delivery.

Each format retains the interactive components (as supported) and lets you control the delivery context.

Pro Tips for Pitching with Gamma

- **Create multiple versions**: One detailed deck for sharing, one short deck for live pitching.

- **Practice transitions**: Use Gamma's "Present" mode to simulate audience navigation.

- **Include backup slides**: Use collapsible sections or buttons to hide bonus material you can reveal if asked.

- **Track engagement**: With viewer analytics, see how much time investors spend on each slide and where they drop off.

Case Study: Gamma-Powered Pitch Success

Let's say you're the founder of "EcoBox"—a startup that creates reusable packaging for e-commerce. Using Gamma, you:

1. Prompt the AI with: *"Create a pitch for a sustainable packaging startup."*

2. Refine the output into a clean 12-slide deck using Gamma's slide layout suggestions.

3. Embed a video of the product in use.

4. Add CTA buttons for a product demo and download of your business model.

5. Share a branded URL with potential investors via email.

The investor opens the pitch on mobile, watches the video, clicks into the "Traction" section, and replies for a meeting—all without needing a Zoom call first.

This is the power of combining strong storytelling with Gamma's flexible, modern platform.

Conclusion of Section

A strong business pitch is both art and science. With Gamma, you have the tools to combine narrative, visuals, and interactivity in one seamless package. By understanding your audience and tailoring your pitch structure accordingly, you increase your chances of leaving a lasting impression. Whether you're raising funds, pitching a new idea, or updating stakeholders, Gamma gives you the flexibility and intelligence to deliver presentations that matter.

6.1.2 Online Portfolios

Creating Online Portfolios with Gamma: Showcasing Your Work with AI Elegance

In today's digital-first world, an online portfolio is more than just a collection of your work—it's your personal brand, your resume, and your voice. Whether you're a designer, writer, marketer, student, developer, or educator, presenting your work in an engaging and modern format is essential for standing out. Gamma offers a unique opportunity to create stunning, interactive online portfolios that feel more like websites than traditional slide decks—no coding required.

This section will walk you through how to build an impactful online portfolio using Gamma. We'll cover what makes a strong portfolio, how to use Gamma's features effectively, and share practical design tips and real-world examples.

1. Why Use Gamma for Online Portfolios?

Gamma isn't just a presentation tool—it's a flexible, responsive, AI-enhanced canvas that helps you tell stories visually and interactively. Here are a few reasons why it's ideal for online portfolios:

- **Interactivity:** Let viewers explore your work, click through projects, or jump between categories.

- **Responsiveness:** Your portfolio looks great on any device—desktop, tablet, or mobile.

- **AI Assistance:** Generate structure, sections, and visual layouts effortlessly.

- **Professional Design:** Use sleek themes and layouts to make your content shine.

- **Easy Sharing:** Share via a link, embed in your personal site, or send it as a microsite.

2. Planning Your Portfolio Structure

Before jumping into Gamma, spend some time planning your content. A portfolio isn't just a gallery—it's a narrative that highlights your strengths and shows how you think and solve problems.

Here's a typical portfolio structure you can adapt to your needs:

- **Home / Introduction Page**: Brief intro about who you are and what you do. A professional headshot and mission statement work well here.

- **About Me**: Share your background, career path, education, and skills. Gamma's layouts allow for a clean visual structure for timelines and experiences.

- **Projects**
  The heart of your portfolio. For each project, include:
    - Project name
    - Objective
    - Your role
    - Tools used
    - Outcome or results
    - Visuals (screenshots, embedded videos, etc.)

- **Skills & Tools**: Use Gamma's visual blocks (icons, tables, badges) to list your competencies.

- **Testimonials (Optional)**: Add quotes or references from previous clients, teammates, or professors.

- **Contact Info**: Include clickable links to your email, LinkedIn, GitHub, or other platforms.

3. Building Your Portfolio in Gamma

Step 1: Start with a Template or Prompt

Gamma offers several templates specifically designed for portfolios. Search for "Portfolio" or "Personal Brand" when creating a new doc. Alternatively, use the AI prompt like:

"Create a professional portfolio for a UX Designer named Maria who specializes in mobile design and has five projects."

The AI will auto-generate a solid starting point with placeholder text and structure you can edit.

Step 2: Customize the Layout

- Use **Page Blocks** to divide sections like About, Projects, and Contact.

- Insert **Image Blocks** for project previews or mockups.

- Use **Text + Icon Blocks** to list skills or highlight achievements.

- Add **Dividers** for a clean visual break between sections.

Keep your layout scannable—avoid long paragraphs. Gamma is great at modular content presentation, so use that to your advantage.

Step 3: Add Interactive Elements

Make your portfolio engaging:

- **Clickable Project Cards** that lead to detailed case studies.

- **Embedded Media**: Insert YouTube or Loom videos showing your process.

- **Hyperlinked Icons**: Link to GitHub, Behance, LinkedIn, etc.

- **Buttons**: Use buttons like "View Project" or "Contact Me" with clear calls to action.

4. Best Design Practices for Portfolios in Gamma

Be Visual First

Gamma is a visual-first tool, so let your work shine with bold visuals:

- Use high-resolution images

- Keep screenshots consistent in size

- Avoid walls of text—use captions and bullet points

Use White Space Strategically

Gamma allows generous padding and spacing—embrace it. White space increases readability and directs attention where it matters.

Stick to a Consistent Theme

Choose one of Gamma's design themes and stick with it across all pages. Customize fonts and colors to reflect your personal branding.

Avoid Clutter

Don't overload with every project you've ever done. Choose 4–6 that best represent your capabilities and provide depth in their presentation.

---

5. Examples of Portfolio Types by Profession

For Designers

- Use image carousels to display UI/UX work.

- Embed Figma prototypes or Dribbble shots.

- Include a design philosophy section.

For Writers / Content Creators

- Showcase articles, newsletters, or blog posts.

- Add previews with clickable "Read More" buttons.

- Use quotes to highlight your tone and writing style.

For Developers

- Highlight projects with GitHub repos.

- Include architecture diagrams or live site links.

- Use "Problem / Solution / Result" format.

For Students and Recent Graduates

- Feature academic projects or internships.

- Add a "What I Learned" section for each project.

- Use Gamma's timeline elements to show progression.

6. Sharing Your Portfolio

Once your portfolio is ready, Gamma makes it easy to share and embed.

- **Publish as a Link:** Gamma creates a unique link you can include in resumes, bios, or emails.

- **Embed in Personal Website:** Use the embed code to place your portfolio inside a website or blog.

- **Share on Social Media:** Post your Gamma portfolio on LinkedIn or Twitter to attract opportunities.

- **Export as PDF (if needed):** While interactivity is lost, you can still create a sleek PDF version for recruiters or offline use.

7. Updating and Maintaining Your Portfolio

A good portfolio is a living document. Set a reminder to revisit it every few months:

- Replace outdated work with recent projects.

- Update your About and Skills sections as you grow.

- Review links and embedded content for broken elements.

- Add new testimonials or feedback.

8. Tips for Standing Out

- **Tell a Story:** Don't just show your work—explain your thought process and how you solve problems.

- **Use Motion Carefully:** Animated GIFs or auto-playing videos can work—but don't overdo it.

- **Get Feedback:** Share early drafts with peers or mentors for suggestions.

- **Highlight Results:** Metrics, user growth, or any quantifiable impact makes your work more compelling.

9. Portfolio Case Study Example (Template)

Gamma allows you to include full case studies in interactive form. Here's a common structure:

Project Title: Mobile Banking Redesign
Client: ABC Bank
Role: UX Designer
Tools: Figma, Gamma, Adobe XD
Challenge: Outdated design with poor mobile UX
Solution: Conducted user interviews, redesigned interface, implemented new navigation
Result: 40% increase in mobile engagement
Visuals: [Gallery of screens], [Figma embed], [Demo video]
Reflection: Key takeaway was the importance of early prototyping and testing.

Create one such Gamma page for each of your key projects.

Conclusion: Make It Yours

With Gamma, building a professional, polished, and interactive portfolio has never been easier. The platform's combination of AI-powered content structuring, beautiful design themes, and flexible layouts gives you the power to tell your story the way it deserves to be told.

Your portfolio is not just a showcase—it's a living, breathing extension of who you are as a creative or professional. Make it clean. Make it engaging. Make it *you*.

6.1.3 Educational Content

Education is rapidly evolving in the digital age, and effective communication of ideas is more essential than ever. Whether you're a teacher, student, academic researcher, or training professional, Gamma offers a flexible, intuitive, and AI-powered platform for creating engaging educational content. In this section, we will explore how educators and learners alike can harness the power of Gamma to create visually compelling, informative, and interactive educational presentations.

Why Use Gamma for Educational Content?

Traditional presentation tools like PowerPoint and Google Slides often come with rigid templates, time-consuming design processes, and limited interactivity. Gamma, however, empowers users to design dynamic, narrative-driven presentations that feel more like digital stories or microsites. The built-in AI tools also reduce content creation time significantly, enabling educators and students to focus more on content quality rather than formatting.

Benefits include:

- AI-assisted content generation and summarization
- Modern, visually appealing templates
- Interactive elements to boost engagement
- Seamless collaboration with students or peers
- Easy web-based access without downloads or software installation

Common Use Cases in Education

Let's take a closer look at how Gamma can be used in different educational contexts:

1. Lesson Plans and Lectures

Teachers and professors can use Gamma to build interactive lessons that go beyond static slides. Incorporate images, videos, and clickable links to make the session more engaging.

Example use:

- A history teacher designs a Gamma presentation on World War II with embedded timelines, videos, and interactive quiz links.

- A math lecturer creates a visually rich guide on linear algebra, with expandable examples and definitions.

2. Student Projects and Assignments

Instead of submitting boring essays or linear slide decks, students can present their work in an interactive format that showcases creativity and digital literacy.

Example use:

- A biology student builds a Gamma microsite on the human circulatory system, with embedded diagrams, video explainers, and clickable terms.

- A literature student creates a comparative analysis of two novels, linking sections and providing pop-up character bios.

3. Online Courses and E-Learning Modules

Instructors can design self-paced learning materials using Gamma's multi-page structure. This gives learners the freedom to explore content in their own time.

Example use:

- A language instructor builds a vocabulary lesson with flashcards, pronunciation audio, and quizzes.

- A coding teacher uses Gamma to teach HTML basics, linking out to live code samples and sandbox environments.

4. Workshops and Training Programs

Corporate trainers and workshop facilitators can use Gamma to create interactive training manuals, onboarding guides, or workshop summaries.

Example use:

- An HR trainer delivers a diversity and inclusion module with clickable case studies and embedded surveys.

- A nonprofit hosts a youth workshop using Gamma to guide attendees through learning activities with downloadable worksheets and interactive tasks.

Design Tips for Educational Gamma Presentations

Creating educational content requires more than just placing information on a page. It requires structure, clarity, and interaction. Here are some actionable design strategies:

1. Start with a Clear Learning Objective

Begin your presentation by stating what the audience will learn or achieve. This helps focus the learner's attention and guides your structure.

Example:
At the start of a lesson on climate change, include a section titled "By the end of this presentation, you will be able to…"

2. Use Section-Based Navigation

Gamma supports multiple pages and navigation styles. For longer educational materials, break them into thematic sections and use buttons or links for progression.

Tip:
Use "Next Section" or "Review Previous Topic" buttons to give learners control over pacing.

3. Combine Text with Visual Aids

Avoid long paragraphs. Use Gamma's block-based editor to add:

- Bullet points and summaries

- Infographics and charts

- Relevant images or diagrams

- Video clips from platforms like YouTube or Vimeo

4. Embed External Resources

Add clickable buttons or links to:

- Articles and PDFs

- Practice problems

- Online quizzes (e.g., Google Forms, Quizlet)

- Google Docs for collaborative notes

5. Encourage Interaction

Educational presentations should not be passive. Use Gamma's features to keep the audience engaged:

- Ask questions (and link to a feedback form or Padlet)

- Use hover-over definitions for complex terms

- Include "Check Your Understanding" blocks

Creating an Educational Presentation: Step-by-Step Walkthrough

Let's go through a basic example: **Creating a lesson on Renewable Energy for High School Students.**

Step 1: Start with a Prompt

Use the AI prompt: "Create a high school-level educational presentation on renewable energy sources."

Gamma will generate an outline with:

- Introduction to energy

- Types of renewable sources (solar, wind, hydro, etc.)

- Pros and cons

- Global usage trends

- Conclusion and quiz

Step 2: Organize into Pages

Create a separate page for each topic. Name them:

1. What is Renewable Energy?

2. Solar Energy Explained

3. Wind and Hydro Energy

4. Comparing Energy Sources

5. Interactive Quiz

Use navigation buttons or a fixed menu for quick access.

Step 3: Add Multimedia

On each page, embed:

- YouTube videos showing how solar panels work

- Infographics on energy consumption

- A bar chart comparing cost-efficiency

Step 4: Enable Collaboration

Invite your co-teacher to review the material or allow students to co-create by adding their own pages (e.g., "My Local Renewable Project").

Step 5: Share and Publish

Share the Gamma link with students or embed it into your LMS (Google Classroom, Canvas, Moodle, etc.). You can also track engagement through analytics.

Collaboration in Educational Settings

One of Gamma's greatest strengths is **real-time collaboration**. This is particularly useful for:

- Group projects

- Peer reviews

- Co-teaching scenarios

- Building a class resource hub

Each participant can edit, comment, or suggest changes. Permissions allow educators to control roles.

Tip:
Use version history to revert or review changes made by students over time.

Accessibility and Inclusivity

Educational materials should be accessible to all learners. Gamma supports:

- Keyboard navigation

- Screen reader compatibility (depending on how content is structured)

- Clean, high-contrast design themes

Best Practices:

- Avoid red-green color contrasts for color-blind learners

- Use alt-text or captions for all visuals

- Keep fonts large and readable

Use Case Spotlight: A Teacher's Experience

Ms. Carla Nguyen, a 7th-grade science teacher, shared her experience using Gamma:

"I used to spend hours formatting PowerPoints. Now I just type my topic into Gamma, and it gives me a whole structure! My students love the interactive diagrams and videos. Even kids who struggled with attention before are more engaged now."

Carla uses Gamma to:

- Present live during class

- Assign self-paced modules

- Share resource links with parents

Her school plans to roll out Gamma use across all departments next semester.

Conclusion: Why Gamma Works for Education

In today's educational landscape, engagement and accessibility are just as important as content. Gamma provides a powerful toolset for:

- Saving time

- Enhancing creativity

- Increasing learner interaction

- Collaborating in real time

- Delivering professional-looking educational experiences

Whether you're a teacher building a lesson, a student creating a digital report, or a training specialist designing onboarding material, Gamma helps you do it all — beautifully, efficiently, and with the support of cutting-edge AI.

6.2 Design and Communication Tips

6.2.1 Consistency in Visuals

Visual consistency is one of the most fundamental yet often overlooked elements of effective presentations. Whether you're pitching a business idea, sharing a portfolio, or educating an audience, maintaining a unified visual style strengthens your message and enhances credibility. In this section, we'll explore why consistency matters, how to achieve it effectively using Gamma, and offer specific design tips tailored to the platform.

Why Visual Consistency Matters

Visual consistency ensures that every part of your presentation feels cohesive. It's not just about making your slides look pretty—it's about creating a professional, polished experience that keeps your audience focused on your content rather than getting distracted by erratic design choices.

Here are a few key reasons visual consistency is crucial:

- **Builds Trust:** Consistent design signals professionalism. It tells your audience that you've put thought and care into your message.

- **Enhances Comprehension:** Repetition of familiar visual elements helps the brain process information more efficiently.

- **Reduces Cognitive Load:** A predictable layout allows your audience to focus on *what* you're saying instead of *how* you're presenting it.

- **Strengthens Branding:** For business users, keeping a consistent color scheme, font, and logo presence supports your brand identity.

In Gamma, achieving visual consistency is both easy and intuitive thanks to its templating system, AI-powered suggestions, and style-saving features. Let's explore how to use these tools effectively.

Setting a Foundation with Gamma's Design Tools

Use of Themes

Gamma offers a variety of presentation themes that come with pre-set fonts, colors, and layout structures. Choosing a theme at the beginning ensures a strong foundation of consistency across all your slides.

How to Apply a Theme in Gamma:

1. From your workspace, click on the presentation settings or "Design" tab.

2. Browse available themes or use the search bar for keywords like "Modern," "Clean," or "Corporate."

3. Apply the theme, and it will automatically update across all your slides.

4. If you change the theme later, Gamma will intelligently attempt to preserve your content structure while adapting it to the new visual system.

Customizing a Theme

Once you've selected a base theme, you can adjust:

- **Colors:** Use your brand's primary and secondary colors. Keep color usage consistent for titles, subtitles, and body text.

- **Fonts:** Stick with no more than two font families—one for headings and one for body text.

- **Button styles:** Gamma allows you to edit the default style for interactive elements so they match the rest of your visual identity.

Use these settings to define your visual "rules"—and then stick to them throughout the presentation.

Typography Consistency

Typography plays a major role in how professional and readable your presentation feels.

Best Practices:

- **Font Pairing:** Choose fonts that complement each other. For example, a bold sans-serif like *Montserrat* for headers and a clean serif like *Lora* for body text.

- **Hierarchy:** Use heading levels (H1, H2, etc.) consistently to signal importance. Gamma makes this easy with built-in styles.

- **Alignment:** Align text consistently—left-aligned for most body content, and centered only when stylistically appropriate.

- **Avoid Text Overload:** Stick to concise sentences or bullet points. Gamma helps with this by offering AI suggestions to condense or summarize text.

Gamma Tip:

Enable the "Typography Guide" feature to automatically check for inconsistent text size, line spacing, and font usage across your slides.

Color Palette Management

Color has emotional weight and communicative power. But used incorrectly, it can be confusing or jarring. Aim to use a limited and consistent color palette throughout your presentation.

Creating a Color Palette:

1. **Primary Color**: Usually your brand or project's main color.

2. **Secondary Colors**: Two to three complementary shades.

3. **Accent Color**: For emphasis (e.g., calls to action or key stats).

4. **Background/Neutral Colors**: White, light gray, or black to support readability.

Gamma Tip:

You can define your brand color palette in Gamma under *Brand Settings*, which allows you to reuse it in all future presentations.

Avoid These Mistakes:

- Using too many colors on one slide.

- Changing your accent color slide-to-slide.

- Using colors with insufficient contrast, which affects accessibility.

Visual Elements: Icons, Images, and Graphics

Images, icons, and illustrations are essential for breaking up text and making your slides visually engaging—but they must follow the same style to feel unified.

Image Guidelines:

- **Style Consistency:** Choose either photography or illustration—don't mix both unless you're intentionally contrasting.

- **Aspect Ratio:** Keep image shapes uniform unless you're creating a visual collage.

- **Borders and Effects:** If you apply a drop shadow or border to one image, apply it to all others too.

Icons and Shapes:

Gamma has a built-in library of icons. When using icons:

- Stick to a single icon set for consistent style.

- Avoid mixing outlined and filled icons.

- Keep icon color aligned with your primary or secondary palette.

Gamma Tip:

Use the "Duplicate Style" tool to replicate the formatting of one image or icon to another, helping maintain a uniform look.

Layout and Structure

Visual consistency also depends on how you structure your slides.

Use Reusable Slide Layouts:

Gamma allows you to create and save custom slide layouts (e.g., title slide, text with image, quote card). Use these consistently for:

- Opening slides

- Section headers

- Lists or bullet points

- Data visualizations

Margins and Spacing:

- Maintain equal margins across slides for clean alignment.

- Avoid crowding elements—leave white space to improve legibility.

Slide Transitions and Flow:

While Gamma presentations are scroll-based (like web pages), consider how each section transitions into the next visually. Use consistent patterns like:

- Alternating background color blocks

- Repeating header styles

- Anchored navigation menus

Bringing It All Together with Gamma

One of Gamma's biggest strengths is that it handles much of the consistency for you—*if* you work within its frameworks. But the real power comes when you learn how to guide the AI and design tools with intention.

Smart Design Features to Leverage:

- **"Apply to All" Edits:** When updating fonts, logos, or button styles, apply changes to all slides with one click.

- **AI Rewrite with Tone Consistency:** Make sure your voice remains consistent—formal or casual—using the AI editing tool.

- **Global Style Settings:** Define and lock in visual rules for headers, buttons, cards, and other components.

Checklist: Maintaining Visual Consistency in Gamma

Before finalizing your presentation, run through this checklist:

✓ Did I apply a consistent theme across all slides?
✓ Are the font styles and sizes unified?
✓ Is my color palette limited to 3–5 consistent tones?
✓ Are images and icons from the same style family?
✓ Is layout spacing consistent across all slides?
✓ Are interactive elements styled uniformly?

Final Thoughts

In a tool as fluid and modern as Gamma, good visual design is not about mastering complexity—it's about making intentional, thoughtful choices and applying them consistently. A cohesive visual presentation doesn't just make your work look good—it makes your ideas easier to understand, more memorable, and ultimately more persuasive.

By understanding and applying the principles of visual consistency, you not only create more beautiful presentations—you create more *effective* ones. And with Gamma, you have the tools to do so at your fingertips.

6.2.2 Clear Messaging

In today's digital age, information overload is the norm. Attention spans are short, and your audience expects clarity, brevity, and value—fast. Whether you are pitching to investors, teaching students, presenting to a team, or sharing ideas publicly, the core of a successful Gamma presentation is clear messaging.

In this section, we will explore what clear messaging means in the context of a Gamma presentation, why it matters, and how you can master it using both the platform's AI-powered features and classic communication principles.

What Is Clear Messaging?

Clear messaging refers to the ability to communicate your ideas in a way that is:

- **Concise**: Gets straight to the point.

- **Understandable**: Uses plain language.

- **Purposeful**: Every word has a function.

- **Structured**: Follows a logical flow.

In Gamma, where design and content creation is fluid and fast, these principles are even more important. With AI tools at your fingertips, it's tempting to generate large amounts of text quickly—but effective messaging isn't about more, it's about *better*.

Why Clear Messaging Is Crucial in Gamma Presentations

1. **Your Audience Skims**: People often skim slides rather than reading every word. Clear headers, key points, and visual hierarchies help retain attention.

2. **AI-Generated Content Can Be Wordy**: While Gamma's AI writing assistant is powerful, its initial output may need refining. You must ensure it aligns with your intent and audience needs.

3. **The Web-Like Format of Gamma Demands Precision**: Because Gamma allows for more interactive, web-style navigation, users may jump between sections. Clear messaging helps maintain coherence no matter where they land.

4. **It Builds Credibility**: A well-articulated message demonstrates professionalism, thoughtfulness, and command of your subject.

Principles of Clear Messaging

1. Know Your Audience

Before you even open Gamma, answer these questions:

- Who am I creating this for?

- What do they already know?

- What are they expecting?

- What is their goal or problem I can solve?

Tailoring your message to the audience is the first step in clarity. For example:

- For investors → focus on benefits, market size, growth, and ROI.

- For students → focus on step-by-step explanations and visuals.

- For teams → highlight decisions, next steps, and timelines.

2. Use the Pyramid Structure

This classic communication technique puts the conclusion first, followed by supporting details.

- **Top**: Your main message (e.g., "Our revenue doubled this quarter.")

- **Middle**: Key supporting points

- **Bottom**: Additional evidence, examples, or data

You can structure Gamma pages accordingly:

- The top section introduces the key takeaway.

- Sub-pages or expandable blocks house deeper details.

3. Write Like You Speak

Avoid jargon, filler words, and overly formal writing. Aim for:

- Short sentences (10–15 words)

- Familiar vocabulary

- Active voice

Instead of:
"Our initiative was executed in a manner that yielded a significant improvement in user engagement."
Try:
"We launched a new feature, and user engagement improved."

Gamma's AI can help rephrase for clarity, but always review the tone and accuracy.

4. Use Headings That Say Something

Bland headers like "Overview" or "Details" waste space. Make your headings part of your message.

Instead of:
"Market Analysis"
Try:
"Why Our Market is Ready for Disruption"

In Gamma, headings are critical because they often act as section labels and navigational guides. Be bold and clear.

5. Cut Ruthlessly

Once you've written a section, review it and ask:

- Does this sentence add value?

- Can I say this in fewer words?

- Can I show this in a visual instead?

Editing is not about removing information—it's about *revealing* the core message.

6. One Message per Slide/Page

Don't try to do too much at once. Every Gamma card or slide should communicate one idea clearly.

One slide = One purpose.

Examples:

- "Problem Statement"

- "Key Metric"

- "Customer Testimonial"

- "Call to Action"

Breaking ideas into separate cards also takes advantage of Gamma's visual structure and navigation.

Messaging and Visual Hierarchy in Gamma

Gamma gives you powerful layout tools. Use them to emphasize your message:

- **Headings**: Use larger, bold fonts to highlight key ideas.

- **Bullets and lists**: Organize content into digestible parts.

- **Bold & Italics**: Use sparingly to highlight critical phrases.

- **Whitespace**: Avoid clutter. Empty space improves readability and draws attention to what matters.

Leveraging Gamma's AI for Clearer Messaging

Gamma's AI assistant can help you:

- Summarize long text

- Rephrase sentences to be more concise

- Generate outlines for sections

- Expand ideas if you're stuck

But remember: AI suggestions are just starting points. It's your job to refine and shape them.

Pro Tip: After generating a block of content, use Gamma's **"Shorten"** or **"Rewrite"** feature, then select the version that is most aligned with your tone and clarity goals.

Examples of Clear Messaging in Gamma

Example 1: Investor Pitch Slide

Weak Slide Title:
"Company Overview"

Better Slide Title:
"Our AI Platform Saves Companies 30% on Customer Support Costs"

Content:

- 3 bullet points on how the AI system works

- 1 chart showing cost reduction across industries

- CTA: "Let's talk about how we can save you time and money."

Example 2: Internal Update Presentation

Weak Message:
"Progress is being made on the feature rollout."

Clear Message:
"We launched Phase 1 of the new dashboard—100% of test users reported improved usability."

Visual Messaging: Show, Don't Just Tell

Where possible, **replace text with visuals**:

- Replace a long explanation with a chart

- Use icons to represent services

- Insert a user testimonial with a photo

- Use screenshots to show product features

Gamma allows embedding multimedia, images, and GIFs easily. Use these to complement your message, not distract from it.

Checklist for Clear Messaging in Gamma

Before publishing or sharing, run through this checklist:

✓ Does each slide/page have **one clear purpose**?
✓ Are the **headings meaningful and specific**?
✓ Have you **eliminated jargon** or unnecessary complexity?
✓ Are you **showing key ideas visually**?
✓ Have you **reviewed AI content for accuracy and tone**?
✓ Would a person who knows nothing about your topic **understand the core ideas in 30 seconds**?

Encouraging Feedback to Refine Messaging

Sometimes, what feels clear to you may not be to others. Gamma makes it easy to **collaborate and gather feedback**:

- Use the "Comment" feature to ask for clarity checks.

- Share with a test audience and ask: "What are your 3 main takeaways?"

- Use analytics (covered in Chapter 5) to track where users drop off or click.

Use this feedback to adjust wording, visuals, or the structure of your content.

Conclusion: Mastering Messaging in Gamma

Clear messaging is a superpower in the digital age—and Gamma gives you the tools to wield it with elegance. By combining traditional communication best practices with Gamma's AI and design capabilities, you can craft presentations that are not only informative, but also persuasive, engaging, and impactful.

Remember: **If your audience doesn't understand it, they won't remember it. And if they don't remember it, it's like you never said it.**

Let every slide you make in Gamma speak loud and clear.

6.2.3 Accessibility Considerations

Creating a beautiful and engaging presentation in Gamma is only part of the story. If your audience can't fully experience your content—due to visual impairments, cognitive limitations, hearing difficulties, or other accessibility barriers—your message may be lost. Accessibility is not just a legal or ethical obligation; it's a powerful design mindset that expands the reach of your ideas and ensures your content is inclusive and effective.

In this section, we will explore practical ways to ensure that your Gamma presentations are accessible to all users. Whether you're building a pitch deck, a product overview, or an educational guide, these best practices will help you reach a wider and more diverse audience.

1. Why Accessibility Matters in Presentations

Accessibility allows everyone, regardless of ability, to perceive, understand, and interact with your content.

Expanding Your Audience

By considering accessibility, you ensure that your content reaches users with:

- Visual impairments (including color blindness)
- Hearing loss
- Mobility or motor challenges
- Cognitive and learning disabilities
- Situational limitations (e.g., poor lighting, using mobile devices, language barriers)

Building Ethical and Inclusive Communication

Designing for accessibility aligns with universal design principles and demonstrates empathy for your audience. It also reflects positively on your personal brand or organization.

Meeting Legal and Industry Standards

In many countries, accessibility is required by law in educational, government, and business settings. Guidelines like the **Web Content Accessibility Guidelines (WCAG)** can serve as a helpful reference.

---

2. Designing Visually Accessible Presentations in Gamma

Use High Contrast Text and Backgrounds

Ensure there is sufficient contrast between text and background colors. Gamma allows you to customize themes and background colors. When doing so:

- Use dark text on light backgrounds or vice versa

- Avoid using red and green combinations (common issue for color-blind users)

- Use Gamma's color picker with care and test your designs using online contrast checkers

Choose Readable Fonts

Gamma offers modern fonts, but not all are optimal for accessibility.

- Stick to simple, sans-serif fonts like **Roboto, Open Sans**, or **Arial**

- Avoid decorative or script fonts for body text

- Use a minimum font size of 16pt for body text and 20pt+ for headings

Maintain a Clean Layout

Avoid visual clutter. Gamma's AI design assistant helps you create clean, spaced layouts. Some tips:

- Use bullet points instead of large text blocks

- Keep plenty of white space between elements

- Avoid overly busy background images

Use Headings and Hierarchies Properly

Organize content using clear heading structures.

- Use consistent heading sizes

- Group related information visually

- Avoid using font size *alone* to indicate hierarchy—consider using bold, color, or layout cues as well

---

3. Accessible Color and Visual Usage

Avoid Relying on Color Alone to Communicate

If you use color to show meaning (e.g., red = stop, green = go), include labels or icons.

- Add text to color-coded charts (e.g., "High," "Medium," "Low")

- Use patterns or icons in charts in addition to colors

Use Descriptive Labels for Charts and Graphs

Gamma lets you embed visuals such as charts and graphs. Ensure:

- Labels are clear and placed near data points

- Use alternative methods of representation when possible (like summary text)

Use Alt Text for Images

While Gamma currently doesn't offer direct fields for alt text like some web builders, you can:

- Add descriptive captions under important images

- Include image context in your surrounding text

Example: Instead of simply inserting a chart, write: *"The chart below shows a 45% increase in engagement after redesigning the landing page, with most growth between Q2 and Q3."*

4. Accessibility for Non-Visual Users

Keyboard Navigation

While Gamma presentations are not yet fully optimized for screen reader and keyboard-only navigation, you can:

- Use clear link text like "Learn More About Our Services" instead of "Click Here"
- Keep interactive elements (buttons, links) large and easy to tab through
- Avoid hover-only elements for key information

Simplified Interactive Flow

Minimize complex navigation paths:

- Use consistent "Back" and "Next" buttons in multi-page presentations
- Add breadcrumbs or clear headings on each page for orientation
- Provide a table of contents or navigation index if the presentation is long

Descriptive Button Text

If you add interactive buttons in Gamma (such as linking to another slide or a website):

- Use meaningful labels (e.g., "View Product Demo" instead of "Click Here")
- Keep button text concise and action-oriented

5. Accessibility for Users with Cognitive and Learning Disabilities

Use Simple Language

Avoid jargon, complex sentence structures, and long paragraphs.

- Aim for a reading level equivalent to 8th grade or lower
- Break up content into sections or steps

- Use lists and visuals to support text

Use Consistent Layouts and Design Patterns

Gamma's templates make consistency easier—choose one and stick with it.

- Use consistent placement for navigation buttons
- Don't move key content around from slide to slide

Include Visual Cues and Icons

Support text with icons, illustrations, or emojis (used thoughtfully).

- Visuals can help reinforce meaning and improve comprehension
- Avoid overloading slides with multiple animated elements that distract from core messages

6. Making Videos and Audio Accessible

Gamma allows embedding multimedia—here's how to make it accessible:

Include Captions for Videos

If you're embedding videos:

- Choose videos that already have closed captions
- If creating your own, use tools like YouTube, Kapwing, or VEED.io to generate captions

Provide Audio Transcripts

For podcasts or voice recordings embedded in Gamma:

- Include a downloadable or inline text transcript
- Label it clearly as "Transcript" and place near the media

7. Testing and Validating Accessibility

Use Accessibility Checkers

Although Gamma doesn't yet offer built-in accessibility reports, you can:

- Export your presentation as a PDF and use Adobe Acrobat's accessibility checker

- Use online tools like **WAVE**, **Color Contrast Analyzer**, or **axe DevTools**

Test with Real Users

Nothing beats real-world feedback:

- Ask colleagues with diverse needs to review your content

- Run through your presentation using screen readers (e.g., NVDA, VoiceOver) or keyboard-only controls

8. Creating an Accessibility Mindset with Gamma

Accessibility should not be an afterthought. Build it into your process:

- **Plan for inclusion from the start**
  Don't "retrofit" accessibility—design with everyone in mind from the beginning.

- **Educate your team or collaborators**
  Share accessibility goals and checklists with anyone working with you on Gamma.

- **Review regularly**
  Make accessibility part of your final review checklist before publishing or presenting.

Conclusion

Gamma empowers creators to make elegant, AI-enhanced presentations—but true effectiveness comes when *everyone* can access and understand your message. By applying these accessibility considerations, you build presentations that are not only visually beautiful, but also inclusive, respectful, and impactful.

In the next section of the book, we'll explore **Common Mistakes to Avoid**—a look at the pitfalls that often hurt content quality, engagement, and yes, accessibility.

6.3 Common Mistakes to Avoid

6.3.1 Overloading Slides

In the world of digital presentations, less is often more. One of the most common—and damaging—mistakes users make when creating slides in Gamma (or any presentation tool) is **overloading slides with too much content**. This includes excessive text, a clutter of visuals, poor layout balance, or even cognitive overload caused by combining too many ideas on one screen.

This section explores why slide overload happens, the risks it brings to your audience engagement and message clarity, and how to avoid it with actionable strategies tailored to **Gamma's unique AI-powered design capabilities**.

! Why Slide Overload Happens

Slide overload is a byproduct of several habits and misconceptions:

- **Trying to say everything at once:** Presenters often attempt to cram all their points into a single slide to avoid "too many slides."

- **Fear of forgetting:** There's a tendency to add large blocks of text as a safety net, thinking it helps the presenter stay on track.

- **Lack of design training:** Without a visual communication background, many users struggle to balance white space, visuals, and text.

- **Transferring documents into slides:** Some treat slides like Word documents, placing entire reports or paragraphs verbatim into a presentation format.

In Gamma, while the tool is designed to create visually appealing presentations, the AI can only do so much if you feed it with dense, unstructured, or overly verbose content. Understanding the risks can help prevent these habits from forming.

☐ The Risks of Overloading Slides

1. Reduced Audience Engagement

When slides are packed with content, viewers often stop paying attention. Instead of listening to you, they start reading. If the text is long, they may read ahead, disengage, or miss the point entirely. Worse, they might become overwhelmed and simply tune out.

2. Cognitive Overload

The human brain can only process so much information at once. When multiple ideas are thrown onto one slide, it can confuse or fatigue your audience. Cognitive overload means they may retain **nothing at all**, regardless of how important the content is.

3. Visual Chaos

Too many elements—charts, images, blocks of text—clutter the design. This not only weakens your brand but also makes your message harder to follow. Gamma's clean layout tools are best used when you let each element breathe.

4. Poor Navigation and Flow

When each slide feels like a mini-essay, it's hard for the audience to follow a logical storyline. Gamma presentations often work like web pages—with flow and interaction. Slide overload kills that navigation-friendly experience.

✅ How to Avoid Overloading Slides in Gamma

Let's walk through **practical methods** to design clean, engaging, and audience-friendly slides with Gamma.

◆ Use One Idea per Slide

Golden Rule: *One key idea = one slide.*

Break complex topics into multiple slides. Gamma makes this easy with intuitive slide duplication and section management. For example:

Instead of this (bad):

Slide Title: "Marketing Strategy"

Paragraph: A 150-word description of goals, channels, KPIs, and budget.

Do this instead (good):

- Slide 1: "Marketing Goals" – Brief bullet list

- Slide 2: "Key Channels" – Icons or visuals

- Slide 3: "Success Metrics" – A chart or numbered list

- Slide 4: "Budget Breakdown" – Use Gamma's chart block

Each slide should visually reinforce *one point*. This boosts memory retention and keeps your audience focused.

◆ Embrace White Space

White space isn't "wasted space"—it's a **powerful design tool**.

In Gamma, choose templates with clear visual spacing and let your AI assistant maintain balance. When editing manually:

- Avoid stacking too many blocks in one layout.

- Use padding around text and visuals.

- Limit font sizes so elements don't bleed into one another.

Tip: Use **Gamma's section blocks** to organize content into expandable areas. This lets you show depth without showing everything at once.

◆ Replace Paragraphs with Visuals

Visual thinking is crucial in modern presentations. If your slide contains more than 3-4 lines of text, ask yourself: *Can this be shown visually instead?*

Gamma Tools to Try:

- Convert data into **bar or pie charts** using AI-generated visuals.

- Use **icons or infographics** to represent concepts.

- Add **illustrations** from the built-in media library.

- Summarize steps or timelines with the **timeline block**.

Example:
Instead of listing 5 benefits of your product in a paragraph, show them as **5 visual cards** or a carousel.

◆ Use Speaker Notes for Supporting Details

If you're afraid of forgetting something during your presentation, **don't dump all the info on the slide**. Use Gamma's **speaker notes section** to guide yourself. This keeps the visuals clean while ensuring you're confident with your delivery.

Alternatively, you can use **pop-out or expandable blocks** (interactive features Gamma supports) to reveal more detail *only if needed*.

◆ Let the AI Help Simplify

Gamma's built-in AI is a fantastic ally in fighting clutter. Here's how to use it effectively:

- **Summarize large blocks of text** by right-clicking and choosing "Summarize this."

- **Split content across slides** using prompts like "Break this into 3 slides."

- **Visualize points** using "Suggest images" or "Convert to graphic" options.

- Use the **Rephrase tool** to shorten verbose text.

Prompt tip: Try writing

"Turn this paragraph into 3 bullet points with emojis"
to make a slide lighter and more engaging instantly.

◆ Apply the 3x3 Rule

This classic presentation rule works well with Gamma's design format:

- No more than **3 bullet points per slide**

- Each point should be no longer than **3 lines**

Gamma layouts usually default to 2–4 content blocks per section. Stick with that natural rhythm for better flow and balance.

Example: Before vs. After (Slide Overhaul)

Original Slide (Overloaded)

- Slide Title: "Q2 Performance Overview"

- 2 long paragraphs

- 3 different charts

- Product roadmap screenshot

- Notes about client feedback

Problems:

- Too many visuals

- Multiple themes

- No white space

Improved Version (Using Gamma Smart Layouts):

- Slide 1: Q2 Highlights – 3 bullet points

- Slide 2: Performance Charts – 1 key chart with notes

- Slide 3: Client Feedback – Carousel block with quotes

- Slide 4: Roadmap Snapshot – Interactive image with notes

This version turns **1 messy slide** into **4 clean, purposeful ones**—each with one story to tell.

━▢ Quick Checklist: Avoiding Slide Overload in Gamma

✅ **Do This**	✖ **Don't Do This**
Use 1 idea per slide	Combine multiple ideas
Add visuals to replace text	Dump full paragraphs
Break up sections	Write like a Word doc
Use Gamma AI to simplify	Paste unstructured content
Embrace white space	Fill every inch with elements

● Final Thoughts

In a tool like Gamma—where design, storytelling, and interactivity blend seamlessly—slide overload disrupts not only clarity but the overall experience of your viewer. Fortunately, the platform gives you smart, intuitive ways to **avoid the clutter**, **focus your message**, and **amplify your ideas** through thoughtful structure.

Remember: Presentations aren't just about information—they're about **communication**. Don't make your audience work harder to understand you. With smart layout, selective content, and a little help from AI, you can turn every presentation into a meaningful experience.

6.3.2 Ignoring Structure

When it comes to creating compelling and impactful presentations, structure is not just a "nice-to-have"—it's a core pillar. In the world of Gamma, where powerful AI can generate content quickly and seamlessly, it can be tempting to focus solely on visual design or AI-generated text and forget about the most important element: **how your content flows and connects**.

This section will guide you through:

- Why structure matters more than ever in AI-powered presentations

- Common structural pitfalls users make in Gamma

- How to design a clear, logical flow using Gamma's tools

- Real-world examples of poor vs. effective structure

- Pro tips for building a strong narrative from start to finish

1. Why Structure is the Backbone of Any Great Presentation

Think of structure as the skeleton of your presentation. It holds everything together. A well-structured presentation:

- Helps your audience follow your message easily

- Makes your content more persuasive

- Allows for better visual and narrative flow

- Reinforces your core message at every stage

Even if you have beautiful slides, interactive elements, and great content, your audience will struggle to engage if the ideas are presented in a chaotic or illogical order.

In the Gamma environment—where design is streamlined and content can be AI-generated—**you are responsible for bringing order to the creativity.** That means thinking intentionally about:

- The beginning, middle, and end

- Section breaks and transitions

- Highlighting key messages at the right time

2. Common Structure-Related Mistakes in Gamma Presentations

Let's break down the most frequent structural mistakes users make while building in Gamma:

2.1 Starting Without a Clear Outline

Many users dive straight into writing prompts or dragging in AI-generated slides without planning the flow. This often leads to:

- Repetition of ideas

- Lack of a coherent storyline

- Weak conclusions: To avoid this, **outline your presentation** before building in Gamma, even just with bullet points or sections.

2.2 Overloading Slides with Mixed Ideas

Each slide should ideally focus on **one main point**. When slides contain unrelated ideas or multiple messages, the audience becomes confused or disengaged.

Use **Gamma's section headings** and layout blocks to isolate key thoughts, and let the AI assist in expanding one idea per slide.

2.3 Missing Logical Transitions

Without natural transitions, even well-written slides can feel disjointed. For example:

- Jumping from problem to solution without explanation

- Presenting data without framing it

- Concluding suddenly without summarizing key points: Use **bridge slides**, transition phrases, or Gamma's summary tool to maintain flow between sections.

2.4 Treating All Slides Equally

Not every slide needs the same level of detail. In poorly structured presentations, users often:

- Spend too much time on minor points

- Rush through important conclusions: Prioritize your content like a story arc— **build tension, provide insight, and resolve clearly**.

2.5 Lack of Thematic Cohesion

Structure also means **thematic consistency**. Presentations that shift tones or messaging midway through without purpose can confuse the audience.

Ensure every section relates back to your **core message or purpose**. If you're presenting a pitch, every section should build toward persuading the audience to say "yes."

3. Structuring Presentations with Gamma's Tools

Gamma gives you several intuitive tools that can help you **build a strong, clear structure**.

3.1 Using "Section Headers" for Navigation

Gamma allows you to create distinct sections. Use these wisely:

- Introduce each major part of your presentation
- Visually signal transitions
- Break up long presentations into digestible chunks

For example: **Introduction → Problem → Solution → Benefits → Case Study → Conclusion**

These can all be section headers, helping the viewer navigate and you to maintain control over the flow.

3.2 Creating a Narrative Flow with Smart Blocks

Gamma's **smart content blocks** help group ideas and layouts together logically. Use these for:

- Comparing two ideas
- Presenting steps in a process
- Showing a timeline or progression

Each block should tell a mini-story that fits into the bigger narrative.

3.3 Outlining Before You Generate

Instead of jumping directly into generation, try outlining using Gamma's built-in text boxes:

- Use bullet points to define the message of each slide
- Run individual prompts for each section to avoid generic flow
- Rearrange content easily before applying design

3.4 Linking Content with Interactive Navigation

Gamma supports internal navigation between slides or sections. Use this feature to:

- Jump between major themes (good for pitches or portfolios)
- Create "choose your path" experiences for viewers
- Make long presentations more manageable

Think of it like creating your own table of contents within the experience.

4. Good vs. Bad Structure: Real-World Examples

Let's compare two sample presentations created in Gamma:

Poorly Structured Gamma Deck:

- Starts with detailed product features before defining the audience's pain points
- Slides alternate between customer stories and technical info without order
- Closes with a vague "thank you" slide instead of a clear CTA

Well-Structured Gamma Deck:

- Begins with a clear agenda
- Follows a logical order: Problem → Solution → Benefits → Testimonials → CTA
- Each section is marked with a visual divider
- Final slide is a compelling call to action with contact info and next steps

Key difference: Structure = Clarity

5. Pro Tips for Mastering Structure in Gamma

✅ Plan Before You Prompt

Even a quick bullet-point plan can vastly improve your final product. Think of Gamma like a creative assistant—it's powerful, but it still needs your direction.

✅ Use "Signposting" Language

Guide your audience by using clear transitions: *"Next, we'll look at..."* | *"Now that we understand the problem, let's move to the solution..."*

✅ Keep Sections Balanced

Avoid spending 10 slides on background and 1 slide on the conclusion. Allocate your slides intentionally:

- 10–20%: Intro & context
- 50–60%: Core content
- 20–30%: Summary & next steps

✅ Think Like a Storyteller

Every great presentation is a **journey**. Your viewer should feel like they've been taken somewhere. Define your "story arc":

- Set the scene
- Introduce conflict
- Resolve with insight or action

✅ Review and Reorder

Gamma makes it easy to **drag and reorder slides**. Use this to refine your structure:

- Are ideas building logically?
- Are you repeating yourself?

- Is the conclusion strong and memorable?

6. Conclusion: Structure is the Invisible Superpower

Structure may not be the flashiest part of your Gamma presentation—but it's what makes everything else **work**.

By taking time to plan your flow, using Gamma's tools smartly, and thinking like a storyteller, you can transform your AI-generated content into truly persuasive, beautiful experiences.

So the next time you open up Gamma and see that blinking cursor waiting for a prompt, take a breath. Ask yourself:

"What journey do I want my audience to go on?"

Then use the structure to take them there—step by step, slide by slide.

6.3.3 Forgetting Your Audience

Creating a presentation using a powerful AI tool like Gamma can be exhilarating—templates flow smoothly, content generates with a click, and design elements fall into place. But amid the excitement of slick layouts and AI-powered copy, many presenters fall into a dangerous trap: **forgetting their audience**.

This section explores the critical importance of **audience awareness** in presentation design and delivery. We'll examine the consequences of overlooking your viewers, provide strategies to refocus your content, and offer actionable tips to ensure your audience remains the centerpiece of your presentation journey.

Why Audience Awareness Matters

Every presentation is a form of communication, and communication requires a recipient. Whether you're pitching to investors, training a team, or educating students, your presentation isn't just about what *you* want to say—it's about what *they* need to hear.

When you forget your audience, even the most well-designed, beautifully written content can fall flat. Here's why:

- **Misaligned content** leads to confusion and disengagement.

- **Overuse of jargon** alienates non-expert viewers.

- **Irrelevant visuals** distract rather than support understanding.

- **Lack of emotional connection** makes your message forgettable.

AI tools like Gamma can assist in streamlining creation, but **you must remain the human filter and curator**—always tailoring for the people on the other side of the screen.

Signs You've Forgotten Your Audience

Let's look at some common indicators that a presentation has been created with little audience consideration:

- **You're not sure who the audience is.** If you can't define the viewer's role, needs, or expectations, you're likely creating generic or misaligned content.

- **Too much content, not enough clarity.** Instead of addressing core needs, the presentation becomes an information dump.

- **Slides packed with internal language.** Using terms familiar only to your team or industry without explanation makes the content inaccessible.

- **Lack of engagement features.** No interactive elements, no questions, no calls-to-action—nothing to make the audience feel involved.

How to Re-Center Your Audience in Gamma

Gamma provides numerous tools to help tailor your presentation to the right viewers. But first, you need to define who they are.

Step 1: Identify Your Audience

Before you even open Gamma, ask yourself:

- Who is going to see this presentation?

- What is their level of knowledge on the topic?

- What are their interests, goals, or pain points?

- What do they expect or hope to get from this presentation?

You can even use Gamma's AI features to help brainstorm content ideas **based on specific audience types**. For example, prompts like:

"Create a 5-slide overview of our startup for investors with no technical background."

This keeps your message aligned from the start.

Step 2: Match Your Language to Your Audience

Use the right tone, terminology, and level of detail. Here's how:

Audience	Preferred Style	Tips
General Public	Conversational, simple	Avoid jargon, explain terms
Business Executives	Concise, results-oriented	Use visuals, highlight ROI
Educators/Students	Clear, structured	Include learning objectives
Developers/Engineers	Technical, detailed	Use diagrams and workflows

Gamma's text editor and AI-powered rewriting features can help **adjust tone and complexity**. You can even prompt the AI to:

"Rewrite this slide in a simpler way for a non-expert audience."

Step 3: Tailor Visuals and Layouts for Your Audience

Design is not just about beauty—it's about *usability*. Gamma's layout blocks, themes, and image suggestions can be used to support comprehension, but only if chosen with the audience in mind.

Here are audience-focused design suggestions:

- **For busy executives:** Use clean layouts, big headlines, and strong key metrics.

- **For visual learners:** Choose diagrams, infographics, and GIFs to support concepts.

- **For technical experts:** Embed deeper content links, code snippets, or data tables.

- **For mobile users or remote teams:** Design in vertical-friendly formats and limit slide text.

Step 4: Make It Interactive and Personal

If you're presenting live or sharing asynchronously, Gamma supports **engagement features** like buttons, embedded links, and feedback forms.

To make your presentation more interactive:

- **Add clickable links** that direct viewers to more information.

- **Insert polls or surveys** (using embedded third-party tools).

- **Include action buttons** with labels like "Learn More" or "Book a Call".

This turns passive viewers into active participants—an especially effective strategy for educators, sales teams, and community organizers.

Real-World Examples of Audience-Focused vs. Audience-Blind Presentations

Let's compare two fictional presentations on the same topic: a new HR software platform.

Category	Audience-Focused	Audience-Blind
Title	"How Our Platform Reduces Your Hiring Costs"	"Features of Talent360 v4.2"
Opening Slide	Short stat: "Companies save 30% in hiring time"	Logo, version number, product name
Language	"You can customize workflows easily"	"Our proprietary TalentSync™ algorithm…"
Visuals	Flowchart showing user journey	Screenshot of code backend

Call-to-Action	"Start your 7-day free trial today"	"Contact us for more details"

As you can see, one speaks to the *audience's needs*, the other focuses on *the presenter's product*.

Tips to Keep Your Audience in Focus Throughout the Creation Process

Here's a practical checklist to refer to as you build your presentation in Gamma:

✔ Have you clearly defined your audience?
✔ Are your examples and analogies relevant to them?
✔ Is your language appropriately complex—or too complex?
✔ Are your visuals adding value for *this* specific group?
✔ Does your layout promote easy scanning or deep reading?
✔ Have you invited feedback or interaction where appropriate?

Gamma's real-time collaboration and preview features are excellent tools to test your material with others before going live.

Final Thoughts: Speak *To* Them, Not *At* Them

AI tools like Gamma have opened up incredible opportunities to create faster, better, and more beautiful content. But the most important ingredient remains deeply human: **empathy**.

To create presentations that inspire, persuade, or inform, you must design with your audience in mind at every stage—from brainstorming to publishing.

When you truly understand your audience:

- Your content feels more relevant.

- Your delivery becomes more confident.

- Your presentation leaves a lasting impression.

Don't just present. Connect.

Let Gamma's AI be your creative partner—but let your audience guide your voice.

CHAPTER VII
Going Beyond Presentations

7.1 Creating Documents and Pages with Gamma

7.1.1 One-Pagers and Reports

While Gamma is widely recognized for its powerful AI-assisted presentation creation capabilities, its potential extends far beyond traditional slides. One of the most impactful yet often overlooked features of Gamma is the ability to create **beautiful, interactive one-pagers and reports** that are web-based, visually appealing, and easy to share. In this section, we will explore how you can use Gamma to create these documents effectively, transforming the way you share information.

What is a One-Pager or Report in Gamma?

A **one-pager** is a single-page document that summarizes a topic, product, or idea in a compact and visually engaging format. **Reports**, on the other hand, are multi-section documents that may span multiple pages but still retain a clean, digestible structure.

In Gamma, these documents aren't constrained by traditional paper formats. They're designed for the web—scrollable, clickable, and interactive. This opens up new possibilities for storytelling, data sharing, and collaboration.

Use Cases for One-Pagers and Reports in Gamma

Before diving into the how-to, let's look at some practical examples of how one-pagers and reports are being used:

- **Product Overviews**: Quickly summarize your product's key features, target audience, and benefits.

- **Marketing One-Pagers**: Highlight your services, company value proposition, or campaign summary.

- **Internal Reports**: Share project updates, performance metrics, or quarterly reviews within teams.

- **Investor Updates**: Present financials, KPIs, and progress in a way that's sleek and professional.

- **Case Studies**: Tell compelling customer success stories with visuals, quotes, and results.

- **Event Recaps**: Showcase photos, statistics, and outcomes from recent events or launches.

Planning Your One-Pager or Report

Before opening Gamma, it's helpful to plan your content using a few simple steps:

1. **Define Your Goal**: Are you informing? Persuading? Summarizing? Your purpose will guide structure.

2. **Identify the Audience**: Internal stakeholders? Investors? Clients? Tailor tone and visuals accordingly.

3. **Outline the Sections**: Common sections include:

   o Header or title block

   o Introduction or summary

   o Key points or sections

   o Data or visuals

   o Call to action or next steps

4. **Gather Your Assets**: Collect necessary data, quotes, charts, logos, or images before you start.

Step-by-Step: Creating a One-Pager in Gamma

Let's walk through how to create a one-pager from scratch in Gamma.

Step 1: Create a New Document

- Click **"+ Create"** in the workspace.
- Choose **"Start from scratch"** or use a **template**.
- Select the **"One-pager" format** or customize a blank canvas for free-form design.

Step 2: Add a Strong Title Block

- Use a **header block** with a clear, bold title.
- Add your logo or company name.
- Use the **subheader** to provide context or a brief summary.

Tip: Use Gamma's AI suggestions to generate a punchy title or tagline if you're stuck.

Step 3: Structure the Page with Sections

Gamma's **block system** makes it easy to divide the document into visual sections.

- Use **horizontal dividers** to separate parts.
- Insert **heading blocks** for each section.
- You can use **columns** for side-by-side comparison, stats, or quotes.

Common blocks include:

- **Text Blocks**: Use for paragraphs, bullets, or brief explanations.
- **Image Blocks**: Upload relevant photos or illustrations.
- **Callout Blocks**: Highlight important facts or figures.
- **Chart/Graph Blocks**: Add visuals to support your message.

Step 4: Add Data and Visuals

- Use Gamma's chart builder or embed charts from Google Sheets.
- Visualize stats using icons, percentage bars, or infographics.

- Add quotes or testimonials in styled quote blocks for social proof.

Pro Tip: Keep the balance between text and visuals. Don't overwhelm the viewer.

Step 5: Customize Style and Theme

- Apply a **visual theme** from the theme selector (brand colors, fonts, etc.).

- Customize individual block styles to match your brand.

- Maintain visual consistency throughout—headings should align, font sizes should harmonize.

Making It Interactive

What makes Gamma unique is the ability to **go beyond static PDF-style documents**:

- **Add Buttons**: Link to your website, social pages, or calendar.

- **Embed Media**: Add videos (e.g., YouTube), animated GIFs, or audio.

- **Enable Comments**: For internal documents, allow collaborators to leave feedback.

- **Link to Sections**: Use anchor links to allow easy internal navigation on longer reports.

Tips for Effective One-Pagers

1. **Keep it concise**: Focus on clarity. Avoid unnecessary jargon.

2. **Use whitespace**: Space is not wasted—it helps guide the reader's eye.

3. **Tell a story**: Even in reports, use narrative structure where possible: setup → detail → conclusion.

4. **Use AI to Your Advantage**: Let Gamma's AI help rewrite, summarize, or expand content. But always edit for tone.

5. **Test readability**: Read through the page from a viewer's perspective—does it flow naturally?

Publishing and Sharing

When your one-pager is ready:

- **Click "Publish"** to make it live online.

- Share via:

    o **Public link** (view-only or editable)

    o **Email invite**

    o **Embed** on your site or Notion page

- You can also export to **PDF** if needed for offline use (though interactivity will be lost).

Note: Gamma's web-native format works best when shared via link. It looks great on both desktop and mobile!

Real-World Example: Sample Marketing One-Pager

Here's a practical example layout for a company's service overview:

- **Header**: Logo + "Our Marketing Services"

- **Intro Text**: Short company bio

- **Section 1**: Services (icons + descriptions)

- **Section 2**: Client logos or testimonials

- **Section 3**: Case study preview

- **Section 4**: Contact button + social links

This one-pager acts like a mini-website that can be shared with potential clients or included in outreach emails.

Collaboration and Versioning

- Use **real-time collaboration** to co-edit with your team.

- Leave **comments** for feedback or revisions.

- Duplicate or version documents for different audiences (e.g., internal vs external).

Adapting for Reports

If you're creating a **multi-section report**, follow the same steps but:

- Use **multiple stacked sections** (Gamma's web layout scrolls smoothly).

- Add a **table of contents** block at the top with anchor links to sections.

- Group related data with titles, visuals, and summary text.

Popular report types include:

- Monthly or quarterly team reports

- Performance reviews

- Annual summaries

- Marketing or campaign reports

Final Thoughts on One-Pagers in Gamma

Creating one-pagers and reports in Gamma redefines how information is shared—bridging the gap between traditional slide decks and rigid text documents. You get the **flexibility of a web page**, the **structure of a slide**, and the **power of AI** all in one tool.

Whether you're summarizing a product, pitching an idea, or showcasing results, Gamma lets you do it in a way that's interactive, professional, and modern. And the best part? You don't need to be a designer or coder.

In the next section, we'll explore how Gamma integrates with your existing tools—so you can plug this power into your broader workflow seamlessly.

7.1.2 Portfolios and Landing Pages

While Gamma was originally designed to reinvent the way we create presentations, its power goes far beyond traditional slide decks. One of its most impressive capabilities is the ability to design and publish **interactive portfolios and landing pages** that look professional, dynamic, and polished — all without a single line of code.

In this section, you'll learn how to leverage Gamma to build stunning personal portfolios and landing pages that are web-ready and optimized for engagement. Whether you're showcasing your design work, pitching a startup, launching a product, or building a personal brand, Gamma can help you create a one-of-a-kind page that feels more like a sleek website than a slideshow.

Why Use Gamma for Portfolios and Landing Pages?

Before diving into the how-to, let's first understand the **why**:

- **No-Code Web-Like Creation**: Gamma allows you to design pages with interactive blocks, smooth transitions, and clean layouts — no need to learn web development.

- **AI-Powered Speed**: You can start from a prompt or let Gamma build a portfolio structure for you, saving hours of design time.

- **Multimedia Support**: Seamlessly embed videos, links, images, GIFs, and interactive charts — all in one place.

- **Professional Look & Feel**: With responsive design and templated styles, your work looks polished on both desktop and mobile.

- **Easy Sharing and Analytics**: You get a shareable link, viewer tracking, and customization options — ideal for pitching or promoting.

Planning Your Portfolio or Landing Page

Before jumping into Gamma, consider the **goal** of your page:

- Are you showcasing your design or writing portfolio?

- Launching a new product or service?

- Pitching your company or idea?

- Promoting your personal brand or resume?

The **structure** and content of your page will depend on its purpose. Here are some common use cases:

Type of Page	Common Elements
Creative Portfolio	Bio, selected works, images, client list, testimonials, contact info
Startup Landing Page	Hero section, product features, call to action, video demo, sign-up form
Personal Brand Page	About you, achievements, projects, blog or media links, social handles
Resume Page	Summary, skills, experience, education, download link to resume

Step-by-Step: Building a Portfolio or Landing Page in Gamma

Let's walk through how to create a professional portfolio or landing page using Gamma:

Step 1: Start a New Page from a Prompt or Blank Canvas

1. **Click "+ New"** from your Gamma workspace.

2. Choose **"Start from a prompt"** and enter something like: *"A creative portfolio showcasing my design projects, bio, and contact info"* OR
Select **"Start from blank"** if you prefer full control.

3. Gamma will generate a page layout with suggested sections — you can customize or delete them as needed.

💡 Tip: Use prompts that clearly mention your audience and purpose. The better the prompt, the smarter the AI structure.

Step 2: Structure Your Page Sections

A great landing page has clear, scrollable sections. Gamma uses **blocks** to represent each section. Some key sections you might want to include:

For a Portfolio Page:

- **Hero Section**: A big image or your personal logo, with a headline and subheading.

- **About Me**: A short bio and what you do.

- **Project Highlights**: Image-based blocks that showcase your work, each with a short description and optional link.

- **Skills & Tools**: Bullet lists or icons representing your expertise.

- **Client Testimonials or Achievements**: Quotes, logos, or quick stats.

- **Contact Info**: Include social links or a call to action.

For a Landing Page:

- **Hero Section**: Product name, bold headline, and CTA button (e.g., "Try it now").

- **What's Inside**: Feature list with icons or short explanations.

- **Video Demo or Screenshots**: Embed from YouTube or upload your visuals.

- **Pricing or Plans**: Use a table or comparison layout.

- **Testimonials or Social Proof**: Add credibility with quotes or case studies.

- **CTA & Contact**: End with a form or clickable button.

💡 Tip: Keep each section focused and visually clean. Gamma thrives on simplicity and modular design.

Step 3: Customize Text, Layout, and Media

With your structure in place, it's time to fine-tune:

- **Text Blocks**: Double-click to edit text. Use Gamma's built-in AI tools to rewrite, shorten, or expand text. You can also apply formatting like bold, bullet points, and headings.

- **Image Blocks**: Drag and drop images or upload from your device. Gamma supports automatic layout adjustments for image-heavy sections.

- **Video Embeds**: Add YouTube, Loom, or Vimeo links, and Gamma will render a native player.

- **Icons and Logos**: Use icons from the built-in library or upload your own SVG or PNG files.

- **Interactive Elements**: Include clickable buttons, links, or collapsible sections for a more dynamic experience.

Step 4: Design and Branding

Your brand identity matters — and Gamma helps you stay consistent:

- **Themes**: Choose a theme or create a custom one with your preferred fonts, colors, and button styles.

- **Brand Logos**: Add your logo to the header or footer block.

- **Consistent Layouts**: Use duplicable layout blocks to repeat sections with a consistent style (e.g., all project entries look the same).

- **Spacing and Alignment**: Gamma automatically handles alignment, but you can manually adjust padding and order for perfection.

💡 Pro Tip: If you already have a visual identity (e.g., brand color codes or a font), apply it early via your theme settings.

Step 5: Optimize for Sharing and Viewing

Before publishing, review the following:

- **Mobile Responsiveness**: Use the preview button to check how your page looks on smaller screens.

- **Custom URL**: Change the share link to something memorable (e.g., gamma.app/janedoe-portfolio).

- **Access Settings**: Choose whether your page is public, private, or view-only with specific people.

- **Call-to-Action**: Every good page ends with something actionable — include a contact link, sign-up button, or download option.

Step 6: Publish and Track Performance

Once ready, hit **"Publish"**, and your Gamma page is now live!

Gamma provides **viewer insights** to help you track engagement:

- Total views and unique viewers

- Clicks on buttons or links

- Scroll behavior and time on page

Use this data to tweak your design, update messaging, or follow up with interested visitors.

Tips for Building a Powerful Portfolio or Landing Page

- **Keep it Scannable**: Most users skim. Use short text, bullets, and headers.

- **Show, Don't Tell**: Rely on visuals, project screenshots, and embeds to demonstrate your work.

- **Be Selective**: Curate only your best pieces. Less is more.

- **Make It Personal**: Let your personality shine through. Use your own voice and story.

- **Update Frequently**: Gamma pages are easy to update — treat them like a living document.

Real-World Examples (Hypothetical)

1. **Freelance Designer Portfolio**

   o Hero with logo

- o Projects with client names

- o Testimonials from clients

- o Embedded Dribbble/Behance links

- o Contact button with Calendly link

2. **Startup Pre-Launch Page**

- o Product teaser with video

- o Features section

- o Email sign-up form

- o Countdown timer

- o CTA to join beta list

3. **Resume + Personal Site**

- o About section

- o Work experience with icons

- o Projects as image links

- o Embedded PDF resume

- o LinkedIn and GitHub links

Conclusion: A Page that Works for You

Gamma isn't just about making beautiful slides — it's about **communicating ideas in flexible, modern formats**. Whether you're a creative showing off your portfolio, an entrepreneur launching a product, or a student building a personal website, Gamma lets you create pages that are **engaging, dynamic, and impactful** — fast.

Best of all, you can build, edit, publish, and share your page all in one place, with built-in AI to help guide the process.

Ready to turn your ideas into reality? Your Gamma-powered portfolio or landing page is just a few clicks away.

7.1.3 Resource Libraries

Introduction to Resource Libraries

Gamma is more than just a tool for presentations—it's a dynamic content creation platform that allows you to build rich, interactive, and highly shareable digital experiences. One of the most powerful, often underutilized features is **creating Resource Libraries**.

A **Resource Library** in Gamma is a curated collection of materials—documents, links, embedded videos, presentations, and even interactive elements—organized into a visually engaging and navigable format. Whether you're onboarding new employees, launching a course, managing client assets, or creating a knowledge base for your team, Gamma enables you to build a professional, branded resource hub in minutes.

This section will walk you through how to build effective Resource Libraries with Gamma, complete with structure planning, content sourcing, design strategy, AI-powered workflows, and publishing tips.

What is a Resource Library?

A Resource Library is a centralized digital collection of materials that users can browse and interact with. Think of it as a hybrid between a microsite, a document repository, and an interactive learning hub.

In Gamma, a Resource Library typically includes:

- Structured sections with text and visuals

- Embedded presentations or video tutorials

- Links to relevant tools, platforms, or downloads

- Navigation buttons for easy movement across pages

- Searchable or categorized content for ease of use

Use cases include:

- Internal training hubs
- Client onboarding kits
- Marketing asset libraries
- Product documentation
- Student learning resources
- Team knowledge bases

Planning Your Resource Library

Before diving into Gamma to build your library, it helps to plan your structure:

Define Your Purpose

Ask:

- Who is this for?
- What kind of resources are they looking for?
- What action do I want them to take after using this?

Organize Your Content

Group your materials into categories or themes. For example:

- For a product onboarding library:
    - Getting Started
    - User Manuals
    - Video Walkthroughs
    - Advanced Use Cases
    - Support Contacts
- For a student resource hub:
    - Class Notes

- o Reference Materials
- o Assignment Templates
- o Exam Prep Videos

Use mind maps or outlines to sketch your content structure.

Gather Your Materials

Before you start building, collect:

- PDFs or documents
- Links to videos or articles
- Gamma presentations
- Logos or brand assets
- Embedded forms or feedback tools

You can link these directly or upload them to Google Drive or another storage platform and embed via Gamma.

Building a Resource Library in Gamma

Once you've planned your library, follow these steps to build it in Gamma.

Step 1: Create a New Page

In Gamma:

1. Click "Create New"
2. Select **Blank Page** or choose a **Microsite-style Template**
3. Give your library a clear title like "Marketing Toolkit" or "Sales Training Hub"

Step 2: Design the Homepage

The homepage serves as the entry point to your library. Make it engaging:

- Add a **hero section** with a title, short description, and an engaging image
- Use **buttons or tiles** to link to different sections of your library

- Embed a short welcome video if helpful

- Add a table of contents or navigation panel on the side

Gamma's **AI layout suggestions** can help arrange this content beautifully with minimal effort.

Step 3: Add Sections or Pages for Each Category

For each category of content, create a **new slide or linked page**. You can structure them like:

- Slide title (e.g., "Tutorial Videos")

- List of resources with thumbnails or preview links

- Embedded media (YouTube, Loom, Gamma presentations)

- Download buttons (linked from Drive, Dropbox, or Gamma assets)

Use **icons, cards, or collapsible blocks** for clean organization.

Step 4: Embed and Link Materials

Gamma supports a wide range of embeds:

- YouTube / Vimeo

- Google Docs, Sheets, Slides

- PDFs

- Loom videos

- Figma / Miro boards

- Forms (Typeform, Google Forms)

To embed:

1. Copy the embed link

2. Add a new block in Gamma

3. Paste the link and select embed format

4. Adjust size or layout for readability

For external links, use **interactive buttons** with clear call-to-action labels like "Watch Now" or "Download Template".

Step 5: Enable Navigation and Searchability

Use navigation aids to enhance user experience:

- Create **top-level buttons or tabs** for major categories

- Add **"Back to Top" or "Home" buttons** on each page

- Use **internal links** between sections for cross-referencing

- Add a **search block** using third-party tools like Google Custom Search (optional)

Using AI to Build and Manage Your Library

Gamma's AI assistant can speed up and enhance your workflow.

AI for Content Generation

- Generate category descriptions from a simple prompt

- Summarize long documents into quick blurbs

- Rewrite technical terms into beginner-friendly copy

- Create suggested resource lists for each section

AI for Layout and Design

- Ask AI to recommend layout blocks based on your content

- Use it to create consistent card designs for repeated resource formats

- Style sections with branded color palettes and font pairings

Smart Updates with AI

When updating a resource or adding new materials:

- Prompt AI to summarize changes

- Use AI to auto-generate titles and summaries for new content

- Ask AI to recommend tags or keywords for easier navigation

Design Tips for Effective Resource Libraries

A beautiful library isn't just nice to look at—it makes information more accessible and memorable. Here are key tips:

Keep It Visual

- Use icons, illustrations, and thumbnail previews
- Break up long lists with headers or cards
- Use consistent visual styling across all sections

Consistency is Key

- Stick to a uniform color scheme and font choice
- Use a fixed layout format (cards, grids, sections)
- Avoid mixing too many design styles

Prioritize Accessibility

- Use high contrast text
- Add alternative text for images
- Keep language simple and readable
- Ensure buttons and links are clearly labeled

Publishing and Sharing Your Resource Library

Once your Resource Library is ready:

Publishing Options

- **Public link**: Anyone with the link can access
- **Private or shared with team**: Control visibility
- **Password-protected** (coming soon in some plans)

Embedding the Library

You can embed the entire library or specific sections:

- On websites

- Inside your LMS

- In Notion or Confluence

- Within other Gamma projects

Updating and Version Control

- Gamma saves versions automatically

- You can duplicate and revise pages

- Use "last updated" notes at the top of your pages for transparency

Use Case Examples

Company Onboarding Portal

- Welcome video

- Company values

- Policies and forms

- Links to training modules

Course Content Library

- Weekly lecture summaries

- Assignment instructions

- Study resources

- Feedback forms

Client Resource Hub

- Contract templates

- Campaign timelines

- Instructional videos

- FAQ and help articles

Marketing Asset Center

- Brand guidelines

- Logos and templates

- Content calendar

- Analytics dashboard embeds

Final Thoughts: Why Gamma is Ideal for Resource Libraries

Creating a Resource Library with Gamma offers:

- **Speed**: AI speeds up everything from copywriting to layout

- **Flexibility**: You can embed almost any content format

- **Ease of Use**: No coding, no plugins, no fuss

- **Interactivity**: Buttons, animations, media, and forms make the library dynamic

- **Professional Presentation**: The end result looks like a polished microsite

Whether you're managing internal knowledge, delivering training, or building community resources, Gamma empowers you to share information effectively and beautifully—all with AI at your side.

7.2 Integrations and Extensions

7.2.1 Connecting to Google Drive

As Gamma evolves beyond its core functionality of crafting AI-powered presentations, one of its greatest strengths lies in its ability to **integrate seamlessly with other tools** that professionals already rely on daily. Among these, **Google Drive** stands out as a powerful companion.

This section will walk you through:

- Why integrating with Google Drive enhances your workflow,

- How to connect your Gamma workspace to Google Drive,

- Ways to import content from Drive into your presentations,

- Exporting Gamma content back to Drive, and

- Best practices for managing files between the two platforms.

Why Integrate Gamma with Google Drive?

Google Drive is a widely used cloud-based storage and productivity platform. For individuals and teams already operating within the Google ecosystem—using Google Docs, Sheets, Slides, and more—the ability to connect Gamma with Google Drive can drastically improve both **workflow efficiency** and **content centralization**.

Key Benefits:

- ☐ **Seamless File Transfer** – Import existing assets (images, videos, documents) from Drive directly into Gamma.

- ☁☐ **Cloud-Based Access** – Always work on the most updated versions of your content without needing to re-upload files.

- ☐ **Cross-Tool Collaboration** – Combine Gamma's stunning AI-generated visuals with data or documents already built in Drive.

- ⬆ **Simple Export Options** – Back up or share Gamma projects through your Google Drive folders.

How to Connect Gamma to Your Google Drive

Before you can begin importing or exporting files between Gamma and Google Drive, you'll need to authorize the connection between the two services. Here's how to do it step-by-step.

Step 1: Open Gamma Settings

1. Log in to your Gamma workspace. https://gamma.app/

2. Click on your profile icon or workspace name in the top-right corner.

3. Select **Settings** from the dropdown menu.

Step 2: Navigate to Integrations

1. In the settings panel, locate the **"Integrations"** tab.

2. Click on it to reveal available third-party service connections.

Step 3: Connect to Google Drive

1. Find **Google Drive** in the list of integrations.

2. Click **"Connect"** or **"Sign in with Google."**

3. Choose the Google account you want to associate with Gamma.

4. Grant the necessary permissions, which typically include:

   o Access to view and manage your files in Google Drive.

   o Permission to upload or export files.

   o Viewing shared documents.

🔒 **Note:** Gamma does not access your files unless you explicitly choose to upload or sync them. You're always in control of what is shared.

Step 4: Confirm and Sync

- Once authorized, Gamma will show a confirmation.

- Your Drive will now be accessible from within the file picker interface in Gamma.

Importing Files from Google Drive into Gamma

With your account connected, it becomes incredibly easy to pull assets directly from Google Drive and incorporate them into your Gamma presentations, pages, or documents.

Supported File Types for Import:

- Images (JPG, PNG, SVG, WebP)

- PDFs

- Google Docs

- Google Sheets (for embedding tables or charts)

- Videos (MP4, YouTube links stored in Drive)

How to Import:

Method 1: File Upload During Editing

1. While editing a Gamma presentation, click **"Insert"** or **"Media."**

2. Select **"Upload from Google Drive."**

3. Browse your Drive folders or use the search bar.

4. Choose the file you want to insert.

5. Gamma will upload and embed it into your current slide or section.

Method 2: Drag-and-Drop (Browser Support Required)

- If your browser supports it and Gamma enables drag-and-drop, you can open Google Drive in another tab or window and drag files directly into the Gamma editor.

Method 3: Copy-Paste from Google Docs

- Open your Google Doc.

- Highlight the section or content you want to reuse.

- Copy (Ctrl+C / Cmd+C) and paste (Ctrl+V / Cmd+V) directly into Gamma's editor. Formatting such as headers, lists, and links are typically preserved.

✅ **Tip:** Embedding Sheets or Docs keeps them live. Any changes made in Google Drive will reflect in Gamma when viewed online (depending on embed settings).

Exporting Content from Gamma to Google Drive

Once your presentation or document is complete, you might want to save a backup to Drive, collaborate further with your team, or simply organize content in your cloud folder system.

Export Formats Supported by Gamma:

- PDF

- PPTX (PowerPoint)

- Markdown or Text

- Image (JPG/PNG for individual slides)

- Shareable Web Link (to embed in Google Sites, Docs, etc.)

How to Export to Google Drive:

Method 1: Download and Upload

1. In Gamma, click **"Export"** on the top menu.

2. Choose **PDF** or **PowerPoint**.

3. Save the file locally.

4. Go to Google Drive and drag the file into the desired folder.

Method 2: Save Directly to Drive (if enabled)

1. In the export modal, if you're connected to Google Drive, you'll see an option to **"Save to Drive."**

2. Click it, choose your folder location, and confirm.

3. Your file is instantly stored in your Google Drive.

💡 **Pro Tip:** You can organize presentations by folders such as:

- /Marketing/Decks/2025 Launch

- /HR/Onboarding Materials

- /Education/Courses/Module 1

Embedding Google Drive Content in Gamma

Sometimes, rather than uploading static content, you might want to **embed a live document or spreadsheet** from Google Drive directly into your Gamma slide.

Embedding a Google Doc, Sheet, or Slide

Step-by-Step:

1. Go to the desired file in Google Drive.

2. Click **Share** > Change permissions to "Anyone with the link" (View or Comment access).

3. Click **File > Embed (if supported)** or copy the **shareable link.**

4. In Gamma, select **Insert > Embed** or paste the link into a block.

5. Gamma will render a preview (interactive when possible).

📊 **Live Data** from Google Sheets can be used to create dynamic charts in your presentations. Just embed the live chart from Sheets or upload CSV data exported from Sheets for styling in Gamma.

Use Cases for Gamma–Google Drive Integration

Use Case	Benefit
Creating a pitch deck using data from Google Sheets	Real-time charts and visualizations
Embedding legal documents or whitepapers stored in Drive	Adds authority and accessibility
Reusing learning materials in Gamma from Google Docs	Saves time in content creation
Backing up all presentations to a team folder in Drive	Organized document management
Collaborative review of Gamma exports via shared Drives	Team feedback & version control

Best Practices for Managing Content

1. Maintain a Clear Folder Structure

Organize your Drive with consistent naming and hierarchy so you can find and link assets quickly.

2. Keep Live Links Updated

If embedding content, remember that changes to the original Google Doc or Sheet will update in Gamma **only if the correct sharing permissions remain active**.

3. Avoid Over-Reliance on Third-Party Files

Whenever possible, upload essential assets to Gamma directly to avoid broken embeds in case Drive files are moved or deleted.

4. Enable Version Control

Use Google Drive's version history alongside Gamma's autosave to track changes over time and maintain backups of key versions.

Troubleshooting Common Issues

✖ I can't see my Google Drive files inside Gamma.

- Ensure you're signed in with the correct Google account.

- Check that you've granted the necessary permissions.

- Try disconnecting and reconnecting the integration under **Settings > Integrations**.

✖ My embedded content doesn't load.

- The shared link may be restricted. Re-check Google Drive sharing settings (set to "Anyone with the link").

- Make sure Gamma supports the content type (some Slides/Forms may not render properly).

✖ I get errors when exporting to Drive.

- Make sure you're connected to the internet.

- Re-authenticate your Google Drive account.

- Try downloading first and uploading manually if needed.

Final Thoughts on Google Drive Integration

Connecting Gamma to Google Drive opens up a powerful set of tools that can help you build, share, and manage your content more effectively. Whether you're creating educational materials, corporate reports, or marketing assets, the integration ensures a **smooth content pipeline**, saves time, and enhances collaborative possibilities.

In the age of cloud-first workflows, Gamma and Google Drive together become a **dynamic duo** that lets creativity and productivity flow side by side.

7.2.2 Exporting to Notion or Docs

In today's collaborative digital environment, flexibility is king. Content is no longer confined to just one format or platform—it flows across apps, devices, and teams. That's why Gamma's ability to **export your content into popular productivity platforms like Notion and Google Docs** is a game-changing feature for knowledge workers, creators, educators, and teams who thrive in hybrid environments.

In this section, we will explore:

- Why exporting to Notion and Docs is useful

- Step-by-step instructions to export Gamma content

- Tips to optimize content formatting during export

- Common use cases and workflows

- Limitations to consider

- Troubleshooting tips

Why Export to Notion or Google Docs?

While Gamma excels in visual storytelling and interactive design, there are times when your audience or workflow requires content in more text-based or structured document formats. That's where Notion and Google Docs come in. Here's why exporting to these tools matters:

- **Notion:** Ideal for organizing knowledge bases, team wikis, project documentation, and collaborative brainstorming. Exporting Gamma content to Notion allows you to repurpose your presentation into structured blocks for ongoing project work.

- **Google Docs:** Perfect for team reviews, content editing, long-form documentation, or submitting reports in standardized formats. Gamma's ability to output your content into Docs ensures continuity in environments that prefer traditional document workflows.

How to Export to Notion

Gamma does not offer a native, one-click "Export to Notion" feature—yet. However, exporting Gamma content to Notion is still quite seamless using the following approaches:

Method 1: Copy and Paste with Smart Formatting

Gamma's content structure is modular and rich in formatting. Fortunately, Notion supports many of the same elements. Here's how to export your Gamma content into Notion manually:

1. **Prepare your content:**
   - Finalize the Gamma page or presentation you want to export.
   - Use the "Present" or "Preview" mode to check for layout flow and completeness.

2. **Copy your content:**
   - Highlight a section, block, or full page from your Gamma workspace.
   - Right-click and select **Copy**, or use **Cmd/Ctrl + C**.

3. **Open Notion:**
   - Create a new page or open an existing one.
   - Use **Cmd/Ctrl + V** to paste.

4. **Clean up formatting:**
   - Gamma's text, headings, bullets, and links typically translate well.
   - Media like images or embedded links may require manual re-insertion.
   - Use Notion's block shortcuts (/) to convert content into appropriate block types (e.g., callouts, to-do lists, tables).

Tips for Best Results

- Use Gamma's **"Text-only mode"** or "Export to Markdown" (if available) before copying to Notion to maintain consistent formatting.
- Avoid pasting overly complex layouts at once; split content into sections.
- Save custom Notion templates to reuse consistent layouts across exports.

How to Export to Google Docs

Unlike Notion, Google Docs works well with document-based exports like PDF, text, or copy-paste workflows. Gamma supports exporting to Google Docs more directly through Google Drive or formatting options.

Method 1: Export as Markdown or Text, then Copy to Docs

1. **Open your Gamma presentation or document.**

   o Click on the "..." (more options) menu in the upper right corner.

2. **Choose the "Export" Option:**

   o Select **"Export as Text"** or **"Export as Markdown"**.

3. **Paste into Google Docs:**

   o Open Google Docs (https://docs.google.com/) in a new browser tab.

   o Create a blank document.

   o Paste the exported content using **Cmd/Ctrl + V**.

4. **Adjust Formatting in Docs:**

   o Use **Headings (H1, H2)** for section titles.

   o Apply bullets, numbering, or tables where necessary.

   o Use Docs' **"Styles"** feature for consistent formatting.

Method 2: Export to PDF, then Import into Docs

This method is best if your visual formatting is critical.

1. **In Gamma, click "Export" > "Download as PDF".**

2. Open Google Drive and upload the PDF file.

3. Right-click the file and select **"Open with Google Docs"**.

   o Google will convert the PDF into a Docs document, with formatting preserved as closely as possible.

Method 3: Use Google Drive Integration (if available)

If Gamma adds direct integration with Google Drive:

1. Connect your Google account within Gamma's integration settings.

2. Choose "Export to Google Drive" from your workspace.

3. Locate the document in your Drive, then open and edit as needed.

Optimizing Exported Content

To make sure your exported Gamma content remains readable and professional:

- **Use clean section headers:** In Gamma, apply clear and consistent heading styles (H1, H2) so they carry over properly.

- **Avoid overusing interactive elements:** Notion and Docs don't support live embeds or animations, so simplify where necessary.

- **Use plain visuals:** Replace interactive blocks with static images (e.g., charts, maps, timelines) that can be interpreted in Docs or Notion.

- **Label sections clearly:** Especially helpful when collaborating across tools.

Common Use Cases for Exporting

Here are a few real-world workflows where exporting to Notion or Docs enhances productivity:

Use Case	Workflow
Team Planning	Build your pitch or idea visually in Gamma → Export to Notion → Share as a project brief
Documentation	Create a training or process presentation in Gamma → Export to Docs → Submit to HR or team

Use Case	Workflow
Client Deliverables	Present ideas in Gamma → Export as Docs for review and sign-off
Blog or Newsletter Drafting	Write in Gamma with AI support → Export to Notion or Docs → Finalize for publishing

Limitations to Be Aware Of

Although exporting is useful, it's not always perfect. Keep these limitations in mind:

- **Interactive features lost:** Buttons, animations, and transitions don't carry over.

- **Formatting differences:** Fonts, spacing, and layout may look different in Docs or Notion.

- **Manual rework may be required:** You might need to realign visuals or fix list formatting.

- **Live updates don't sync:** Once exported, changes in Gamma won't reflect automatically in Docs/Notion.

Troubleshooting Tips

Issue	Solution
Bullet lists not rendering properly in Docs	Paste in plain text mode and reapply bullets
Images missing in Notion	Download from Gamma and manually upload to Notion
Text too condensed or broken into odd blocks	Use "Export as Text" instead of copy-paste from visual mode

Issue	Solution
Long presentations crash Google Docs	Split into smaller sections or export as PDF instead

Future Outlook

As Gamma continues to evolve, we can expect even more seamless integrations. Potential future enhancements include:

- One-click exports to Notion or Docs

- Two-way syncing with Notion pages

- Live embedding of Gamma pages in Google Docs

- Templates optimized for Notion export

If you're a heavy Notion or Docs user, keep an eye on the **What's New** section of Gamma or join their **community forums** to request features and share feedback.

✅ Summary

Exporting your Gamma content to **Notion** and **Google Docs** empowers you to expand your communication toolkit beyond visual storytelling. Whether you're repurposing a presentation into a technical report, building a knowledge base, or collaborating with teammates in Docs, Gamma gives you a strong starting point with AI-assisted content creation. From there, these integrations ensure your work stays fluid, flexible, and team-friendly.

7.2.3 Embedding in Other Platforms

In today's interconnected digital ecosystem, content creation tools like Gamma aren't just about building standalone presentations—they're about creating versatile, shareable, and embeddable digital assets that live seamlessly across your workflow. Gamma's ability to embed presentations, documents, and interactive pages into other platforms is a game-changer for creators, educators, marketers, and business professionals who want to extend the reach and accessibility of their content.

In this section, we'll dive deep into the embedding capabilities of Gamma, explore how to embed your Gamma creations into different platforms, discuss the technical and strategic considerations, and walk through real-world use cases that show how embedding can amplify your communication efforts.

📌 What Does "Embedding" Mean?

Embedding means inserting content (like a Gamma presentation) into another digital environment—such as a website, blog, learning management system (LMS), or collaboration tool—so it can be viewed and interacted with directly within that platform, without needing to open a new browser tab or external application.

Unlike sharing a link, embedded content becomes a native part of the viewer's experience, making your message more cohesive, interactive, and immediate.

🔲🔲 Why Embed Gamma Presentations?

Before we jump into the technical how-tos, let's understand the **value of embedding** Gamma content:

- **Seamless Experience**: Viewers stay on the same page or platform, reducing friction.

- **Visual Impact**: Gamma's sleek design and interactive layouts stand out within static environments.

- **Real-Time Updates**: Embedded Gamma files remain live, so when you update the original content, the changes are reflected instantly wherever it's embedded.

- **Better Engagement**: Interactive slides, clickable elements, and media-rich content drive deeper engagement.

- **Multi-Platform Consistency**: You can ensure your branding and messaging remain consistent across platforms.

🔧 How to Embed Gamma Content

Let's walk through the **step-by-step process** of embedding your Gamma content into a range of platforms.

1. Get the Embed Code from Gamma

1. Open your Gamma presentation or page.

2. Click on the **"Share"** button on the top right corner.

3. Select the **"Embed"** option from the sharing menu.

4. Gamma will generate an **HTML <iframe> embed code**.

5. Copy this code to your clipboard.

You can often customize the **size (width and height)** of the embed, depending on where you want to place it.

☐ Popular Platforms You Can Embed Into

A. Websites and Blogs (HTML editors)

Platforms like **WordPress, Wix, Squarespace, Blogger, Webflow**, and even custom-coded sites allow you to embed Gamma content using the HTML embed block or a code editor.

Example (HTML):

```
<iframe src="https://gamma.app/embed/presentation-link" width="800" height="600" frameborder="0" allowfullscreen></iframe>
```

Tips:

- Adjust width and height for responsive design.

- Place the embed within content blocks or modals for smoother integration.

B. Learning Management Systems (LMS)

Embedding Gamma in LMS platforms like **Moodle, Canvas, Blackboard, or Google Classroom** enhances learning experiences by enabling **interactive, visually engaging lesson content**.

Steps:

- Access the LMS content editor.

- Switch to **HTML view** or use an **Embed/Code block**.

- Paste the Gamma embed code.

- Save and preview to ensure functionality.

Use Case: A teacher can embed a Gamma-created lesson plan or assignment brief inside a course module, letting students interact with the material directly.

C. Notion

Though Notion doesn't support iframe embeds natively, you can still share Gamma links as visual previews or embed them indirectly using third-party tools.

Workaround:

- Paste the Gamma link directly.

- If allowed, use the /embed block with the Gamma link (some features may be limited).

- Alternatively, use a service like **EmbedNotion.com** or **Apption.co** to wrap Gamma in a viewable block.

Note: For a fully interactive experience, Gamma content may need to be opened in a new tab from Notion.

D. Google Sites

Google Sites supports iframe embedding, making it easy to insert Gamma presentations.

Steps:

1. Open your Google Site and click "Embed."

2. Choose the **Embed code** tab.

3. Paste the Gamma iframe.

4. Resize as needed and publish.

Use Case: A small business could embed a Gamma pitch deck directly onto their company website or product launch page.

E. Microsoft Teams and SharePoint

Embedding Gamma in enterprise platforms like Teams or SharePoint can bring **dynamic presentations into team environments**.

Teams:

- Paste the link in a chat or as a tab.

- While iframe may be limited in some contexts, the **link preview** is still usable.

SharePoint:

- Use the **Embed web part**.

- Paste the iframe code from Gamma.

- Adjust size and permissions as needed.

Pro Tip: Always make sure your Gamma presentation is shared with the correct visibility (e.g., public or organization-only) to avoid access issues.

F. Email Campaigns (Limited Embedding)

Due to security restrictions in most email clients, **direct iframe embedding is not supported**. However, you can:

- Add an image preview or thumbnail of your Gamma presentation.

- Link the image to the presentation URL.

Tools to Consider:

- Mailchimp

- HubSpot

- ConvertKit

Use Case: A marketer sends a newsletter with a "Watch Presentation" button linking to a Gamma sales deck.

⚠☐ Important Considerations When Embedding

- **Permissions**: Set your Gamma file to **"public"** or **"anyone with the link can view"** if embedding externally.

- **Responsive Design**: Use CSS or dynamic width settings (width: 100%) to make your embedded presentation look good on mobile.

- **Load Times**: Large presentations with media may take longer to load. Optimize for speed.

- **Privacy and Access Control**: Avoid embedding sensitive content unless it's behind authentication.

- **Fallback Plans**: Always provide a direct link alongside the embed in case the viewer's platform doesn't support iframes.

☐ Embedding Strategy: Real-World Use Cases

✅ Startup Pitch Deck on Landing Page

A startup embeds its Gamma pitch deck on its homepage to attract investors. This approach eliminates the need for PDFs and allows real-time updates to the deck as the business evolves.

✅ Portfolio for Designers or Creators

A designer uses Gamma to build a sleek portfolio and embeds it on a personal website built with Webflow. Viewers can flip through designs interactively without leaving the site.

✅ Online Course Materials

An educator embeds Gamma-created micro-lessons within each unit of their online course hosted on Moodle. This makes content more engaging and modern.

✅ Interactive Knowledge Base

A company creates internal training docs using Gamma and embeds them into its SharePoint knowledge base. This approach makes onboarding more dynamic and unified.

✅ Sales Enablement Pages

A sales team embeds Gamma one-pagers into HubSpot or CRM landing pages for client education. Instead of sending PDFs, they now share a live, interactive, and brand-aligned experience.

☐ Updating Embedded Gamma Content

The beauty of embedding Gamma files is that they **automatically reflect any changes you make** in the original file.

Tips:

- Make changes in Gamma anytime.
- No need to replace the embed code.
- Use this for evolving content like feature updates, schedules, or dynamic reports.

📈 Tracking Engagement on Embedded Content

While Gamma does not yet offer native analytics per embed, you can use third-party tools to track user behavior around embedded content:

- **Google Analytics + Events** (if on your own site)

- **Hotjar or Microsoft Clarity** for heatmaps and click tracking

- **UTM parameters** if linking via buttons

🚀 Final Thoughts on Embedding with Gamma

Embedding your Gamma creations opens up a world of possibilities beyond static slides and downloadable documents. Whether you're building a **modern website**, managing an **online course**, **onboarding a new employee**, or just sharing your ideas more effectively, Gamma's embedding functionality allows you to **meet your audience where they are—** in the context they're already engaged in.

By mastering this integration layer, you're not just using Gamma—you're turning it into the **nucleus of your content strategy**.

Conclusion

Recap and Final Thoughts

Key Takeaways

As we come to the end of our journey exploring **Gamma**, it's a perfect moment to reflect on everything you've learned and accomplished. Whether you are a beginner stepping into the world of AI-powered presentations or a creative professional seeking a fresh, streamlined way to build interactive content, Gamma offers you a powerful, flexible, and intuitive tool.

In this section, we'll walk through the key takeaways from the book so you can revisit and reinforce your understanding, keep best practices top of mind, and confidently begin applying Gamma to your real-world projects.

1. Understanding What Gamma Is

One of the first and most important takeaways is understanding what Gamma is and what it isn't. Gamma is not just another presentation tool—it's a dynamic content creation platform powered by AI that enables users to create presentations, documents, landing pages, and digital experiences in a fraction of the time traditional tools require.

You learned that:

- Gamma is browser-based—no software download required.

- It combines AI-assisted writing, design, and layout with manual editing for full control.

- It enables presentations, documents, and microsites to exist as interactive, responsive content—ideal for web-native audiences.

- Gamma supports real-time collaboration, interactive elements, and easy sharing or embedding across platforms.

☐☐ 2. Mastering the Basics: From Sign-Up to Your First Presentation

We walked step-by-step through:

- Creating a Gamma account and exploring the dashboard.

- Starting a new presentation using either:

    o AI-generated content from a text prompt.

    o Pre-designed templates customized to your needs.

    o Or building a project from a blank slate, giving you full creative control.

You've gained familiarity with the workspace layout, learned how to manage your pages, edit content blocks, adjust design elements, and organize your content intuitively.

☐ 3. Harnessing the Power of AI

Gamma shines through its smart use of AI. Key takeaways in this area include:

- Using AI to generate outlines, structure arguments, summarize ideas, or fill in details quickly.

- Leveraging smart text tools like:

    o Expand, to elaborate ideas.

    o Rewrite, to offer alternative phrasings.

    o Summarize, for condensing long content.

- Gamma's AI is not just about text; it can also assist in design suggestions, layout structure, and content refinement.

- The AI assistant is best used as a partner. You remain the creative driver, while the AI provides options, inspiration, and efficiency.

Pro tip: Always fact-check AI-generated content, and rewrite it to match your brand voice or communication style. AI is a tool—not a final editor.

☐☐ 4. Creating Visually Stunning, Interactive Presentations

Throughout the book, we emphasized design simplicity and impact. You've learned to:

- Choose and customize themes and visual styles.
- Use blocks to insert and manage content: text, images, embeds, videos, buttons, etc.
- Avoid overcrowding by applying visual hierarchy, negative space, and consistent font and color choices.

More importantly, we explored interactive elements that turn static content into engaging experiences:

- Internal links and buttons to guide flow.
- Embeds (videos, GIFs, forms) to keep audiences engaged.
- Multi-section layouts that feel like navigating a website instead of flipping through slides.

This chapter showed you how to shift your mindset from "slide-by-slide presentations" to interactive storytelling experiences.

☐ 5. Collaborating and Sharing with Ease

In modern work environments, collaboration is key. Gamma supports:

- Real-time co-editing, similar to Google Docs.
- Commenting and feedback tools to streamline review cycles.
- Role-based permissions to control who can view, edit, or share.
- Easy sharing via:
  - Public or private links.
  - Embeds for blogs, websites, and online portfolios.
  - PDF or PowerPoint exports (when needed).

You also discovered that analytics are built-in, allowing you to:

- Track views.

- Understand user behavior (clicks, scrolls).

- Optimize your content based on engagement data.

☐ 6. Going Beyond Presentations

One of the most empowering takeaways is that Gamma isn't just for slides.

You now know how to use Gamma to create:

- One-pagers and company reports.

- Landing pages and personal portfolios.

- Resource hubs and knowledge libraries.

This flexibility makes Gamma a compelling tool not only for presentations but also for content marketing, internal documentation, product announcements, and more.

With integrations like:

- Google Drive (for syncing files),

- Notion or Google Docs (for exporting/repurposing),

- Embeds into any webpage or intranet, you're set up to scale your workflow and eliminate content silos.

🔍 7. Looking Ahead: The Future of Gamma

Gamma is an evolving platform, and one key lesson is this: It will only get better. You've seen a preview of what's coming:

- New AI features for smarter suggestions and deeper automation.

- Community templates and plug-ins.

- User-generated resources and learning libraries.

It's not just a tool—it's becoming a content ecosystem where users can share, collaborate, and grow together.

🎞 8. Best Practices to Remember

Before you leave this book behind, keep these core principles in mind:

- Start with clarity. Know what your presentation is trying to accomplish.

- Let the AI help—but don't rely on it blindly. Review and revise.

- Keep it simple. Gamma shines when used with intention and clean design.

- Use interactivity to serve your audience, not distract them.

- Practice, share, and get feedback. You'll grow with every project.

🏁 Final Words: You're Ready

You've made it through the complete journey—from understanding what Gamma is, to using it effectively for a variety of professional and creative tasks. You now have a **powerful new toolset** and a mindset shift that will enable you to create smarter, more engaging content faster than ever.

Whether you're a teacher creating a lesson, a founder pitching a product, a marketer launching a campaign, or a student presenting a research project, Gamma can help you do it better—with **style, intelligence, and impact**.

So what's next?

Use Gamma.
Test your ideas.
Share your voice.
And most of all—**create fearlessly.**

Acknowledgments

First and foremost, **thank you** for choosing to read *Getting Started with Gamma: Create Stunning Presentations with AI*. I am truly grateful that you've invested your time, attention, and trust in this book.

Whether you're a curious learner, a creative professional, or a team leader seeking smarter ways to communicate, your interest in exploring innovative tools like Gamma reflects a spirit of growth, adaptability, and forward-thinking. This book was written with people like you in mind—those who are not only eager to learn but also to create meaningful, impactful work.

Your support means more than you might realize. By purchasing this book, you're not only supporting independent authorship but also fueling a mission to make modern tools and technology more accessible, practical, and empowering for everyone.

I hope this guide has inspired you, helped you gain confidence in using Gamma, and opened new doors for how you share your ideas with the world. If even one tip, tool, or concept made your creative process easier or more enjoyable, then this book has done its job.

Thank you once again—and here's to your continued success in every presentation, project, and idea you bring to life.

Warm regards,